ISBN 978-1-331-48572-8
PIBN 10196582

This book is a reproduction of an important historical work. Forgotten Books uses
state-of-the-art technology to digitally reconstruct the work, preserving the original format
whilst repairing imperfections present in the aged copy. In rare cases, an imperfection in
the original, such as a blemish or missing page, may be replicated in our edition. We do,
however, repair the vast majority of imperfections successfully; any imperfections that
remain are intentionally left to preserve the state of such historical works.

English
Français
Deutsche
Italiano
Español
Português

www.forgottenbooks.com

Mythology Photography **Fiction**
Fishing Christianity **Art** Cooking
Essays Buddhism Freemasonry
Medicine **Biology** Music **Ancient
Egypt** Evolution Carpentry Physics
Dance Geology **Mathematics** Fitness
Shakespeare **Folklore** Yoga Marketing
Confidence Immortality Biographies
Poetry **Psychology** Witchcraft
Electronics Chemistry History **Law**
Accounting **Philosophy** Anthropology
Alchemy Drama Quantum Mechanics
Atheism Sexual Health **Ancient History**
Entrepreneurship Languages Sport
Paleontology Needlework Islam
Metaphysics Investment Archaeology
Parenting Statistics Criminology
Motivational

MEMOIR

OF THE

REV. JOSEPH SANFORD, A.M.

MEMOIR

HENRY PERKINS, CHESTNUT STREET.

BOSTON: PERKINS & MARVIN.

1836.

MEMOIR

OF THE

REV. JOSEPH SANFORD, A.M.

PASTOR OF THE SECOND PRESBYTERIAN CHURCH, PHILADELPHIA.

BY ROBERT BAIRD.

" Soldier of Christ! well done ;
Praise be thy new employ ;
And while eternal ages run,
Rest in thy Saviour's joy."
J. MONTGOMERY.

PHILADELPHIA:

HENRY PERKINS, CHESTNUT STREET.

BOSTON: PERKINS & MARVIN.

1836.

I. ASHMEAD AND CO. PRINTERS.

INTRODUCTION.

It can scarcely be said that this volume is intended for the public eye; for it has been prepared especially, and almost exclusively, for the gratification and benefit of the numerous friends of the subject of it.

It became known to several individuals, shortly after Mr. Sanford's death, that he had left numerous letters and other papers, which bear record of his uncommon piety; and which, if published, might, with the blessing of God, be instrumental in doing good. And a desire was expressed, that the author should undertake the task of their selection and arrangement. But incessant duties prevented his attempting the work whilst he remained in America. And it has only been by seizing the few hours of leisure which other duties have allowed him, since his arrival in Europe, that he has been able to accomplish the undertaking. He is conscious that the work has been prepared under many disadvantages. With all its imperfections, however, he commits it to the divine blessing, with the hope that it may contribute to the promotion of that blessed kingdom which it was so much the desire of the subject of it to advance, whether living or dying.

To those who enjoyed the privilege of living under the ministry of Mr. Sanford, and especially to those who were connected to God, through his instrumentality, this Memoir of their late excellent pastor is respectfully dedicated. That it may be the means of forcibly reminding them of his earnest and faithful sermons, and his unwearied efforts, on their behalf, and of stirring them up to follow, with more alacrity and constancy, the example of his faith and patience, is the prayer of,

THE AUTHOR.

Paris, March 7th, 1836.

MEMOIR.

———◆———

THE REV. JOSEPH SANFORD was born on the sixth day of February, 1797. He was the youngest of three children. His parents were originally from the town of Southbury, Fairfield county, Connecticut. His father was the son of Joseph and Ann Sanford. His mother was the daughter of Thomas and Sarah Strong, all of Southbury, Connecticut. It is believed that both his father and his grandfather were soldiers in the memorable war which resulted in the establishment of the independence of our beloved country. His parents, a few years after their marriage, removed from Connecticut to Vermont, where the subject of these memoirs was born. Shortly after that event they removed to Saratoga county, in the state of New York, where they continued to reside until July 1816, when they again removed, and settled in Cayuga county, in the same state. They were both, there is good reason to believe, savingly acquainted with the Lord Jesus Christ, and they carefully instructed their children in the principles of the Christian religion. His father died in the year 1826; his venerable mother is still living.

The work of divine grace seems to have been commenced in the heart of the subject of these memoirs at a very early period. On this point he himself remarks, in some of his writings—"From my earliest recollections I had always a peculiar veneration for serious persons and things." There is reason to believe, that at the age of eight years his heart had been renewed by the Spirit. His convictions of sin were deep, and distressing, and long; but he found peace and hope through faith in the Lord Jesus Christ. He did not, however, make a profession of religion, by uniting with the visible church, until his thirteenth year. At the age of fourteen he taught a district school, to the entire satisfaction of his employers.

When in his eighteenth or nineteenth year, he began to pursue classical studies, with the view of obtaining an education at college, in order to qualify himself, so far as human knowledge constitutes a qualification, for the holy ministry. These preparatory studies seem to have been pursued chiefly at the academies at Granville, in Washington county, and Ballston, in Saratoga county, New York. Even at that early period, it is the testimony of excellent men who resided at that time in those villages, his piety had attained an uncommon degree of maturity. He was very active in every effort which was made to do good. At the request of the proper persons, he took a prominent part in the prayer meetings, and in the meetings for religious inquiry. And decided testimony is borne to the acceptableness and usefulness of his exercises and labours on these occasions. The uncommon talent for popular addresses which he possessed in so large a measure, and which he began even then to display, rendered his exhortations at the small assemblages of the people for religious purposes extremely acceptable. And there is reason to believe, during this his earliest period of preparation for preaching the everlasting gospel, he was the instrument of great spiritual good to many persons. At the same time it is abundantly shown, by testimony from the most competent sources, that his diligence in study was unremitting and his success great. Both in Granville and

Ballston, as well as in the neighbourhood of Milton Academy, where, when he was very young, he spent some time in teaching the younger classes of that institution, his memory is most affectionately cherished by those who witnessed his exemplary and Christian deportment, and his zealous and discreet efforts to promote his Master's kingdom.

That Mr. Sanford, whilst labouring for the souls of others, was not unmindful of his own soul, and its progress in grace, is fully proved by the numerous memorials on that subject which are to be found among his papers. To this class belong the striking and appropriate reflections which he was in the habit of making at the juncture of the past and coming year. The first record of these reflections which is to be found among his papers, is that made of the last day of 1815 and the first of 1816. It is full of pious and solemn meditations, befitting that interesting crisis. The succeeding one is here subjoined, and cannot, we think, be read without profit.

" *Ballston,* 31*st Dec.* 1816.

" This is truly an interesting moment. Another year is just at its close. A few moments, and 'twill be numbered with the years beyond the flood, and my account for it will be sealed up to the judgment. My God, what an important moment! How stand my accounts with God? Are my sins repented of? Is the pardon for my transgressions sealed? Have I given myself away to God? Am I Christ's by the covenant of grace? Is he mine, really mine—entirely mine, eternally mine; the Lord *my* righteousness, all my salvation and all my desire? Am I clothed with his righteousness, and have I been washed in his blood? Have I ever made an entire surrender of myself to God, soul and body, for time and for eternity? Oh, eternal, unchangeable, omnipotent, all-wise, all-holy, self-existent, uncaused, omni-

scient, omnipresent, heart-searching, sin-hating, sin-avenging,
prayer-hearing, prayer-answering, sinner-pardoning God! at
whose incommunicable name the devils tremble, and at whose
awful voice the earth quakes—by the breath of whose displeasure the wicked are slain, and the universe melted down
—from whose presence the heavens flee away,—wilt thou
be pleased, in and through Jesus Christ, to look down through
the confounding interval which lies between us, upon a sinful
worm, and behold me in Christ with pity and compassion.
For Christ's sake alone wilt thou pardon my sins, blot them
from thy book, and fold down the leaf for an eternal con-
cealment when they are recorded.   Enable me to give myself in a covenant to thee; and here, on the evening of the
31st December, 1816, in the full exercise of all the powers
and faculties of my mind, desiring the assistance of thy
grace, do solemnly dedicate myself, soul and body, uncon-
ditionally and eternally to thee.

> Thine would I live, thine would I die,
> Be thine through all eternity:
> The vow is past, beyond repeal,
> And now I set the solemn seal.

Ratify in heaven, oh ever-blessed and glorious Trinity, that
which has now been done upon earth.   And oh, holy Father,
wilt thou be my reconciled Father and my covenant-keeping
God!   Oh, Jesus, Master, wilt thou be the Lord my righteousness and the Lord my strength, all my salvation and all
my desire!   Oh, Holy Spirit, wilt thou be my sanctifier
and comforter!   And oh, mysterious union of persons, in-
comprehensible Jehovah God, wilt thou guide, guard, direct
and protect me during the year upon which I now have entered; and, if consistent with thy holy will, wilt thou spare
my life, continue my health, the use of my reason and my
limbs, and make me useful in my day and generation.   But

prepare me for all thy will concerning me, and whether living or dying may I be the Lord's. May God grant it for Christ's sake. Amen. *Jan. 1st, 1817.*"

On the 19th day of September, 1817, Mr. Sanford entered the Sophomore class in Union College, Schenectady, New York. Of the events of the three important years which he spent in that excellent institution, and the spiritual blessings which he enjoyed under its distinguished president and professors, he has left the following memoranda.

First session. College duties arduous. No opportunity for social intercourse. Few religious acquaintances. Spent my few hours of relaxation in solitude and retirement, although surrounded by a multitude. Find no congenial souls. Actuated by a sense of duty, I had the misfortune to offend my class, by reciting, contrary to their wishes. A part of them were, for awhile, very insolent; some threatened violence; but I stood in silent, unheeding, self-approving confidence, and the storm blew quickly over. Nothing of importance took place. My health, which was poor when I entered, began to improve. I think that I had much joy and peace in believing. Some hours, long to be remembered, in the stillness of midnight, when the noisy, thoughtless crowd were locked in slumber, and through " globe's dark solitude no mortal wak'd but me." Then my soul seemed to stretch her pinions for the heavens, and to hold communion with her Saviour. Delightful seasons, oh, return! Examination took place on the 16th and 17th of December. Vacation of three weeks. Spent it in Ballston very pleasantly. Returned to Schenectady, January 9th. Roomed with Bishop.* Staid

---

* At present a very worthy and devoted minister and missionary in the Sandwich Islands.

1*

at college four weeks; returned to Ballston to spend the remainder of the term.

" Ballston, February 9th, 1818.

"MY DEAR SIR,

"Being very providentially in Ballston to spend the Sabbath, I had the happiness to hear from Granville by Mrs. O. Believe me, my dear sir, it afforded me no ordinary degree of satisfaction to learn that your esteemed family were well. And although my last has not been answered, I cannot forego the pleasure of forwarding a line; and a line is all this momentary opportunity will allow. My health, since I last saw you in Salem, has been good. I entered Union College on the 19th of September last, where I have been mostly since confined. And if God should spare my life, and continue my health, I shall not complete my collegiate course until the April of 1820. But this period will soon be gone. Time's mighty current rolls the wheel of man's existence; and the spring of childhood, the summer of youth, autumnal manhood, and wintry age, are alike affected by the movement. The little moments which compose our life, on wings unnumbered flit away. Each pursues its predecessor, and is swiftly pursued by its successor, and soon the last will fly. Oh, to be wise to improve them! 'Heaven's on the wing.' Let us fix the citadel of our hopes far above the commotions which agitate this lower world.

"I am very anxious to see you all, and speak face to face; but I cannot tell when I shall enjoy that happiness. A conveyance is hard to be obtained, and my studies are pressing. I now expect to spend the remainder of the term in Ballston. I can study here to advantage. It will be about six weeks. Do let me hear from you. Give my best respects to your family. May God throw around you the arms of his protecting providence, and bless you with his free and rich salvation."

March 9th. On account of an increasing debility laid aside my studies. I am almost distracted with pain in my head.

Went to New York about the last of March, and returned the last of April; but·was advised by Dr. Nott and other officers not to resume my studies. Spent May in Ballston. Went west in June, and visited Geneva, Canandaigua, and Rochester, and returned to Schenectady, on the Monday before commencement. Spent the succeeding vacation at Milton, and returned with improved health to college, September 18th, and recommenced my studies. Oh God, make me grateful for past mercies!

Junior year. Studies more agreeable. Was able to pursue my studies far beyond my expectation. Had several short seasons of illness, but they did not, in all, hinder me more than ten days. Have abundant reason to adore the goodness of Almighty God for the mercies I enjoy, numerous as the moments of my existence, and rich with immortal hopes. Examination took place, December 17th. Vacation was spent in Ballston.

TO MR. H. D., OF BALLSTON, N. Y.

"*New York, October* 24*th*, 1819.

"I can mingle my thanksgivings with yours, my dear friend, that your health is so far restored that you have been again up to the house of the Lord, and have renewed your vows in his holy temple. Oh, may he grant you grace to fulfil them. My soul can say with yours, 'that it is good to be afflicted.' Oh, how it softens the heart, sweetens the temper, revives the drooping graces of the Christian. It improves his views of earthly and heavenly things, by removing the dust that collects around him, from being 'of the earth—earthy,' and having so much to do with earthly things. Oh, we not only know but feel that these very afflictions are for our immediate good. The rod is a branch from the tree of life, and it is in the hands of our Redeemer; and we will bless him for every stripe, and every smart; we will kiss the rod, and the hand that holds it, and endeavour by his grace to say with David, 'Before I was afflicted I went astray, but now have I kept thy word.'

"I have had some blessed seasons lately, some seasons when I felt that God was near, that I could call him my Father. Oh, what a privilege, to be admitted not only into the audience-chamber, but into the very banqueting-house of the King of kings, to feed on children's, yes, on angel's food.

'Oh, to grace how great a debtor
Daily I'm constrained to be.'

We are the King's soldiers, and if he permits us to sit at his table, how faithful ought we to be.

"I have been through the New York hospital. The sight was painfully interesting, to see so much poverty and wretchedness, and yet to see it rendered comparatively happy by kindness and care. The lunatic department presented less that was loathsome, but more that was affecting. To see persons in the vigour of life and health, with reason dethroned, is an awful spectacle. Let age and disease crumble down the body, it is not so difficult to be borne. But when the *immortal mind* is in ruins, it is a more awful calamity, it is of more tremendous import. But what amazing debts of gratitude do we owe the Preserver of men, that we enjoy the use of all the powers of the mind as well as the body. How we should improve them! To-morrow we may be the prey of disease. The air we breathe may contain the seeds of death—some accident may derange the curious and complicated mechanism of the body. The torch of reason, of intellect, may be at once extinguished, and we may be virtually blotted out from the records of the living; and as to all purposes of usefulness or enjoyment, be as though we had never been. Oh, let us seize the passing hour—improve the moments as they fly."

December 31*st.* In the enjoyment of blessings which I can neither number nor name, I am brought near the close of another year—a year commenced in the best of health, but in the course of which I have been brought to contemplate wasting disease and an opening sepulchre. It has witnessed my prospects clouded, my hopes blighted, my studies interrupted, my health declining, and all my highest, fondest earthly expectations sinking to the earth. But the Lord Jehovah reigns, and reigns a God of consolation. And he is as kind and compassionate, when mantled in more than chaotic darkness, as when we behold him looking down upon us in all the tenderness of suffering sympathy, and all the ardour of a Saviour's love. Now, at the close of the year, I am enjoying health and happiness; and a thousand arguments combine to call forth heart-felt acknowledgments of purest, warmest gratitude. Here will I raise my Ebenezer. Lord, thou hast been my helper through all the dangers of another year. But in that year which is just ending I have done nothing for thee, thou Creator, Preserver, and Redeemer of men. Oh Jesus, Master, wash me afresh in thy blood; forgive all my sins; forgive my coldness, my ingratitude. May this year not bear testimony against me in the court of heaven. Seal not up its report for the great day, but cancel all my iniquities and my frailties with thy most precious blood. And, oh God of eternity, have mercy upon me, a poor sinful creature here, in time, and may I live to thy glory, and as one of thy children. In the course of this year I have witnessed——but the clock strikes—it is gone—hid in the mighty caverns of the past.—Another to that eternity which has gone by! But I shall see this mighty volume all unrolled—mighty volume, rolled *back*, rolled *onward!* Dreadful, delightful day! Jesus, Jesus, be thou my friend!

Read Numbers xxi. 5—9, in connexion with Rev. v. 6—14. John i. 29 : "Behold the Lamb of God, which taketh away the sin of the world." The passage in numbers is all a type, and Jesus Christ is the great antitype—looking on the brazen serpent represents believing on Christ. He himself says, "As Moses lifted up the serpent in the wilderness, so shall the Son of Man be lifted up."

Returned to college January 18th, and recommenced studies as usual. Roomed alone. Some seasons of serious illness; lost as much as ten or twelve days during the term. Examination early in April. Visited New York; returned and visited Salem, Granville, &c. Session began early in May. Studies very agreeable. Health good during the first few weeks of the term, but declined with the approach of warm weather. Discontinued study almost entirely three weeks before the end of the term. Commencement on the 28th of July. Spent the vacation in visiting Albany, Water-ford, Lansingburg, Cambridge, Salem, Granville, &c. &c., and returned to college in good health.

Senior year—September 24th, 1819. The last year placed me under tremendous obligations to devote myself to God. What a mass of this world's population did it carry from the earth, while I was left behind! Oh, may I inscribe *"Jehovah Jireh"* upon some monument of gratitude, and may it appear on earth and in heaven that I was not spared in vain. The weather is very fine, health very good, studies agreeable. Have my dearest friend on earth, for a room-male. Dr. Nott's recitation interesting. Dr. M'Auley goes to Malta to-day, to organize a church; very flattering appearances of a revival of religion.

Dec. 15*th.* Went to Ballston and Malta, saw what wonders the Lord is doing, and, blessed be God, hope that I felt some of the celestial fire. Saw things new and glorious. A communion season at Malta; about thirty were added to the church. Dr. M. seemed inspired, and spoke in strains more than mortal. Attended anxious meetings, where from fifty to one hundred and fifty were most deeply agitated under a sense of sin.

Milton, Dec. 31*st.* A few more hours, and another eventful year will have fled for ever! I have enjoyed mercies which I cannot enumerate. While death has made more than ordinary ravages in the ranks of human society, my unprofitable life has been spared. Oh, that there were a heart in me to acknowledge God's goodness. Oh, that this departing year might not leave me with my sins unrepented of, but that it might carry, along with its record of my mercies and my crimes, my gratitude and my penitence. I have been too cold and inactive in the cause of Christ; but, blessed be God, I feel somewhat awake, not only to a sense of God's goodness in sparing me through another year, but of my guilt in loving him no more and serving him no better. May I never again become so stupid and so indifferent in the cause of my Master, and never so attached to a fleeting, fading world. Several of my acquaintances and friends have gone during the last year to eternity. Yesterday I saw L. M.; she appears to be going. A few days ago she was in health; now, a confirmed consumption has faded the rose on her cheek, wasted her frame, blighted her hopes, blasted her earthly prospects. May I have faith to present her case before the throne of grace, where Christ, the healer of the Gentiles, sits to hear and save. What an affecting insignifi-

cance does such a providence stamp on all things below the
stars. Oh God, teach me how short my life is, and give me
grace to prepare for death, and to improve for eternity. If
consistent with thy most holy will, spare me through the
coming year, prepare me for the ministry of reconciliation.
Warm my heart, purify my motives, quicken my zeal,
strengthen my faith; and may thy Spirit cherish all my
Christian graces, and lead me into all truth. Oh, do not
suffer me to be deceived; but wilt thou search my heart,
and try my thoughts, and establish me on the rock of ages.
Accept my gratitude for the mercies of the past year, and
assist me to commit the keeping of my frail body and my
immortal soul to thee for the time to come. Do thou accept
and bless me for Christ's sake. Amen.

January 12*th*, 1820. Returned to college. Felt a desire unusually ardent that God would pour out his spirit on
the college. Some of the brethren feel actually more engaged.

February 2*d*. God has made an awful visit to us. Mr.
A. C. H. of Shaftsbury, Vermont, died suddenly after an
illness of only three days. Prayed that the mighty power
which dealt the blow would sanctify it to the good of souls.
The officers, Dr. M'Auley in particular, improved the previ-
dence. The corpse was carried into Dr. M'A.'s study-room,
who, in language more than mortal, urged those to repentance who came in to see it.

God was pleased to bless these timely warnings, and to
awaken many to make the inquiry, " What shall I do to be
saved?" Oh, that men would praise the Lord for his goodness and for his wonderful works to the children of men.
About the last of February the work was at its height. New
instances of awakening and conversion were heard of every
day. But unable to pursue my collegiate studies, and my
exertions, though feeble, being needed in other places, 1 left

college and went to Saratoga county, where God was open-ing the windows of heaven and raining down spiritual bless-ings in overwhelming abundance. At the same time the work was going on powerfully in Stillwater, Malta, Ballston, Galway, Amsterdam, and Schenectady.

March. Spent some time in Galway, and witnessed scenes never to be forgotten. Miss W. apparently near her end. Made a short visit to Granville, returned and called upon her for the last time, the day before she died. Found her sweetly reposing her confidence on the arm and the mercy of Jesus, and calmly waiting till her change come. She died in peace: she sleeps in Jesus; and her ransomed spirit, released from its earthly prison, climbs unfettered the heights of the celestial city, and mingles in the anthems of eternity.

Passed immediately to New York—found my friends in good health. Spent three or four days, and then, for the first time, visited Princeton, N. J., in company with my friend and benefactor, D. S. Lyon, Esq. While at Princeton attended the ordination of Mr. Chapman, one of the mission-aries to the Osage Indians. Mr. Woodhull preached. Dr. Miller gave the charge. Dr. Alexander made the couse-crating prayer. Returned to New York. Preparations are making to fit out the mission and family. Never did a holier enthusiasm animate the minds of the good people of New York. The mission family consists of 21 persons. They met for the first time in the Middle Dutch Church, the next evening in the Brick Church; at both places appropri-ate prayers and addresses were made. The next day, the day of their departure, they met in the Consistory of the Garden-street Church. From thence they went to the boat, in waiting to receive them. Here parting hymns were sung, parting hands were given, parting prayers were offered, and they left their native land amid the supplications of thou-

2

sands; amid the shouts, no doubt of exulting angels, and the smiles of approving heaven.

Spent a few days with the Rev. T. Osborne, at West Farms. Returned to Schenectady to finish my collegiate course. The session ,unusually pleasant. Lectures on chemistry, &c. very interesting. The session ends July 26th. Verily, the Lord has been my helper. Oh, that my future life may be more devoted to the service and glory of God. Left Schenectady in less than two weeks after the commencement, to visit my dear aged parents. Found them in health, on the evening of the 8th of August, after an absence of more than two years. Passed through Geneva, Canandaigua, to Rochester, and thence to Niagara Falls.

September. Took leave of my parents; returned to Schenectady; spent about a week at Dr. M'Auley's, and came to New York the last of the month. Spent the month of October in the hospitable and dear family of Mr. L. Blessed be God for some degree of deadness to the world. Oh, suffer me never more to feel it to be my continuing city; but may I seek one to come, made without hands, where the inhabitants shall never say "I am sick," and where friends never part. Oh, may I there meet those friends who have died in the Lord. A good work of grace seems to be beginning in Dr. Spring's congregation. Attended some interesting meetings. Really, God seems to be in the midst of them. Conversed with some of the hopeful subjects of it. Oh, how Christians speak the same language, have the same hopes and fears, joys and sorrows and prospects.

November 4th. Left New York for Princeton, to commence my theological studies. Oh God, wilt thou not go with me and bless me? else suffer me not to go hence. I renewedly cast myself upon thee. Through Jesus own me for a child, and may 1 be obedient and jealous for thine honour.

It is proper to remark here, that Mr. Sanford maintained, throughout his entire course at college, a high character for sound and ardent piety. He was greatly respected by the members of the faculty of that college, and beloved by his fellow students; and although his studies were pursued under some disadvantages arising from the want of continued health, yet his standing in his class was very respectable.

After leaving college, Mr. S. addressed the following letter to his friend, Mr. H. D., of Ballston, N. Y.

TO MR. H. D. OF BALLSTON, N. Y.

"New York, Sept. 28th, 1820.

"I was unable to obtain a seat at Schenectady on Tuesday, and so could not leave until Wednesday morning at five—and this morning, at half past six, arrived in this city.

"The state of the fever in Savannah has become less alarming, but it is still dangerous to visit those southern towns. The Rev. Sylvester Larned, of New Orleans, is no more; he fell a victim to the fever about the 19th of September. So pass away the hopes of men! The remark is often made, that genius is almost always short in its career.

"Where the mind is ardent, whatever may fire that ardour, it will soon exhaust the body. Our bodies at best are decaying tabernacles, the tottering tenements of rebellious souls. But while we can say by one part of our nature to 'corruption, thou art my father,' and to the 'worm, thou art my mother, and my sister,' by another part of that nature we are allied to angels, and if born again, are heirs to crowns and kingdoms. Not crowns that will fade, and kingdoms that some ambitious and successful rival may take away, but crowns of immortal glory, kingdoms of unfading grandeur and beauty, to which our title deed is the promise and the oath of the everlasting God. Oh, how I pity the thoughtless worldling, who aims at no inheritance but his heaps of shining dust—dust, to be sure, of some relative value; but to him with that contracted heart, and with that sleepless, grinding avarice, mere contemptible trash. Verily, a 'soul immortal,' spending, all her 'fires' about the paltry business of the world, resembles

> ——'ocean into tempest tost,
> To waft a feather or to drown a fly.'

"I had no design of giving *you* useful hints on the subject of loving the world. I well know your ideas on that subject, and I highly approve them, and sincerely hope, that you will not only practise upon such correct opinions, but endeavour to disseminate them, since there are so many excellent men, who seem to think that 'to be rich' is the chief end of man.

"But, blessed be God, we have higher and nobler aims. We hope that we have tasted too often of the love of God, to relish the husks of time and sense. In the course of the last winter we often found ourselves in the banqueting-house of the King of kings, while 'his banner over us was love.' Have we not, my brother, been often fed with children's food, while we were unworthy of the falling crumbs! Verily, the grace of God is so rich and so free, the love of God is so deep and so broad, the arm of the Lord is so mighty, and his favour so immutable, that when we are satisfied that he, with all his fulness, has become ours, and that we, in spite of our unworthiness, have been made his, we may bid a bold defiance to all the attacks of Satan, and the world without and around us, and Satan and the flesh within us. Jesus Christ is indeed a 'strong tower, to which the righteous flee and are safe,' whatever may befall them. Satan may vent his rage, the malice of men may seize and confine my body, they cannot confine my soul from communion with God. They may break my body on the wheel, suspend it on the gibbet, burn it in the fire, and scatter my ashes to the winds and the waves, I am safe, blessed Jesus, and my sleeping dust is under the notice of thine eye, and its scattered particles are safe under' thy protecting care; and whether it flies in the air, floats in the ocean, or vegetates on the earth, the voice, that voice that wakes the dead, will start it from its slumbers, and, refined and purified by the resurrection, it will bloom in immortal youth and beauty, a fit tenement for a blood-washed spirit, and a fit inhabitant for the city of Zion. Oh, my brother, let thoughts of God and glory fill our minds, and animate us on our journey. Let the past time of our lives more than suffice us to have lived in stupidity, for our veriest zeal has been little less than stupidity. And while here in this world, let us animate and provoke each other to love and good works; and if we are so happy as to meet before the throne, we will emulate each other in swelling the immortal anthems of eternity.

"Make my best and warmest wishes to my dear friends. Since I began to write, the morning paper has been put in my hands, and I learn that the fever at the south is as violent as ever. Mr. Larned died on the 19th of September, after an illness of four days. Mrs. Larned has lost her mother, brother and child, and now her husband, in less than twelve months."

————

In the autumn of 1820 Mr. Sanford entered the Theological Seminary at Princeton, N. J., with the view of prosecuting his studies for the holy ministry. In that distinguished institution he remained three years, under the instruction of its eminent professors. During this whole period he was remarkably attentive to his duties as a student, preparing for the high office which he had in view. He was most assiduous in his efforts to acquire the knowledge which the sacred office demands, and which that institution so richly

2*

furnishes. His time was most conscientiously devoted to his studies. Nothing was slighted. The opinions and suggestions of his beloved and venerated teachers were always listened to by him with profound regard and consideration. In this respect few men have passed through a theological seminary with greater, if equal, propriety of deportment. For although he was far from being deficient in self-respect and independence of mind, yet he was modest, respectful, and most dignified, in all his intercourse with his professors. He went to the institution to *learn.* He had entire confidence in the qualifications of his instructers; and no man ever left that institution more respected by those revered teachers. He left it, giving abundant evidence that he had well employed his time and opportunities. His standing as a scholar was highly respectable. The essays which he wrote, in compliance with requirements of the institution, display a vigorous mind. On one or two occasions he was chosen by his fellow students to perform the highest offices which their associations prescribe. One of these was the delivering of the annual or semi-annual oration before the Society of Inquiry on the subject of Missions.

But, however respectable Mr. Sanford's standing was as a student and a scholar, his ardent piety was far more prominent. He was, during the whole period, distinguished for his dignified, consistent, holy and devoted life. All who knew him were deeply impressed with his serious and most exemplary deportment. He was a man of much prayer. He was solemn, habitually serious, but not morose. There was a spirituality, a holy unction, pervading his conduct and conversation, which made it manifest that he was a holy man, conversant with the heavenly, the hidden life,—the life of God in the soul of man.

Respecting this portion of Mr. Sanford's life the reader will find ample and interesting details in the following extracts from his letters and journal.

Theological Seminary, Princeton, N. J.
November, 1820.

Here I desire to erect my Ebenezer. The Lord has indeed been my helper. When difficulties and embarrassments lay across my path, he has removed them. When danger threatened, he has been my deliverer. When I have been wasted by sickness, and brought nigh unto death, he has been my healer. When I have been in darkness, he has caused his face to shine. He has given me friends and benefactors; he has fed and clothed me; he has soothed my sorrows, and wiped away my tears; he has carried my burdens; he has chosen the changes, regulated the events, and managed the little concerns of my hitherto useless life. Oh, what was I, that he should watch over my childhood, when my careless footsteps had not learned to run in the way of his commandments? What was I that he should give me pious parents, through whose tender care and instructions, with the blessing of the Spirit, my mind was early called to the business of preparation for death and improvement for eternity? What was I that he should bear with the follies, reclaim the wanderings, and restore the backslidings of my earlier as well as my later years? What was I, that he should early implant a desire in my heart to be employed in the holy office of the Christian ministry, and that in spite of my indigence and obscurity, he should afford me the means of education, and place me now in this seat of sacred science, thus granting one of my most ardent wishes? I am his by every tie that can bind a creature to the throne of its Creator, that can endear an unworthy, a rebellious child, to the kindest and best of Parents. And oh, thou Preserver of men, am I indeed thine by a living and a life-giving faith, though the most unworthy of thy children? It is all of grace, from first to last. And wilt thou enable me to enter on a course of immediate preparation for the gospel ministry? Wilt thou

grant me thy special blessing in all my studies? Wilt thou
dwell in me as a spirit of wisdom, of humility, of illumina·
tion, of sanctification, of consolation? Warm my heart,
purify my motives, and, if it might please thee, spare my
life, continue my health, and in thine own due time permit
me to enter the field clad in thy might, armed with the whole
armour of God; and permit me to perform some humble
part in thy service in the glorious cause that thou art carry·
ing forward on earth; and finally grant me grace that I may
not dishonour thy cause in death, but may I depart in peace,
yea, in triumph. Take me in mercy under thy special care;
I desire to commit my way unto the Lord, and do thou direct
my paths; and whatever in thy providence may be in reserve
for me, whether prosperity or adversity, long life or early
death, I desire to rejoice only and continually in the assurance
that thou wilt do all things well.

TO MR. H. D., OF BALLSTON, N. Y.

"*Princeton, Nov.* 16*th*, 1820.

"Yours by Mr. G. came duly to hand in this place, where
I have already spent more than a week. To say that your
letter afforded me much pleasure would be useless, for you
know that already. But were I not selfish, I could not pos·
sibly find time to answer it so soon. My time here will be
completely occupied in performing the various duties that devolve upon me as a student of theology—a candidate for that
holy office, under the weight of whose responsibilities a man
or an angel would sink, without the supports of God's grace.
Oh, I never before had such overwhelming views of that
sacred office! For an unworthy sinner like me, who have
been for more than twenty years a transgressor of God's
law; with a heart so vile, affections so earthly, faith so weak,
so much fear of the world and conformity to it, with so much
impurity in my best motives, and so much imperfection in

my best services,—in a word, so very a wretch in the sight of God, to think of speaking in his name! Oh, why does he not make the confounding challenge, 'Who hath required this at your hands?' He is a God of matchless condescension, to suffer such rebels against his government to live; to devise a plan of salvation; to come as the 'man of sorrows;' to redeem those that were under the law; to suffer in our name; to pay the debt we owed to that law; to blot out the hand writing against us; to come as the Holy Spirit; to raise us from death to life, from sin to grace; then to give us grace for grace, change our state hereafter from grace to glory, and then from glory to glory! Oh, it is compassion like a God, it is a theme too high for angels. And when the ransomed of the Lord are gathered in, it will be sounded in strains higher and nobler than ever rung from a seraph's lyre. Oh, my brother, we will weep together for our astonishing coldness and apathy; but we will rejoice together too, for such great and precious promises. We will try in God's strength to live more to his glory. We will think more and more of the scenes of Gethsemane and Calvary, and clinging more closely to the bloody tree, will cry to that Jesus who once hung thereon, but is now enthroned on high, to keep us from falling, and to present us at last as redeemed sinners, glorified before his Father and our Father, his God and our God."

TO Z. S., ESQ.

"*Princeton, Dec. 1st,* 1820.

" You once told me that I must not pass debtor and creditor with you on the scale of correspondence. I therefore write as often as I can make it convenient. My letter from Schenectady in September last must have miscarried; but my only regret is, that I have been deprived of the pleasure of your answers. When I call to mind the history of our friendship, I almost pant for that state of being when it will be consummated.

"My situation here is peculiarly pleasant, associated with about seventy young men, all preparing for that sacred office under the weight of whose responsibilities a man or an angel would sink without the support of God's rich grace. Oh, my dear friend, in your happiest moments, when you are in the exercise of a lively faith—when the distance between earth and heaven seems annihilated—when God is sensibly near, and you feel him yours, and tell him all your wants with the confidence and the fondness of a child, and are so filled and melted with his love that you feel your heaven be-gun,—oh then remember me, unworthy me. Pray that God would enable me to live to his glory; that he would arm me for the field of battle; make me, sinner as I am, a herald of the cross; that I may be enabled to consecrate every energy to his service, and be willing to sacrifice and suffer all things, if it be necessary, for him; to give myself exclusively to him, that I may live in him, and in death not dishonour him. Do not think that I have been disgusted with the world; no, it is God's world, and although fallen, it is not forsaken; though abased, it is not abandoned. I am too much attached to it; yet I feel its emptiness when com-pared with Jesus Christ. I desire to live above it, for other-wise it will constantly mar my peace and interrupt me in a divine life.

"God has been pleased to grant me some precious seasons lately. I confess that this does give me a disrelish for the world which I wish I could always feel. But if the world, and the flesh, and the adversary were overcome, where were the warfare? It is one of the articles of the new covenant 'that we walk by faith, not by sight;' so that although we may enjoy seasons when faith is almost lost in vision, yet in mercy to our frailty those seasons are short. Flesh would sink—a walk of faith is best adapted to our circumstances and our duties."

Sabbath, December 31*st*, 1820. This day brings with it many manifestations of the love and goodness of God. He has spared me almost through the events, and changes, and desolations of another year. Oh, that I could begin and end every year with a sabbath, and with a sacrament! To-day I hope to meet Jesus at his own table, and there, while I take and taste the symbols of his body and his blood, may I have such views of his fitness and fulness as I have never had before. Jesus, Master, grant me the preparation of the heart. May the world be left behind; may no thought be suffered to wander to improper objects; but do thou possess my heart and sway my affections.—I have taken another oath to be thine for ever. Oh, maintain thine empire in my heart, thou blessed Spirit, and carry on the work of sanctification. Subdue all the corruption of my nature. Take of the things of Christ, and show them unto me. Set thy seal upon my heart unto the day of redemption. Jesus, Master, let me fly to thy bosom; "hide me, oh my Saviour, hide me beneath the shadow of thy wing." The year is almost gone: many who commenced it with fair prospects of longevity, have been long sleeping beneath the clods of the valley. I have seen my friends sinking in the arms of death, and so read the loud admonition to be also ready. Oh, may I not forget the impressions made upon my mind by death-bed scenes. May I never again be attached to the world. May I keep the end of my short journey in sight; and when I face the king of terrors, wilt thou stand by me to be my support; and may I pillow my head, my sinking head, upon thy compassionate bosom, and sweetly sleep in thee!

During the last year I have seen a glorious revival of religion, in which hundreds began their immortal song. Oh, my Saviour, carry on thy cause in my heart and throughout the world.

Conversation this afternoon on the best method of closing the year. Many good remarks were made on the subject of humility, penitence, and new resolutions to live to God's glory. My Father in heaven, make me humble, penitent; and in thy strength may I live more to thy glory. May my loins be girt about with truth, and my lamp be trimmed and burning, so that I may always be ready for the coming of the Son of Man. Oh, wilt thou blot out the sins of the past year, before it shall be numbered with the years beyond the flood, before it shall bear off in its flight my uncancelled accounts to the day of judgment. Accept of my thanks-givings for the signal mercies of the past year, which have been more than I can name or number; and while I adore thee for the past, may I trust thee for the future, and thus launch forth into the awful uncertainties of the time to come. But whether I live, may I live to thee; or whether I die, may I die to thee; so that living or dying I may be thine. Grant it, Lord, for Christ's sake.

Saturday evening, January 6th, 1821. This evening almost completes one week of the new year. I have been already immersed in its cares and its duties. But in what-ever circumstances I may be placed, oh my Saviour, keep me near thee. I desire to live in thee and for thee. This is a most tempestuous night, and how many poor travellers are exposed to these wintry blasts, to this angry storm! Oh God, preserve them. Remember all the children of indi-gence in this inclement season. Shelter them from the storm, feed them and clothe them; especially feed them with the bread of life, and clothe them with a robe of righteous-ness. How should I praise the Lord for the comforts that surround me. Comfortable room and fire, lamp and closet. May my closet bear witness to my gratitude, first to God who is loading me with benefits, and next to those kind friends to whom, under Him, I am indebted for all the comforts that surround me. Oh, reward them for their faith and labour of love; and may my life be such as becomes the recipient of such distinguished mercies.

Sabbath morning, January 12th, 1821. Welcome, sweet day of rest; sweet pledge of rest on high. Oh, my soul, be awake to improve the sacred hours. Indulgent Father, thy goodness has been still manifested on my account during the past week, and I desire to praise thy name for any degree of deadness to the world and engagedness in thy service. Oh,-may I spend this sacred day as becomes an expectant of glory. Grant me fervour in devotion. Tune my heart to sing thy praise. Enable me to come near thee in communion, to draw large draughts from the wells of salvation; to eat of heavenly, spiritual manna, and acquire a disrelish for what the men of the world call pleasure. Oh, strengthen my faith. Wean me from the world. Grant me that peace, and joy, and confidence in Jesus, that will enable me to look on death with a tranquil gaze. May I often dwell on the closing scene of my life. Some of my dearest friends with whom I have often knelt around the domestic altar, had sweet converse of our common hopes and fears, have often mingled hearts and voices in songs of praise to thee, are this day swelling the anthems of eternity around thy throne. They are freed from sin, they worship thee no longer in temples made with hands, they no longer mingle tears of bitterness with the offerings, and sing thy praises with a faltering tongue. No, the temple is made without hands, tears are for ever wiped away, their songs know no discord and never end. No darkness comes across the soul. No intervening cloud to hide the face of Jesus. Oh, my Saviour, draw thine image on my heart. Make the lines thereof deep and broad, that I may know that I am thine.

Sabbath morning, Jan. 26th. Heard Dr. Miller from 1 Cor. xv. 55, "Oh death, where is thy sting?" His object was, first, to show that death has a sting; 2d, that Christ takes away the sting of death, which is sin. Oh, that I might habitually look upon death as having lost its sting. Mr. Perkins in the evening spoke of spiritual life and spiritual death from Eph. ii. 1: "And you hath he quickened who were dead in trespasses and sins."

Sabbath evening, Feb. 4th. Thus far the Lord has led me on, through dangers seen and unseen, by day and by night, at home and abroad. Surely I may say with the greatest propriety, "Goodness and mercy have followed me all the days of my life." God has led me by a way I knew not. Oh, what a mercy that the veil which conceals futurity is impenetrable. While God sheds light upon my immediate path, it is all I have need of, and even without that I can walk by faith. But he does cast light upon my goings, and the luminous path in which I now walk and rejoice, appeared once dark and gloomy; and while I adore my God for the past I will trust him for the future. One day only remains to me of twenty-four years. All have been crowned and crowded with the mercies of my heavenly Father. If I should or could count them, they are more in number than the sands. I do bless my kind, and tender, and bountiful Father, for the signal mercies of the past year, and especially for the lessons he has taught me of the world's emptiness, of life's uncertainty. How our brightest prospects may be blighted, our fondest hopes disappointed. The scene of every plan of happiness substantial must be laid beyond the grave. Oh, my God and Father, there wilt thou enable me to build my hopes where all is substantial and sure. Grant me more deadness to the world, and may I live in thee and to thee, and for thee alone. My heart is prone to search for some earthly idol, but do thou take possession of my heart, and reign without a rival there, and be the object of my warmest affections and my most intense desires.

"Come, Heaven, and fill my vast desires,
    My soul pursues the sovereign good;
She was all made of heavenly fires,
    Nor can she live on meaner food."

TO MR. H. D., OF BALLSTON, N. Y.

"Princeton, February 6th, 1821.

" My situation here is still very pleasant; health was never better, and on the whole I think I never enjoyed myself so well as it respects situation, prospects, employments, and spiritual exercises, as since I came here.

" But truly my whole life appears worse than a blank. I know of nothing that I have done for God. There is so much that is unholy in our purest motives, when we are engaged in the service of God, that it must at best be abominable to a being who sees and hates the very least sin.

" And oh, how much of our lives have run to waste; and should we be called suddenly to the bar of God, how could we expect to hear said of us, ' Well done, good and faithful servant?' When I think of this, I am impatient to finish my studies, and to be engaged, soul and body, in the service of the great Head of the church. But then I think the inquiry should rather be what is my duty here, where God has placed me, and not what would it be in other circumstances; and so I feel convinced, that to apply my mind diligently to my preparations for the gospel ministry is my present duty.

" Oh, what a resting place is the Rock of-ages! What a support is the arm of Omnipotence! What a master is the King of kings! What a prize is an immortal, unfading crown! And do we serve such a master, rest on such a foundation, expect such an inheritance? ' What manner of persons ought we to be!'

"There is a revival of religion about ten miles from this place, in Trenton, where thirty or forty are already hopeful subjects of it. But Princeton, highly favoured Princeton, is cold and stupid; the church is, I may say, asleep. God grant it may not be the sleep of death. I have just heard from Cayuga county, where my father lives. There, God is working wonders of mercy in the salvation of sinners. My letter stated, that 'the whole town seemed to be electrified with the Spirit of God. In some respects, the work is the most remarkable I have ever heard of since the days of the apostles. Sinners are made to tremble, and saints to rejoice.' "

February 22d. A day set apart for prayer and fasting, by the members of the seminary. Oh, how much need of humiliation before God! on account of the low state of religion in our own souls, the hardness of our hearts, the weakness of our faith, our earthly mindedness, our conformity to the world. Oh, may we not wish to appear unto men to fast; but wilt thou grant us what is the object of fasting— deep humility of heart, and a melting sense of our sins and short comings in every duty, and, in some, of our failure altogether. Oh, Redeemer of my soul, let the remaining part of my life be spent more to thy glory: Accept of my thanksgiving for any spiritual enjoyment, for any degree of deadness to the world. Carry on thy work in my soul, and make me a more ardent, fervent, Christian.

TO MR. H. D. OF BALLSTON, N. Y.

"*March 8th*, 1821.

"Your long and welcome letter came to hand on the morning of the 22d ultimo. I shall not attempt to tell you how much pleasure it afforded me. I did not really think you had forgotten me; but I felt lonely and forsaken, and often thought of other days and distant friends, and sighed ; and could not conjecture what could keep you so long silent; and so my fancy and my apprehensions put it at the worst, and my full heart, breathing out its melancholy, found partial relief. I look upon the friends of my heart as so many gifts from God, as such I love them, as such I make them a subject of my morning and my midnight prayers. In my thoughts by day, and in my dreams by night, I mingle in their dear society, and feel their warm and fond embrace. But when I wake, 'the vision is fled, mountains rise, and billows roll between us.' But it is well we have something always to remind us, what we all acknowledge, 'that this is not our rest.' We are so earthly, so fettered to the world, that even with all the providences and revelations of God, and all the hard-earned lessons of sad experience, and all the high hopes beyond the grave, we can scarce rise for a moment above this earth.

" But, dear brother, I hope your poor unworthy friend is learning, though slowly, to draw upon heaven and heavenly things, for his substantial comforts. Oh, I hope, and trust, I desire sincerely to bless and praise God, for weaning me, in some measure, from the world ; that he is enabling me to lay the scene of my plans of happiness beyond the swellings of Jordan; that every day seems to strengthen my resolutions to live for God, to God, and none other. I mention these things because you were so kind as to inquire about my spiritual affairs, and because I know you will rejoice with me in the goodness of God.

" My brother, I hope we know something of the communion of saints, and these are certainly antepasts of heavenly joy. We rejoice and weep together; we bear each other's burdens, share each other's joys; and our prayers mingle around the same throne. And what if we meet there next? Should such a thought make us sad? Should

3*

it start a solitary tear? No, no. There is Jesus waiting to receive us; the mansions are prepared, ' all things are ready.' There, is the church of the first-born; there, are our dear friends, who have died in the Lord, with whom we have often knelt around the domestic altar; with whom we have walked to the house of God, and surrounded the table of Christ's dying love ; with whom we have often held sweet converse about heavenly things, and wept over our coldness in the cause of Jesus. There, are no darkness and doubts; no bitter tears, no sins, no partings, no backslidings, but all is perfect love, perfect worship, perfect happiness there! Oh, is it possible? There, we shall wear immortal, starry crowns, and triumph in our Saviour's love for ever. Oh, who would shun the hour that cuts from earth, and fear to press the calm and peaceful pillow of the grave? Oh, God, make us fit and willing to live, and may we not live in vain; but may we perform our humble part in thy cause, and have grace to live to thy glory.

"It affords me satisfaction to think I am remembered when you make your nearest approaches to the throne of grace. Oh, continue to pray that I may have grace and strength to improve all the high privileges I enjoy, and that I may at last, in God's time, enter the holy ministry, armed with the whole armour of God, and that I may be an humble, but an undaunted, champion of the truth.

"Dear brother, I wish to exhort you, and yours, and all that love the Lord Jesus Christ, to be more engaged. We have not yet the spirit of the times; we want that zeal and devotedness that fired confessors and martyrs, and missionaries. Oh, for the zeal and the tongue and the wings of an angel, to herald the everlasting gospel round the world.

"If my health is spared, and circumstances unforeseen do not prevent, I hope to visit Ballston in October next. But that time is distant; thousands will sleep in death before it arrives, and we may be among the number. But let us live to God; and rest assured that all the circumstances of our lives and of our deaths will be regulated in the best possible way.

"Last evening the Rev. Mr. Ward, missionary from Serampore, in India, preached here. You know he is on a visit to this country to collect funds for the college at Serampore. He related many interesting facts of the mission, and of the prevailing superstitions of the Hindoos. The fact of his being an eye-witness gave his relations a peculiar interest, although I had read the statement before. To-day the Osage mission family is to pass through this village; so that missionaries from the extremities of the globe will meet in Christian fellowship, and sing and pray together."

March 9th. To-day the Osage mission family passed through Princeton. We met in the church, sang two hymns, and had two prayers; the first of which was offered by the Rev. Mr. Ward, missionary of Serampore. At the close of the service the mission family sang "Farewell my friends, we must be gone." The whole service was inexpressibly solemn. To see a family of nearly forty persons, devoted soul and body completely and actively to God, and actually on their way to the wilderness of the west, and to join in prayer with a dear missionary from the east, a distance of 17,000 miles—I trust it made the subject of missions seem real. Oh, God of grace, make it the means of exciting a missionary spirit. May the wretchedness of those that know not God lie continually upon our hearts, that we may cry without ceasing to God for the extension of the Redeemer's kingdom. May we all be willing and wishing to devote ourselves exclusively to God, to be used when, and how, and where he pleases. Verily, there is nothing worth living for

but to serve and glorify God.   Oh, God, I do desire to give myself away renewedly to thee.   Use me for thy glory.
  Sabbath, 18*th.*

> "Seasons and months and weeks and days
> Demand successive songs of praise."

I rejoice in the high privilege of uniting to-day with the worshippers around the throne in praising God on this Sabbath of ours, and this eternal Sabbath of theirs.   We will sing the song of redeeming love in Christ.   Oh, God, may my sinful heart not be a discordant string to join the grand chorus; but attune my heart and my voice for thy worship, and may I forget the world and the things of the world, and spend the sacred day alone with thee.

  March 25*th.*   During the last week I have been reading the lives of Samuel J. Mills and Henry Martyn, both eminently devoted to God, and who are to-day praising him around the throne in his immediate presence.   Oh, for some of that fervour that glowed so eminently in their bosoms. They counted not their lives dear; they acted nobly, consistently.   Fondly hope, I do feel something of the love they felt, and I pray God to grant me more.   I am sure there is nothing worth living for but to serve God.   That man is certainly happiest who lives alone for God.   It is my reasonable duty to devote myself a " living sacrifice" to God.   Oh, what an expression—to *live a dying life*, and to *die a living death for God*.   To deny myself and take up every cross and follow where my master leads, through good report and bad report; and by the assistance of his grace this I will do; this I am willing to do, if I can promote his glory and the good of souls.   It is but a little to lay down all I have, even my life, for Christ, which, in this age of the world, is scarcely possible.   How worse than criminal to withhold myself and all my time and power from God!

Oh, grant me grace to live to some purpose. To live for thee, to live for eternity. Come, Holy Spirit, take possession of my heart and sway all my affections, and make them holy.

April 1st, 1821. Communion Sabbath. Thanks everlasting be unto God for the institutions of his word, and for the blessed privileges which this delightful day brings with it. Oh, to be seated in the banqueting house of Zion's King, to sit at his table, to see the King in his beauty, to feel his love! We commemorate the death of the Friend of sinners, that death that purchased everlasting life for us.

> " With joy we tell the scoffing age,
>   He that was *dead* has left the tomb ;
> He lives above their utmost rage,
>   And we are waiting till he come."

We, yes I, even I, whose sins drove the nail, and pointed the spear ; I, who have lived far from God, who have been conformed to the world, a captive of Satan, and a willing captive, brought nigh by the blood of Christ. " Oh, to grace how great a debtor." Lord Jesus, bind my heart to thy throne, clothe me with thy righteousness, be all my salvation and desire.

TO MISS A. J.

" *April 25th*, 1821.

" Oh, I do love to come near, even to his seat, and call him ' Our Father,' yours and mine. He is kind, he has been always kind ; he has followed us with mercies ; he has filled our cup with blessings, and our souls with hopes of immortal life and glory. And shall we receive these good things at the hand of the Lord, and shall we shrink from his chastising hand? Especially, when we are sure that he chastises those whom he loves, that the ' rod is a branch from the tree of life,' and that it is in a Father's hand. Oh, no, let us kiss the rod; let us humble ourselves before God, implore his Spirit to sanctify all his dealings, and to assist us to live more to his glory while we live, be it longer or shorter, and to prepare us for that blessed world ' where the inha-bitants shall no more say I am sick.' Whither all our dear friends, who have died in the Lord, have gone; there, where sin and death can never enter; there, where the King of Heaven holds his court; where Jesus intercedes and reigns; where our ransomed souls shall be unclothed of this cum-brous clay, and expand and expatiate, amid all the unclouded splendours, and the unutterable glories of the New Jerusa-lem; there to see God without a veil, to bow down before him; to adore, with cherubim and seraphim; to catch the notes of Abel, and Adam, and Enoch, some of the first re-deemed sinners that ever passed from earth to heaven, and who have been stretching onward and onward, in their ca-reer of rapture, for almost six thousand years; there, to re-view our pilgrimage below; to know that all the storms are past, that all our tears are dried up for ever; to be filled with all the fulness of God; to see eternity opening before us, an endless range of progressive blessedness, and no pos-sibility of a change but from glory to glory! Oh; God of grace and glory, strengthen these desires after a holy heaven! How poor is human language to express the views which, even here, we are permitted to entertain of the society and employments and enjoyments of heaven.

"I did not think of saying half so much. You will not think it ostentation. I am ashamed that my heart is so hard and cold; but when I meditate on this heavenly theme, I seem to breathe another air. My soul struggles under con-ceptions altogether unutterable. Oh, to be an angel, to have the powers and the harp of an angel, when we dwell on this theme of angels, this subject of eternal transport!

'When Gabriel speaks these mighty things,
He tunes and summons all his strings.' "

April 8th. News from the Sandwich Islands. Blessed be God for what he has done by the might of his own arm. That at a blow he has crushed the system of their idolatry and opened the way for the gospel of God our Saviour. That through the long, long wastes of waters and of wilderness that lie between us and our heathen brethren there, the cry is heard, "come over and help us." Oh, may it not be heard in vain.. Oh, Head of the church, work wonders to-day in Zion.

TO THE SAME.

"*April* —, 1821.

" But what a privilege to accompany the child of God in the last day's journeyings of his earthly pilgrimage; to mark the progress of disease; to see the tenement of clay dissolve; to mark the imprisoned blood-bought spirit struggling to be free; to see the value of religion; to learn the insignificance of the world—these are some of the privileges you were permitted to enjoy at the bed-side of your much-loved uncle.

" I have often told you, the most profitable scenes I have ever beheld, have been death-bed scenes. My soul would ever hold them in warm remembrance. They come across my mind with all the power of a charm; and exert, I trust, a holy, heavenly influence. They do not make me sad, but they make me solemn. They check the ardour of youthful enterprize, and assist me when 1 wish to pause and commune with my own heart, and to think of the closing scene of life, of the narrow house, and of heaven beyond it.

" You say, you read to your uncle, as he is able to bear it. If you have not read the Obituary of Mrs. Poor, as contained in the Missionary Herald for April, I wish you would obtain it. It will refresh your soul; and it is peculiarly appropriate to such a case as your uncle's. ' Oh, how she longed to have her passport sealed and be released.'

" My dear A., what is the world? It groans under its Maker's curse. It is reserved unto fire. It is not our rest, it is ' polluted.' It will be burnt up; the decree has gone forth from the throne of God, . ' Let us arise and depart,' quit our hold upon the world, and lay hold on the hope set before us. Let us cling to Jesus ; there, is safety no where else in the whole universe of God. And while we hope in Christ, and feel our feet firmly placed upon the Rock of Ages, let us strive, by our prayers, precepts and example, to influence those whose feet stand on slippery places to beware! In our several spheres, and in various ways, we may be useful to the church of Christ, in promoting the salvation of our fellow creatures ; and when we come to lie on a bed of death, and our career of activity is ended, the recollection of earnest, honest endeavours to do good will be sweet to our minds, while we lie in calm expectation of our departure.

" And in anticipation of that solemn, awful hour, let us be more diligent; let us give all diligence to have our work done, and well done ; to be sure that our peace is made with God, our heaven secure ; for clouds and darkness will be unutterably dreadful in the ' swellings of Jordan.' "

May 4th, 1821. Praised be God that my life has been spared and my health and comforts continued until now. Thanks be unto his holy name for any degree of deadness to the world, and for any sense of his presence, for any increasing love to him, for any deeper and more humbling views of my heart's corruptions, for any greater sense of my unworthiness, weakness, and complete, entire dependence. Oh, God, carry on thy work in my soul. Search me and try me, cleanse my heart of all its abominations, cleanse it and claim it, oh, Holy Spirit, and make it thine abode. How dare I ask it? Pardon my presumption; I ask it in my Saviour's name.

> "Unworthy dwelling, glorious guest,
> Favour astonishing, divine."

May I have an increasing love for thee, thou fairest among ten thousand. May I obey thy precepts, imitate thy illustrious example, bear thine image on my heart, and may I remain in time and through eternity a monument of the efficacy of thy Gospel and a trophy of thy victorious grace. Carry on thy cause in every part of the world. Employ me to act some humble part in this cause. Saviour of sinners, use me for thy glory.

May 13*th.* The last Sabbath of the session. It seems scarcely possible that more than half the year has passed since I became a member of the seminary. Verily, "time rolls its ceaseless course," and I am insensibly, though rapidly, borne along upon its wave. How it steals away the moments of my life. How death is posting on.

> "Oh let me catch the transient hour,
> Improve each moment as it flies."

Every day may I feel that I am acting for eternity, and every day may I perform some business for eternity. "So teach me to number my days, that I may apply my heart unto wisdom." Grant me the wisdom that comes from thee.

June 3*d.* Three weeks have passed since I have made any record of thy goodness. But how strikingly have those weeks been marked with thy goodness. I trust I have felt gratitude though my pen has failed to record it. I have long endeavoured to commit my way unto thee, to ask counsel of thee, and not to lean to my own understanding. I

4

have been enabled to trust in thee, and now, blessed be thy name, thou hast fulfilled thy promise and given me the desire of my heart. Oh, grant me thy blessing in the enjoyment of thy gifts; may I never forget the source of all my comforts, and may the richest, tenderest mercies, instead of weaning my affections from thee by usurping thy place in my heart, lead me constantly to love thee more and serve thee better. May I feel the increasing obligations which thy repeated and diversified favours involve, and henceforth may I feel that I am doubly thine. Grant me more of thy love, more love for souls, more zeal for thy cause, more deadness to the world, more entire, sincere devotedness to thy cause and kingdom.

June 24th. Still thy mercies are repeated with every moment of my life. In my visit to New York thy goodness has followed me at every step, and notwithstanding one disappointment, unpleasant in itself, but which already works for my good, every occurrence is calculated to fill me with gratitude and humility. Oh, God, grant me humility. Let not the honest but imprudent remarks of my friends make me vain, or give me occasion to think of myself more highly than I ought to think. May all my strength and influence be consecrated to thy cause. May I lie low at the foot of the cross. May I never desire the honour that comes from men. Deliver me from a man-pleasing, a man-fearing, and world-adoring spirit; but, oh, wilt thou purify my heart and my motives, and enable me to perform some humble part in thy cause. May I live nearer to thee, be more dead to the world, and be making constant advances in a divine life, becoming more and more devoted to thee and thy cause, more heavenly minded.

" *May* 15*th*, 1821.

" To-day our long session ends, and I can assure you I am glad of an opportunity of relaxation. I wish I could go to Ballston, and then ride to Granville, to spend part of my time where God is pouring out his Spirit. I heard of the revival when I was in New York about three weeks ago. Dr. M'Auley told me it had commenced powerfully. About ten days since I received a letter from R. Shepherd, Esq. giving me further particulars.

" You will learn all the news from this region from the brethren whom you will probably see in the course of the vacation. I expect to leave the seminary only for a short time, just to recruit my strength, and then to return to my studies. There is so much before me to learn, and the time is so short, that there is really not a moment to spare.

I wish to be remembered particularly to all my friends. I should be happy to see them this vacation but cannot. I hope to visit you in October. I long since learned a little ' ode to disappointment,' which has often since been the best language in which my feelings could be expressed. You will see it in the first volume of Kirk White's Remains. You know, my brother, how to be grateful for afflictions.

> ' Trials make the promise sweet,
>   Trials give new life to prayer;
> Trials bring me to his feet,
>   Lay me low, and keep me there.'

" Blessed be God, tribulation is a part of the legacy our Saviour has left us. Oh, may we improve them, and all our numerous blessings; and live more to his glory."

TO MISS A. J. OF TRENTON, N. J.*

"*Philadelphia, May 18th, 1821.*

" MY DEAR A—,

" You will doubtless be surprised to receive a letter from me so soon, and especially when I have the pleasing prospect of seeing you in town in a few days. But I will not attempt an apology. I regretted much that I came so early to town, since there will be nothing that I am anxious to hear or see in the Assembly until Monday. I presented the letter your mother was so kind to give me to Mr. Henry, but I have not yet become acquainted with the family."

*   *   *   *   *

" True, genuine affection, must always be founded upon merit, solid merit, and is therefore as immutable as the principle on which it depends. Circumstances may change, summer friends may fail, the world may frown—but distance of place, nor lapse of time, nor change of circumstances, can break the tie that binds heart to heart, when human friendships are sanctified by religion.

" But how important that we should be cultivating more and more the spirit of the gospel, and be endeavouring to live more and more to God. Oh, should any earthly object come between our hearts and Jesus, he would remove it in mercy to our souls. Let our high ambition be to lie at the feet of Jesus. Let our most ardent wishes be to promote his glory. And let us endeavour to do every thing with a reference to eternity."

* This letter, and many of those which follow in this chapter, was addressed to Miss Anna Jackson, of Trenton, who afterwards became his wife.

TO THE SAME.

" Princeton, June 1st, 1821.

" Last evening I went to the office after ten o'clock for your letter, just exactly in time to be caught in a tremendous shower, that already blackened all the heavens when I left the house. The earth was shaking with its thunders, and my path was rendered luminous by its lightning. You may perhaps think me rather romantic, but I can assure you it was a *stormy reality* before I reached Dr. Alexander's : I had engaged to spend the night there."   *   *   *

" How much danger that our ' dearest joys and nearest friends' will usurp the place that Christ Jesus ought to hold in our affections. Let us guard against it and pray against it, and by cultivating a keener relish for spiritual enjoyments become more and more dead to the world. Our happiness depends on the presence and favour of God, whether we wish it or not. No matter whether we soar in honour or sink in disgrace—no matter whether we roll in affluence or beg our morsel from door to door, the presence of God alone can make us happy. And were I called on for a choice of contrasted miseries, I would much rather endure the misery of the peasant than that of the prince. The wretchedness of the cottage is far more tolerable than the wretchedness of courts. And so in proportion I would say of all the different grades in life and classes of society.

' When winds the mountain oak assail,
  And lay its glories waste,
Content may slumber in the vale,
  Unconscious of the blast.'

" I do not know when I can see you, but intend to before I go to New York. Thanks to your mother for the interest she takes in my health. I hope Miss B. is improving in health, and especially that she may experience the tenderness and skill of the Physician of souls. Let us live nearer to God and more for his glory. Let us love our Saviour more, and give ourselves no rest in his absence—no joy until he return to bless and cheer our hearts by the light of his countenance. Into his hands I commit you. May you be blessed indeed. Live near to him and be happy."

TO THE SAME.

"*New York, June 14th,* 1821.

————" Arrived here at ten o'clock this morning. Dr. Neil, of Philadelphia, one of the passengers.

" Oh, let us cultivate more intercourse with heaven, and endeavour to feel that our happiness depends on God's presence alone, even when we are surrounded by our dearest friends. By what a ' precarious tenure' we hold them ! Let us try to have our conversation in heaven, even while we dwell upon the earth, and as much as possible hold ourselves loose from the world. ' Lean not on earth.' Oh, how important the admonition. The freshest rose may wither on its stem even before our eyes, and always has its thorns; the brightest morning may conceal a thunderbolt; and the stateliest oak is most in danger of being riven by the lightning. Oh, let our highest, noblest, fondest hopes be fixed on God, and they will never disappoint us.

" I saw brother Chester, but he did not engage to attend the meeting on Friday evening at your house. Possibly some other members of the seminary may be there. I expect to hear Mr. Somerville speak this afternoon in behalf of the society for promoting the gospel among seamen."

"*New York, June* 16*th*, 1821.

———— " May the present sabbath bring rest, and joy, and peace, and strength to my soul. I expect to sit again at the table of our dying, risen, reigning Redeemer, in Dr. Romeyn's church. Oh, that I may see the King in his beauty, and be feasted with the provisions of his house. How much we stand in need of heavenly food. We are daily careful to provide for the body, but how our souls famish for the bread of life. What do we more than others? What are we more than others? And then to think what we ought to be. We, upon whom God has lavished so many favours; we, whom his providence has lately so tenderly affected; we, who profess to link our earthly career with the cause of Christ, with the glory of God; we, who expect to spend our lives and to yield up our breath in the promotion of Zion's interests, and for the honour of Zion's King,—oh, what manner of persons ought we to be? Let us, in the strength of Jesus, break off our fetters, and rise above the world, and live nobly independent of its opinions and practices. Whatever others do let us serve the Lord, with our life, our health, our comforts, our influence, with all our talents, and with all our strength. Wherever we are, let the light of our godly example shine. Let us improve every opportunity of visiting the chamber of sickness, of kneeling around the bed of the dying, of instructing the ignorant, of reclaiming the wanderer, and of soothing the sufferer.

" While thus active in the cause of Christ, and endeavouring to promote the everlasting welfare of others, let us not neglect our own souls. Oh, let us dig deep, and be firmly established on the Rock of ages. Let us cultivate more and more communion with God, and learn the temper and disposition of the heavens. Then we can enter with confidence on the uncertainties of life, assured that God will do all things well. Then death will only interrupt our songs for a night, and we shall resume them with our immortal powers in a brighter world, on that unchanging morning that ushers in an everlasting day. Oh, to-day may we mingle our notes with the notes of cherubim and seraphim, and with all the armies of light, and all our friends who have died in the Lord, around God's throne. May we catch something of their ardour, and zeal, and love, and may we have large antepasts of heavenly joy, and drink and refresh our souls with the river of life that flows from the throne of God."

TO THE SAME.

" *Princeton, July 2d,* 1821.

" You are aware, my dear A., that I received your letter directed to New York; it came to hand on Thursday morning.—We have not really commenced business yet, as this is the first Monday of the month; and as Wednesday will be the anniversary of our country's independence, we shall not do much until Thursday. I should go to Allentown and Trenton, Tuesday evening and Wednesday, were it not for an essay that calls imperiously for my attention.

" My health has improved since my return. I sincerely think, as far as tranquillity of mind is concerned, I have never been so well situated for application. Oh, to be assured, (nay, I trust you are already assured,) and know, by happy experience, that there is an unutterable sweetness in feeling that you are in the hands of God, an omnipresent, omnipotent God; and that although he holds up the planets and measures eternity, yet his arm never sinks down exhansted, but directs and guards the meanest insect that crawls upon his footstool. This God is our God, and we will praise him; we will devote ourselves to his service, and he will be our guide even unto death.

"What is fortune, and what is fame, when placed in the scale against the Christian's duties, hopes, and prospects! How affecting, to see beings upon whose brow are drawn traces of a mortal and an immortal nature, bestowing all their thoughts and wishes upon trifles of a day, and making no provision for eternity!

"If we differ from such, it is by the grace of God we are what we are. Let us manifest sincere gratitude to God for his goodness to us, by endeavouring to persuade others to become partakers of the same goodness and abounding grace.

"In attempting to live more to the glory of God, we shall do well to maintain. an holy, hourly watchfulness over our thoughts and affections. By thinking more of heaven and heavenly things, and by spending more time in self-examination and prayer, we shall, by the blessing of God our Father, cultivate more of a holy, heavenly frame. Earth and earthly things will sink in our estimation, and communications of heavenly joy and peace, frequent and abundant, will flow into our souls, that will nourish them and invigorate them for enduring all the trials of life, and at last for enduring and enjoying the unveiled face of Him whom mortal eye hath not seen.

"I shall not finish my sheet until after the Missionary Society meets this afternoon, as there may be some interesting intelligence of battles fought and victories won for King Immanuel.

"P. M., 4 o'clock.—There has been less intelligence than I expected, and the most of it you have heard. One circumstance of a revival that commenced at a wedding, in a Baptist church, and resulted in the conversion of several of the guests. Brother H. Pratt returned while we were in the

Society, and gave a few interesting facts respecting his missionary labours this past vacation; and his brother gave me some good news respecting Connecticut.

"The United Foreign Missionary Society has lately been requested to find two missionaries, to go out with a colony of two hundred or three hundred persons, at the expense and under the protection of government, to settle at the mouth of Columbia, river, that empties into the Pacific, in latitude about 46° north; and to be sent out in the course of next year. And the Society itself wishes to send a missionary to take charge of the mission among the Seneca Indians, near Buffalo village, New York. Oh, this missionary cause is a glorious cause, it is the cause of Christ, it will prevail. The earth shall be filled with the knowledge of the Lord, for his mouth hath spoken it. Let us think, and pray, and then we shall feel more on the subject; and wherever in the church of Christ we may spend our days, let us be missionaries in earnest, determined to fight and to fall in our Master's cause.

"You said in one of your letters that I appear to have no inward conflicts. You are mistaken. I only have not spoken of them. I may tell you hereafter some, to convince you that your trials are by no means peculiar."

TO THE SAME.

"*July 12th*, 1821.

———— "I wished to spend an hour with you last Sabbath evening. I had a delightful day, and no doubt my enjoyment was heightened by the thought that you were seated at the table of the Lord, even admitted into the banqueting-house of the King of kings. My wicked heart, hardened by more than twenty years' transgression, was in some measure softened; and, with an eye of faith, I trust I beheld our Saviour, looking down in all the tenderness of suffering sympathy, and in all the ardour of his unchanging love, pitying our weakness, healing our backslidings, and in his own name presenting our petitions at the throne of his Father and our Father, his God and our God.   The language of my heart was,

> ‘Begone for ever mortal things,
> Thou mighty molehill earth, farewell.’

Oh, the bliss of that moment, when we are enabled to rise above the things of time, and mounting upward in communion, can leave the mists, clouds, and storms below, and breathe the atmosphere of heaven! But alas, one short hour will often plunge us in gloom again.   Yet notwithstanding my unfaithfulness, the week thus far has been a pleasant one.   Oh, to love God more and serve him better!   I hope you are walking in the light of his countenance, and that in the multitude of your thoughts his comforts are the delight of your soul.

“I do not know when it will be in my power to see you. My health is not good; that is to say, I feel an unpleasant weakness when the days are warm and duties arduous; but you need not apprehend illness when I am silent.   I shall always indulge the melancholy, painful pleasure, of telling you all my sorrows and my joys; and let our intercourse be such that the review of it will be sweet, and will mingle with the anguish that kneels at the grave the glorious hope that triumphs in the resurrection.   My warmest, highest esteem for Mrs. H.   I am glad you can beguile for her many a lonely hour.   Never indulge a melancholy that cankers every comfort, but exhort her also to stay herself on God.”

July 22*d.*   Still the goodness of God is continued as the moments of my life; how many blessings he crowds into my cup!   What do I deserve, and what do I want?   Surely I deserve nothing but his displeasure and his unmingled wrath; and as for my wants, I can almost say I want nothing but gratitude for his unnumbered mercies. I long for more love, more zeal, more entire devotedness of heart to God. With temporal comforts my cup runneth over, but oh how much leanness in my soul. How little of my time do I enjoy the sensible presence of God, and that burning zeal for his honour and his cause which I so much desire. And I will praise him, that he ever permits me to call him mine. I will rejoice, that he affords me any evidence that I have been born again, and grants me so many kind expressions of his everlasting love. Oh, my soul, in his strength march humbly but boldly on. I must walk by faith; it is my heavenly Father's will. And if he is pleased to afford me some occasional, transient glimpses of his face, I should not murmur, but adore. Oh, blessed Jesus, throw around me thine everlasting arms, and they will secure me from all the ills of life and fears of death. Oh, Holy Spirit, be pleased to take up thine abode in my heart, and sway all my affections, and wean them from the world. I do feel grateful for diseases, and infirmities, and providences, which admonish me to set my house in order, for death may be near, and for faith which points to a better, brighter world.

TO MR. H. D., OF BALLSTON, N. Y.

"*August* 17*th*, 1821.

"I received yours by Mr. G., and should have written before this time, had I not supposed you were on your visit to Beverly. I could not suppress the sympathetic tear, when I learned the cause of your journey. But the first thought, 'it is the Lord, let him do what seemeth him good,' silenced every murmur. Oh, our heavenly Father is so kind, he mingles so much mercy with the cup of sorrow, that we can scarce taste its bitterness.

"I did hope you might be induced to write me while on your journey, but I am aware that the fatigue and necessary confusion of travelling unfits one for writing. I hope by this time you have returned, with rich experience of the goodness and the sparing, healing mercy of God. We have a safe retreat and a quiet resting place beneath the spreadings of the covenant of grace, to lean on the bosom of our Saviour, to cast all our cares upon him, to commit our dearest, mortal and immortal concerns to his management. Oh, what a blessed privilege! And then to call him our Saviour, in all his fulness! To feel the eternal Spirit influencing our lives and sanctifying our natures, dwelling in our sinful hearts— to call God our Father, with the confidence, and affection, and humility of a child,—oh, these are some of the richest blessings of the new covenant, earnests of coming glory.

" I know I am addressing one who can understand me, one who is by no means a stranger to these exercises ; whose heart still holds in warm remembrance many blessed seasons when the rock within seemed to be completely melted, and to pour itself out like water; when the sweet tears of penitence could flow ; when the soul seemed to rise above the fogs, and clouds, and storms of life, and to breathe the air of paradise. Surely such a one will not, cannot murmur at the afflictive hand of God. It is a blessed thing that we are admonished of our frailty ; to feel the body, a frail tenement of a rebellious soul, tottering to fall; to feel pains, and diseases, and infirmities, pointing us to a better world, and warning us to ' set our house in order;' to be called by the death of friends to quit our hold upon the world, and to be warned by the disappointment of our expectations and the prostration of our hopes, that this is not our home, and thus to be induced to lay up provision for passing over Jordan ; to cultivate the disposition of the heavenly inhabitants ; to learn the song of Moses and the Lamb, and have our hearts and voices tuned to join that concert ; to plume, and spread, and try our pinions, in preparation for our heavenward flight

5

—these, these are our blessings and our privileges.   Let us listen to the voice that invites us home to glory.

"Excuse me for running on so long at random; I was not aware how much of my sheet I had occupied; and please take a hint from it to write on at random long enough to fill your paper.   I think the excellence of letter-writing is to imagine we are in the society of our friends, and addressing them orally.   And now and then I am so fortunate as to forget for some time to mail a letter, feeling that I have communicated all I have to say to my friend.

"The weather is extremely warm; the thermometer at 92° and 94° for several days.   My health fails during the warm season, as usual.   Were it near the end of our session, I would visit Ballston Spa for a few weeks.   But our studies are very important, and besides, fortunately, there is one other impediment of a serious nature.   However, I hope to see you all in health and happiness by the first of October, or before; and though I may be utterly unable to liquidate any debt, yet I will endeavour to increase none but that of gratitude.   My kindest love to Mrs. D. and all friends, as though named.   May all the blessings of the new covenant be yours; and may Jesus, Jehovah, encircle you both and all in his everlasting arms."

TO MISS A. J., OF TRENTON, N. J.

"*August* 18*th*, 1821.

———— "May I never think so much of the creature that God will see fit to remove it, to bring my affections to himself.   Oh, that our esteem for each other, as it rises and strengthens, may become more and more sanctified.   That we may keep constantly in view the object of our being, not to live, and love, and enjoy domestic bliss, but to glorify God, to live for God and to him, to devote ourselves to the gospel of Christ Jesus, and through all the toils, hardships, poverty and persecutions we may meet in our course, we must press onward, fighting to fall, and falling to conquer. Study your own heart in the light of God's word; cultivate more and more intercourse with heaven; study the precepts, promises, doctrines of the Bible, and by all the means in your power endeavour to prepare yourself to become the wife of one who hopes and determines to know nothing but Jesus Christ and him crucified; who hopes to follow Jesus through good and bad report; and who, drawing the sword to fight the battles of the Lord, must throw away the scabbard and die on the field. I trust you will be the means of strengthening my hands, of encouraging my heart, of trimming the lamp of domestic piety, of dividing the sorrows and increasing the joys of life. See 1 Thess. v. 16—23."

September. The same unvaried course of blessings attend me every step. God is good to me, who deserve no good at his hand. Oh, were he as unmindful of me as I often am of him, how soon should I fall and die! The throbbing heart, the heaving lungs, would cease to move; the crimson fluid would freeze in my veins; all the functions of life would at once be suspended, and this curious, complicated, frail machine fall to ruin. And on a large scale of observation, were the nice adjustment of all the elements of the atmosphere to be neglected, how fatal to animal life! Were the degrees of heat in summer or cold in winter less nicely arranged and apportioned, how miserable would they render the inhabitants of the earth. Should he neglect, suspend, or abrogate the laws by which the universe is governed, continents would be scorched or deluged, systems would be at once dismembered.

> " Earth would, unbalanced, from her orbit fly,
> Planets and suns run lawless through the sky,
> And ruling angels from their seats be hurl'd,
> Being on being wreck'd, and world on world."

But God reigns over all; he made all by his power; governs all by his providence; inspects it at a glance, and can
crush it at a word.   But he overlooks not the meanest creature that crawls upon the earth; and he upholds alike, by
his almighty power, the ephemera of a summer's morning
and the cherubim around his throne.   Oh God, how good
art thou!   I am not overlooked nor forgotten, but all my
wants are supplied, my cup is filled with blessings, my days
are crowned with loving kindnesses.   Oh, add to all thy
other gifts a grateful heart: that must come from thee.
Enable me to believe on the Lord Jesus Christ, through
whom all these blessings are conferred; and may he be indeed my Saviour.   Oh, destroy the power of my indwelling
corruptions, and sanctify my nature, and be my covenant-
keeping God.

TO MISS A. J., OF TRENTON, N. J.

" *September* 3d, 1821.

" It storms most tremendously; the rain beats against my
window so that I can scarcely think of any thing.—All the
elements of nature are God's agents; heaven, earth and hell
are distinct provinces of his empire; and if he is our Father
and our Friend, what have we to fear?

" Yesterday was a profitable Sabbath to my soul.   I have
had much calmness and peace in believing, and the experience of every day strengthens my conviction, that the more
we draw our happiness from heavenly fountains, the richer
and the more constant and abundant will be our supply.
God can make his creatures happy, and he alone.   Lodge
me in the darkest corner of the earth, on the loneliest island
of the sea; tear away every thing that is dear to the human
heart, and break off all the tenderest ligaments of the soul,
I can be happy in God, ' in whose presence is fulness of joy,
and at whose right hand are pleasures for ever more!' And

yet I can relish the society of those I love. Let us lay the scene of all our schemes of happiness beyond the swellings of Jordan, beyond its farthest surge-washed shore. In that happy land where storms never beat, chilling winds never blow, disease never spreads its ravages, distance never separates beings closely entwined, where prospects are never blasted. No intervening cloud hides the face of Jesus, but all is peace, and joy, and heaven, and immortality.

" May we be as peculiarly pious as we are peculiarly privileged ; and whether we are to live long or short lives, fill stations of eminent usefulness or to sink down into insignificance, let us cling to the cross of Jesus, cast our anchor within the vale, and we shall outride all the storms of life and make the port of peace.

" Amid this elemental strife how many miserable beings may be struggling for life upon the wave, but the struggle soon is over—the mountain billow dashes over them and they are seen no more. Oh God, have mercy on the beings thou hast made, especially those upon the mighty deep. And may those ' whose home is on the mountain wave,' and who see so many of thy wonders in the mighty waters, become thine in the covenant of grace.

" What are you reading? wish you could commit Practical Piety to memory."

TO MRS. J., OF TRENTON, N. J.

" Princeton, Sept. 8th, 1821.

" I take this opportunity of acknowledging the receipt of your kind, affectionate letter by Mr. H. It afforded me much pleasure, although at that time I was expecting a line from another hand.

" I sincerely thank you for all the important hints and kind feelings your letter contained. And I hope I shall profit by the one, and never become undeserving of the other.

5*

" Accustomed as I have been to watch the leadings of a kind providence from my very childhood, and sometimes enabled to feel the sweet meltings of gratitude to the God of all my mercies, I cannot describe the sensations of my heart when recollecting my first introduction to your family, and especially when I thought I had found in its bosom that friend for whom I oft had prayed, and in regard to whom the confidence of my soul for years has been ' Jehovah Jireh,' the Lord will provide.

" God be praised for all his goodness, and may the lives that he has made his care be devoted entirely to him. We are young adventurers, ere long to enter (should our lives be spared) on the uncertain, tempestuous sea of active life. Oh, to begin aright! It is the desire of my soul that Jesus Christ might reign in us and around us, over all our feelings and affections, all our plans and projects, over our whole lives; and that he would enable us to glorify him in death, and finally receive us to himself, there to recognise and consummate that friendship in the heavens which in his providence, and under his approbation, I trust we have been permitted to commence on earth.

" I received the letter you mailed on Wednesday about ten o'clock the same evening.

" Our session is drawing to a close, and we are reviewing for examination, two weeks from Monday next. My health is good, and I never hailed the approach of autumn with more pleasure. The flight of time always associates melancholy ideas. Oh, to be always ready for the close of life, that death may not surprise us.

" May God bless you abundantly, and all that are dear to you."

TO MISS A. J., OF TRENTON, N. J.

"*New York, Sept.* 29*th*, 1821.

" You will receive this on the morning of the holy Sabbath. Oh, that your soul may have much peace in God,
and may be filled with the strong consolations of the gospel.
I expect to spend the Sabbath here. God grant it may indeed be a Sabbath. Oh, how important to keep up intercourse with heaven.

" On Thursday evening I attended Dr. Spring's lecture.
He spoke upon the subject of death, from these words, ' Death
hath passed upon all men, for that all have sinned.' He had
just seen the remains of a man committed to the earth who
only twenty-four hours before was in the vigour of life and
health. The same evening two cases of the yellow fever
had been reported ; and with all these circumstances to affect
the mind, he asked the solemn question, ' Are you prepared
to die?' a question that ought to be settled before we sleep,
for our sleep may be the sleep of death, the sleep of ages.

" Oh, how fast the population of the earth is changing—
how fast the king of terrors carries on the work of desolation ! How important to be always ready, since at such an
hour as we think not the Son of Man may come."

TO Z. S., ESQ.

" *Philadelphia, Nov.* 4*th*, 1821.

" I am now spending a few days of relaxation in this city,
before the beginning of our winter session, and it affords me
the opportunity of resuming my correspondence with you.

" It is a relief to suspend the routine of even important
duties, and hold intercourse with those we love, and whom
we hope, when the changes of life are past and its duties
done, to meet in heaven and spend an everlasting Sabbath.
It will surely make our heaven the sweeter to enter upon its

glories after having struggled with temptation and our spiritual foes, and with the duties of a life of active toil in the cause of our Redeemer.

"You have often mentioned, in conversation and in your communications, your dissatisfaction with the active duties of your profession, even with much of the necessary intercourse with men of the world. I am becoming more and more convinced that we can carry our religion into every situation in life, and into all our official duties. No doubt we live far below our privileges, and are ourselves the means of beclouding our sky and darkening our path. Oh, when shall we learn to live near to God, and maintain a constant, holy watchfulness, lest we should grieve away the Holy Spirit by which we are sanctified? It seems almost a year since I heard from you last. How is your family? Does God continue to shed his rich spiritual blessings around you with an unsparing hand? Is he giving you, now and then, a glimpse of the promised land, refreshing you by a breeze of the air of Paradise? Does your love to God flow in a deeper, broader channel, and in a more pure, rapid and constant stream? Oh, do you not long to climb the everlasting hills, and there stand above this atmosphere of death, and look down, with gratitude to your Deliverer, and with joy for your deliverance, upon the world of sin and suffering, of darkness and storms you have left behind you, and upward to an endless career of glory, of which, in this narrow vestibule of our existence, we can form no conception? Well, the hour draws nigh, the journey shortens, the conflict will ere long be over, the grave—the home of ages—will surrender up its tenantry of dust, and the glorified body and the purified ransomed spirit will enter on the bliss of heaven. But, Oh! to be found in the attitude of faithful servants when our Lord shall come. To have done something for God, something for souls, something for the Redeemer's kingdom, and then our ephemeral existence will not be spent in vain.

"I hope to hear from you soon. Have your sons given up their studies for the ministry? I wish F. was prepared to come to this seminary."

November 11th, 1821. After an interval of several weeks I am again permitted to return to this beloved institution with some sweet sense of God's goodness. He has made my life his care. He has lengthened my span, filled my cup with blessings, given me kind friends, and profitable enemies, to confer favours which the partiality or the tenderness of my friends prevent them from conferring. Above all, he has given me a Bible which is filled with the record of a Saviour's love, and permitted me to hope that that Saviour is mine; and all this for what? That my final condemnation may be aggravated, and that I should become doubly a reprobate by sinning against all these mercies? I cannot think so, and yet it may be. Capernaum was exalted high by privileges and cast down to hell for abusing them.

"Jesus, thou Son of David, have mercy on me." Make me wise unto salvation.

TO MR. H. D. OF BALLSTON, N. Y.

"Princeton, Nov. 20th, 1821.

"I have been unable, ever since my return from Ballston, to find a moment to devote to you. But this afternoon I studied myself into so violent a head-ache, that I feel it my duty to stay out of recitation, and shall have to beg your pardon for employing the exhausted energies of my mind and body to discharge the duties and the delights of friendship.

"As for my general health, it was never better than at present, and my head-ache is only the temporary effect of

rather too close application.   Indeed it is a season of unusual health in the seminary.   Your acquaintances and
friends are all well, and all are pursuing the arduous, though
interesting and important studies which, by the blessing of
our heavenly Father, will qualify them to preach the everlasting Gospel of God our Saviour.   My studies are more
pressing, as well as more important than they were last
year.   But, 'I can do all things through Christ strengthening me.'   Oh, that every thought, and every faculty of
my nature, may bear upon it, ' *Holiness to the Lord.*'   It affords me much comfort and encouragement to know I have
so many praying friends.

"If my health be spared I do not now expect to visit you
again until I have finished my studies.   And before that
time, you, and all that are dear to you, may have entered
into rest.   Oh, what a changing, fleeting, dying world.   A
few days ago we heard of the death of one of our brethren,
(M. Searle), in Indiana.   This morning, by the Recorder,
we have heard of Mr. Newell's* death, and also Mrs. Poor's,
both useful in their different stations, and in their proper
spheres.   But God is on the throne.   The cause of missions
is his cause.   It will prosper.   Oh, pray that he would raise
up more missionaries, that he would pour out the spirit of
missions upon our churches, and that the full flood-tide of
salvation might bear off upon its waves the ignorance, the
darkness, the corruption, and the misery of the world.

"May you all grow in grace, in usefulness, and in meet-
ness for that world of glory.   There, as ' *sinners saved by
grace*,' may you meet your unworthy friend, and there, together, may we sing the songs of the redeemed, and triumph
in the fulness of God."

* A missionary at Bombay.

TO Z. S., ESQ.

" *Princeton, Dec.* 2d, 1821.

" You will perceive by the date of this letter that this is the Sabbath of the Lord. How I should like to sit down with you at your fire-side and talk of the goodness of our kind heavenly Father. Such a subject would befit the sacredness of this day, and indeed it should be the theme of every day.

> ' When all thy mercies, O my God,
>   My rising soul surveys ;
> Transported with the view, I'm lost
>   In wonder, love, and praise.'

" The whole hymn expresses the feelings of my soul, and I have sometimes thought it might be one of the songs of the upper temple hereafter.

" Tell me, my friend, if my experience is peculiar. Sometimes, when no other consideration will move me to think of God's goodness, my base ingratitude will melt me down. He has healed me when I have been sick, protected and delivered me when in danger. He has resolved my doubts, sanctified my affections, supplied my wants, raised me up kind friends, generous benefactors, profitable enemies. Afforded me the means of education and the prospect of some usefulness. Oh, that I had a heart to love him more and to serve him better. But he will give his Spirit to those who desire it. Oh, that his renewing and transforming influences might descend and rest upon me continually. I bless God for praying friends. It is not an idle, fashionable request I make when I desire to be remembered in their supplications. No, far from it. I do feel the need of their prayers now, and shall need them, if possible, still more if I am spared to complete my preparatory studies.

" We have upwards of seventy students here from various parts of the Union. I hope the spirit of missions is increasing here as well as in all our churches. Mr. Ward's remark cannot be repeated too often. ' That the spirit of missions must evangelize the church before the church can evangelize the world.' If we *think* and *pray* more we shall *feel* more on this subject.

" I regret to hear that Mrs. L. is in poor health. I had hoped her residence at Saratoga would have been the means of establishing her health. ' God seeth not as man seeth,' and he will do what he please with his own, and blessed be his holy name. Oh, for grace to inscribe ' holiness to the Lord,' upon all we have, friends, health, comforts, privileges. A line from your hand and heart is always like cool water to a thirsty soul. I am, indeed, happy to reciprocate your affection, and do believe it will be recognized and consummated in eternity."

December 2d. Almost to the close of another year. How is mercy written upon all the dealings of my God towards me. The record of each succeeding day is only a renewal and recapitulation of his goodness.

> " Why is my heart so far from thee,
>   My God, my chief delight?
>   Why are my thoughts no more with thee
>   By day, no more by night?"

Oh, let quickening, sanctifying grace, come into my soul; revive me by thy sacred influences. Strengthen the principle of spiritual life within me, if it has ever been planted there. Warm and animate all that is cold; sanctify all that is unholy; cleanse all that is impure. Give me joy and peace in believing, and keep me under thy renewing, restraining power. Condescend to take up thine abode within me. Take of the things of the Father and show them unto me. Rest upon me as a spirit of supplication, of illumination, of consolation, and may I cultivate more and more of the spirit of the heavens, hold more intercourse with heaven, have more deadness to the world, and a stronger, keener relish for heavenly enjoyments. May I mortify the flesh with its affections and lusts, and live soberly, righteously, and godly in this present world. Redeeming the time, knowing that the days are few and evil.

December 16*th.* I desire this evening to record my gratitude, blessed Saviour, that thou didst hear my prayer and hast manifested thyself to me, this day, in the breaking of bread; and that, notwithstanding my unworthiness and wandering thoughts and cold affections, thou, blessed Spirit, didst condescend, in mercy, to touch my heart. Oh, renew the impression. Cleanse my heart, and then claim it; and may it be a temple for thee; and may I live with a holy watchfulness lest I should grieve thee to depart. Oh, may rich, free, sovereign, almighty grace keep me from falling, keep me in the path of duty; and after thus solemnly renewing the oath of my allegiance to thee, may I ever feel that I am wholly thine; and may I live for thee alone.

> " Do thou assist a feeble worm,
> The great engagement to perform;
> Thy grace can full assistance lend,
> And on that grace I dare depend."

TO MISS A. J. OF TRENTON, N. J.

" *Princeton, Dec.* 24*th,* 1821.

" I feel every day more and more that I am not my own, but the Lord's; and every thing must bend to his service and to the great object before me. I have been thinking, this morning, on the shortness of life. How soon all our plans and projects will be interrupted by the King of Ter-

rors! How insignificant (comparatively) is every thing not
connected with the glory of God! Nothing here is worth
our attention but religion. 'Tis but a little while, and all
this busy, bustling race of beings that now occupy the the-
atre of life, will be sleeping beneath the clods of the valley.
All our arduous preparations for the gospel ministry, even
with the ordinary length of human life, will be only for the
exertions of a few years. Then death will end the strife,
close the warfare, and set the seal of eternity to our destinies
and our hopes. These little, fleeting moments make up the
time in which heaven is to be secured; in which God is to
be glorified by our activity and zeal; in which sinners are
to be saved.

> ' Then let us catch the transient hour,
>   Improve each moment as it flies ;
> Life's a short summer, man a flower,
>   He dies!—alas! how soon he dies.'

" Present my particular regards to Miss S. I regret that
I cannot avail myself of this opportunity of seeing her. However, I will hope to see her in Philadelphia. Ever since you
informed me of the late loss Mr. N. has sustained, I am
more anxious than ever to visit Philadelphia. I know they
have the strong consolations and supports of the Gospel, and
fondly trust they have a blood-bought title to an inheritance
' that never fades away' in heaven.

" Brother M. presents his best wishes to the family.
Please give my kind regards to all. We warmly express
the compliments of the season, though in anticipation, and
wish you all the happiness that flows from the sweet intercourse of beloved Christian friends, with all the immortal
hopes that religion presents and secures.

" May God have you always in his holy keeping, and
prepare you for great usefulness."

TO THE SAME.

" Princeton, Dec. 27*th,* 1821.

" I felt confident that you would have a happy little circle on the 25th.

" You are aware that all your good Trenton people are
rather anti-Presbyterian for celebrating the 25th of December as the birthday of our blessed Redeemer. It is very
far from being certain that that is the day, so far that few
will speak with confidence on the subject. And, though I
highly approve of religious services, on almost all those
days that are called *holidays,* yet I am not prepared to say
I would celebrate the 25th of December any more than I
would the 25th of January, or the 4th of July, or the 1st of
January, as times peculiarly sacred.

" Next Tuesday will commence the year, and the month
(of course); and, as it is a day when our society for inquiry
on the subject of missions has a regular meeting, and as I
hold the office of First Corresponding Secretary, and have
some reports to make, it will be my duty to be present. I
should be glad to begin the year with you ; but as that will
probably not be practicable, let us regard it as a day of renewed and special dedication of ourselves to God—adoring
and thanking him for the past, and solemnly giving ourselves
to him for the future. Let us thus enter upon another year,
big with the eternal destinies of thousands, and perhaps the
last year we are to number on the records of the living.
Soon our accounts for the expiring year will be closed, sealed
up for eternity. Oh, let us see well to it, that they are all
cancelled by the blood of Jesus, and that they carry no sin
unrepented of to the court of heaven against us. And while
we stand upon the ' grave of the year,' and weep, and adore
at the recollections of the past, oh, let us remember, that in
that grave lie the mortal and immortal hopes of millions

who entered upon the year with hopes as high, and pros-
peets as bright, and as precious as ours. And so let us
breathe a heart-directed prayer, that God would keep and
guide our feeble bark, while we launch it upon the ocean of
eternal scenes. And while we weep at the wrecks of human happiness and human hopes, that cover the ocean of the
past, let us maintain an unshaken trust in God, who sits in
high authority over all these desolations, and has brought
them about for his own glory; and who will be our God for
ever and ever, and our guide even unto death. Let Jesus be
our friend, our Saviour, and all will be well, all will be safe.
Then no matter how short or how tempestuous the voyage
of life; Jesus will be our pilot, and our port will be sure.
And though the next year should prove our last, though we
should not see another summer's sun, nor the flowerets
of another spring; nay, though the blasts of the present
winter should howl over the frozen clods that hide our ashes
from the world, yet we will hope in God. There is a world
that opens bright and glorious, beyond the darkness and the
gloom of the sepulchre; there is a voice sweeter than the
melody of angels that proclaims ' a rest for the people of
God.' May God give us grace to secure that rest, and to
his name shall be the glory."

December 30*th*. The last Sabbath of the year. The year
is almost gone. How have I misimproved every Sabbath,
sinned every hour, forgotten God, and loved and served the
creature; and still I have been spared; spared amidst unnumbered wrecks of human hope, amidst groans and graves,
and " miseries that groan for the grave's shelter." Lord
reform my spared life; may it be more entirely thine. May
I love to commit all the dark, unknown of futurity to thee.
Lord Jesus, grant me a stronger faith.

TO THE SAME.

" Princeton, Jan. 3d, 1822.

" Your letter was peculiarly acceptable, as well as peculiarly excellent, on Tuesday morning. Its length, though a very considerable thing in its favour, was not the most endearing characteristic. Nothing, dear A., affords me more pleasure than indications of deeper spirituality, and more devotedness to God. Oh, that this new year, upon which we have already entered, may be a year of much growth in grace, much victory over sin, much increase in the knowledge of God's word and character, and much knowledge of our own hearts and characters. And may every day bring us nearer and nearer to God, raise us higher and higher above the world, give us more and more energy in our spiritual conflicts, and dispose us to sing from the heart,

' Oh, to grace how great a debtor.'

" We have a missionary meeting in the afternoon; some cheering intelligence of the progress of the Redeemer's kingdom. A letter was read from brother H. P., mentioning the storm encountered at sea, on his passage from Baltimore to Savannah, &c.

" Brother L. reached Charleston in four days from New York, and is preaching to the blacks in the city.

" It would be grateful to my feelings, when the duties of the day are over, to kneel with you before the dear domestic altar, and offer to our kind and Heavenly Father, the effusions of our grateful hearts.

" But God is making our lives his constant care, and granting us many blessings, which we forget to acknowledge—our lives, health, reason, kind friends, food and raiment, the privileges of the Gospel and hopes full of immortality. May he give us gratitude, and sanctify all our enjoyments and hopes, and use us for his service."

6*

TO THE SAME.

"*January* 15*th*, 1822.

"My health was never better; and, without doubt, all the better for my walk yesterday. I feel uneasy about Mr. Armstrong's health. Oh, may God restore and long preserve it. Oh, how many things to remind us that

'Our life is ever on the wing,
And death is ever nigh.'

"And he may now be filling his quiver with arrows to destroy some life we hold most dear. Oh, that our lamps might be ever trimmed, and burning, and we always ready."

TO THE SAME.

"*Princeton, Feb.* 19*th*, 1822.

"In the review of my last visit, the only thing I have to regret is that we did not take more time in the family, and alone, to converse on a subject that ought to lie nearest our hearts. Oh, it is more important than any thing else, that the business of our souls be attended to; for we know not how soon, nor how suddenly, we may be called to the eternal world. When I arrived here on Saturday, I found Mr. T. extremely ill. He was taken on Friday with a severe cholic, which continued for six or seven hours with the most indescribable severity, and was followed by an inflammation; and now it is thought that in a few hours he will be in eternity. While I am writing these words I can hear the gasp of death, although he is in another story of the building, as his room is directly over the one that is adjoining to mine. His convulsive groans pierce my very heart.

"Oh, to be always ready. To have our lamps trimmed, lights burning, loins girt, work done! Oh, God, may I be prepared for that solemn hour. Mr. T. said, a little while ago, ' No father, no sister here.' His mother is not living; and these are, probably, some of his keenest recollections, that his friends are absent. Mr. Wilson, of the seminary, is distantly connected with him by the marriage of some of their friends.

" How important it is that such solemn warnings should be improved. I have tried to imagine myself in his place.

" Have we not reason to be alarmed when our love to God is growing cold, while the love of the creature is intense and ardent? Let us humble ourselves in the dust before him and confess our sinfulness; not that we love the creature so much, but for loving him so little.

" It is a profitable exercise to take the holy law of God, as it is admirably exhibited and illustrated in the Larger Catechism, read it over with prayer to God for the influences of the Holy Spirit, that we may see more and more of its extent and spirituality, feel how it condemns us, and let it perform its office of driving us to Jesus Christ, who has fulfilled its every precept, and suffered its heaviest penalty '*for us;*' yes, for us, if we are Christians. Oh, that his willingness to save may be a matter of faith, and not a mere matter of opinion. That we may have a living, operating, purifying faith on the blessed Redeemer, and that we may feel sensibly the influences of the Holy Comforter and Sanctifier in our souls, moulding every faculty, and every feeling into subjection to his sacred will.

Wednesday morning. Mr. T. is still alive. His desire is for more *light,* and more *resignation* to the will of God. And that the ' *rod* and *staff*' of the ' *Great Shepherd*' of souls may comfort and support him through the ' *dark valley.*'

" I shall not close this letter until evening. Saturday next is proposed as a day of special humiliation and prayer to God.   It is usual to observe such a day about the middle of the winter session.

"I still love to remember twelve o'clock.   Sometimes, on Saturdays and Wednesdays, our recitations interrupt ; but I always remember the hour, and love to send up the desires of my soul towards the throne of grace.

"*Wednesday evening.*   There is no change in Mr. T. for the better ; but Dr. V. C. thinks that if he should con‐tinne in this state for thirty-six hours longer, there will be some hopes of his recovery.   He has been in less pain all day than he was last evening.   Then his hiccough and groans were enough to break almost any heart.   Only a few are permitted to attend him, and those, generally, his particular friends.   You will, doubtless, hear of the issue of his disease in two or three days without my writing."

February 24*th*, 1822.   Almost two months of another year have gone.   How imperceptibly have they fled ; but, oh, what events have they evolved.   Death has removed one of our number* to the eternal world !   "That conqueror of conquerors" and lord of desolation has made a breach in our ranks.   Nothing can divert his aim ; youth, health, sci‐ence, and even piety itself afford no security against his shafts.   Oh, God, who givest life and takest it away, sanc‐tify to us this afflictive providence.   Unless thou dost bless it to us, we shall sink into a more awful stupidity, and be‐come the readier and riper for a severer blow.   Oh, may it be the means of arousing me to more activity.   May the death scene ever live in my lively recollection, and influence all my future life.   May I profit by the melting exhortations of our departed brother—by living nearer to God, more in constant preparation for death.   I do desire to bless thee for

* Mr. Turner, fiom Kentucky.

all that was consoling in the departure of our brother : that his faith was firm, and although he did not, at all times, enjoy as much light as he wished, yet that it pleased thee to chase away the clouds, and that we were permitted to hear his note of triumph and his shout of victory before his eyes closed in death. Oh, God, may the solemn lessons and exhortations he gave us, in his last moments, be the means of more usefulness than his life could have accomplished; and, as an individual, may I not only be quickened in duty, and be led deeper than ever into my own heart, but live always with my lamp trimmed and burning, loins girt, work done, and be ready for the coming of the Lord.

Friday, March 1st. A day of special humiliation and prayer. I have a long catalogue of sins to confess. Oh, God, enable me to forsake them. Faith and repentance are both thy gifts ; oh, bestow them upon me. I have reviewed, and endeavoured to renew, my covenant engagements to be the Lord's. One of a private nature, the other the public formula, adopted by the church. I have broken them many times! Oh, God, if thou shouldst strictly mark my iniquity I must be condemned for ever. But, be pleased, through Jesus Christ, to accept of my imperfect and impure service, and own it as a surrender of myself, renewedly, to thee. I desire to be thine upon thine own terms; to accept of salvation just as it is offered, freely, " without money and without price." I desire to bless thy name that I am shut up to this sweet necessity, that of myself "I have nothing to pay," though " I owe ten thousand talents." Enable me to accept thy salvation with all my heart, and may I exercise a living faith upon a living Saviour; and may I find comfort in this act of self-dedication while I live, and when I enter the *" swellings of Jordan."* Oh, then may I feel the support of thine everlasting arms, and thy blessed presence, Father, Son and Holy Spirit.

TO MISS A. J. OF TRENTON, N. J.

"*March 4th*, 1822.

" We had a solemn season, on Saturday, in following the remains of our departed brother to the grave. It was judged advisable to defer the day of fasting till Friday last, the first day of the month.

" You have, probably, heard the particulars of brother T.'s death. I cannot describe them to you now, if you have not, as the hour has come for me to carry my letter to the office. I can only say, he did not enjoy as much light and assurance of the favour of Christ as he could wish, though his faith in the promises and faithfulness of God remained firm to the last. We think, however, that the clouds cleared away, and that he caught a glimpse of glory before he expired, for his countenance beamed with joy, and he exclaimed, 'Glory,' and afterward, 'My Jesus,' quivered on his dying lips. He gave us many solemn exhortations, and took a most affectionate and affecting leave of Drs. Alexander and Miller, Mr. Hodge and Dr. Vancleave. Dr. Miller has prepared an obituary notice; this you will probably see.

" I hope and pray that this solemn providence may be blessed to us all. May we learn' to work while the day lasts, and to listen to the voice from the grave, that tells us to set our house in order. And may our loins be girt, our work done, and we be thus waiting and watching for the coming of the Lord.

" Nothing could afford me sincerer pleasure than to know that the candle of the Lord is shining brightly around you. May it continue to shine, and may you become more and more dead to the world, and more and more devoted to that Saviour who, I fondly hope and trust, has loved you and given himself for you.

" I think I can say, for one, I have been for several weeks learning new lessons on the humiliating subject of the depravity of my heart, its hardness and its unbelief; though I could humbly hope, not without some sense of the greatness of the love that has provided a Redeemer for sinful men.

> ' How glorious is that righteousness,
> That hides and cancels all our sins.'

" Oh, for more love to God, more faith in him, more active devotedness to him, and for a more constant sense of his presence.

" The bell is this moment ringing for prayer meeting. 'Tis an interesting season. May this be Zion's favoured hour. May God hear the cries of a prostrate church, and have mercy upon Zion. May he enable us to prefer Zion to our chief joy.

" There is a prospect of glorious things in New York. If they continue to become more and more interesting I shall hope to spend the most of the next vacation there, perhaps, after the General Assembly.

TO THE SAME.

" Princeton, March 19*th,* 1822.

" I already feel the benefits of my ride to Trenton, and have quite got over all the unpleasant sensations it occasioned.

" I presume you will have a call from Mr. M'N. and Mr. C., two invalids of our class.

" I was interrupted in my presumptuous strain by company; and before my company retired, the horn was blown for recitation. And now, in about thirty minutes, it will blow again for prayers, (at five); then, in thirty minutes again, for tea; and then, again, in thirty minutes, for the Theological Society (at six). This is the way our time goes here. But every place has its peculiar interruptions: But all, all we have to do, in any situation, is to fill up present time with present duty, and in the midst of all the business and the bustle of the day, I can find many sweet moments to think of God. Oh, that I could improve them as I ought. How much could I then grow in grace! How near could I live to heaven! How sweetly swift the hours would fly! Oh, to be able to say, even should I kneel in anguish over the grave of my last earthly hope, ' My all is not laid here.'

" It is our glory, as well as our duty, to live for God, whom angels worship, and who governs all worlds.

" In one week from next Sabbath, I expect to sit down again at the table of the Lord. May it be such a season as I have never enjoyed before—an antepast of the bliss of heaven. And yet I have scarcely a right to pray for such a season, I live so far below my privileges. God have mercy upon me, and keep me near himself!

" I can give no interesting particulars of the state of things here ; indeed appearances are so delusive. But God is able to grant us all a blessing. New Haven is again gloriously refreshed from on high.

" And how is it among you? Oh, that I could hear the glorious news of sinners born of God and for glory among you. The work in New York is going on, though I have heard no particulars."

May 5th. On such a morning, at this season, it is gratifying to behold the heavens serene, and to see the sun shining in his strength, and to hear the commingled melody of all created nature—fields, floods and forests, with the notes of birds of every wing, rising up in a sinless concert to the great Eternal. On the contrary, the heavens are black with showers, and nature, though in her greenest robes, seems drenched in sorrow at the mute ingratitude of man. Oh, how aptly does this picture represent the state of my heart. On this blessed morning, when every bosom should be peace and every thought should be praise, I find a load of sin press-ing upon my conscience and drinking up my spirits ; and the language of my soul seems to be, " Oh that my head were waters, and my eyes a fountain of tears," that I might weep day and night over a sense of my sinfulness and my ingrati-tude. Oh, may the showers descend, and may they be floods of genuine sorrow for sin. Let them wash away the dust of sin and death that has settled upon my soul. Lord, may I hold sweet intercourse with thee to-day ; let my heart and hopes revive, let my devout affections rise and soar. Let faith take stronger hold, let hope have brighter prospects. Let the world recede from my contemplations, let earth sink down into insignificance, let heavenly views and heavenly glories pour in upon my soul, let the melody of angels and of saints made perfect fall upon my delighted ear, and let my heart be tuned to join the concert. Glory be to the Father, Son, and Holy Ghost, for such high, such blessed hopes, even in this world of sin and death. Father in heaven, glo-rify thy name in my salvation, purchased by the Son, and applied by the Spirit. Work great things to-day in Zion. Give energy and efficacy to the preaching of thy word. Use the earthen vessels to-day so that the excellency of the power may appear to be of God and not of men.

TO MISS A. J., OF TRENTON, N. J.

" *New York, June 2d,* 1822.

" I arrived here on Saturday at 11 o'clock, as I expected, and am happy to be able to sit down and fulfil my engage-ment of writing. I went in the carriage you saw me enter to Princeton, and then took a seat in that which Dr. Rice and company had left. Mr. Bethune was one of our com-pany, and Mr. and Mrs. Fitch joined us. It was twelve before we reached New Brunswick. I was glad to keep still on Saturday afternoon, as I was quite fatigued.

"Yesterday I heard Dr. Romeyn twice; his discourses were excellent, upon the second chapter of Acts, and on the subject of revivals. I do believe he longs for a revival, pure and powerful, free from improper feeling. I never saw appearances so flattering here in general, or in our church* in particular. Called to-day at Mr. C.'s—he was not at home; saw Mrs. C. and Miss C.

"This evening we shall be allowed again to mingle our prayers with many Christians at the throne of grace, for the general outpouring of the Spirit for the conversion of the world. Oh, may God give us the spirit of prayer in large measure.

"*Tuesday morning.* I trust the prayers that ascended to God during the last twenty-four hours, went up like a cloud of acceptable incense, and will be had in remembrance before God. The time will come when Jesus Christ shall reign from sea to sea, and from shore to shore.

"There is a great want of rain in this city; they had no rain on Friday, when you were refreshed with showers. But there is greater need of a rain of spiritual blessings, and for the reign of righteousness; for though there are many children of God here, and many houses of public worship, yet here verily Satan has fixed his throne, and holds his court, and sways a stern and cruel sceptre over thousands of willing subjects. Oh God, break up these strong holds of sin and Satan, and abolish these abodes of corruption and crime.

"My health is better than it was before the vacation. I still spend the morning of each day in my study, and go out in the afternoon and evening.

---

* He was a member of Dr. Romeyn's church.

"I spent a happy Sabbath. I hope I enjoy something of the presence of God, and that I feel his sustaining and directing hand upon me. May he use me in his service here, and admit me to his blissful presence hereafter, and there may I meet all that my heart holds dear."

TO THE SAME.

"New York, June 10th, 1822.

———— "When feeling prompts you to perform any action, pause and inquire if the motive is God's glory. Actions are well to be weighed, by considering the present effect, and the ultimate or remote influence. I might pursue a course of duty, or what should seem to be duty on a partial examination, with a pure desire to promote the kingdom of the Redeemer on the earth, and at the same time be undermining my health slowly and insensibly, but certainly and fatally, and so disqualifying myself for that sphere of usefulness to which I trust God has called me, and in preparation for which, seeking the direction of my Master, I must make every principle, and every faculty, and every feeling bend.

"May God guide you and preserve you, and enable you to let your light shine here below in the kingdom of his grace, and hereafter may you shine as a star of the first magnitude in the firmament of glory.

"Yesterday was another precious Sabbath to my soul. I heard Dr. Spring in the morning from these words: 'For thy name's sake, oh Lord, pardon my iniquity, for it is great.' In the afternoon Dr. Romeyn, from 'Behold the Lamb of God, which taketh away the sin of the world.' And in the evening an old gentleman, from 'Unto you, therefore, who believe, he is precious.' You see the subjects were well calculated to refresh the soul, and truly I can say my soul was refreshed. Between services we read the obituary of Mrs. Poor. It is a precious morsel. Oh, how religion shines in the 'dark valley.' Let me live like the righteous and die like the righteous. My health is very good. I have caught a slight cold in the humid evening air, but shall know how to guard against it in future. I am spending my time pleasantly, and I hope profitably, with access to Mr. Lyon's library, also to Dr. Romeyn's. I know not when I shall leave the city."

TO THE SAME.

"*New York, June 17th,* 1822.

" I have nothing new or interesting to write, my dear A., this morning, except to record the continued mercies of God, which are new every morning, and fresh every evening. Every day I find more and more to interest my feelings and heart in regard to God's work of grace in this city. I do believe, should Dr. Romeyn and his elders go through the congregation and deal faithfully with every soul, whether professors or non-professors, God would own and honour their efforts as the means of exciting this people to such a state of engagedness as they have never seen or felt. Meetings are well attended and solemn ; ten or fifteen are known to be inquiring the way to Zion, weeping as they go ; and I do believe many more are unusually thoughtful. Oh, that God would visit this city in proportion to its inhabitants. If God is angry with one sinner every day, and hates every sinner, how, oh how must his long-suffering patience be tried by the ten thousand abominations of this city ! How must he be insulted by the black cloud of incense that rises daily from a thousand altars consecrated to the prince of darkness ! But he is gathering in his chosen ones, here and there on every side ; and when they are all gathered in, how soon will the cloud of vengeance, red with uncommon wrath, pour down its horrors upon this guilty population. ' The day of their calamity is at hand, and the things that shall come upon them make haste.'

"Oh, to feel more deeply and constantly the worth of souls, and to be more engaged for their salvation.

"I am glad to hear that Mr. A. has been assisted in his present delicate state of health. I do believe he has suffered his anxiety for his people to prey upon his health. Anxiety may rise to a height that will make it sinful. But oh, may God gratify the desires of your soul, and revive his work among you.

"I saw brother Moore just before he left this for Albany. Brother Chester called on me; he is on his way home, where he will spend the summer, and return to Charleston in the fall.—I expect to leave this for Princeton on Wednesday next. I shall not go to Somerville nor Elizabethtown, the vacation is so nearly spent. I must be in Princeton a few days before our duties in the seminary commence."

June 30th. First Sabbath of the summer session. Nearly two months have gone since I have made any record of thy goodness, oh my kind and indulgent Father. Thou hast followed me with thy kindness wherever I have been, and thou hast permitted me to hope and to rejoice in thy mercy. I have seen the traces of thy power, the influences of thy spirit, the movements of thy mercy. I have seen the trophies of thy grace, and would hope I have felt something of thy presence and of thy love wherever I have been. Oh, I desire to begin anew to serve thee, to love thee. Lord, make me entirely thine, for ever thine.

> "Prone to wander, Lord, I feel it,
> Prone to leave the God I love."

Oh, restrain my wandering feet, bind me to thy throne, fill my soul with longings after thy blessed presence—

> "Constrain my soul thy sway to own,
>   Self-will, self-righteousness dethrone."

Lord, make the prayer sincere, and answer it for the sake of Jesus, the sinner's hope, the sinner's friend.

TO MISS A. J., OF TRENTON, N. J.

" *Princeton, July 1st,* 1822.

"I have just returned from a meeting of the Missionary Society; and at this moment a fine shower is beginning to fall, though like many other promising clouds, it may pass with but little rain.

"The weather is intensely warm, every one seems enervated. We have now, however, some thunder, which, with the attendant shower, will greatly purify the air. Oh, that we should think so little of the goodness of our heavenly Father, who is so mindful of our weakness and our wants. He is, in a very gracious manner, sending showers of spiritual blessings to water the barren and thirsty parts of his vineyard. We have heard to-day of many revivals to the north of us; and indeed I have never known a time when such a spirit seemed to be diffused, and is diffusing itself, among those who profess to love the Saviour, and also among those who are far from righteousness. Oh, that this encouraging influence may extend, until every town and hamlet shall be plentifully watered by showers from on high, and every abode of darkness and of death shall be demolished from under the whole heavens, and our Redeemer be exalted in all the earth.

"I have not time to give you the particulars of our missionary meeting. Brother P. gave us an interesting address, and they have taken the liberty of electing your humble servant to deliver one at the beginning of the next session.

Brother S. has just called—says he preached for Mr. A. yesterday. I hope you had a precious season. Dr. Alexander
gave us a very solemn discourse from these words, ' How
shall we escape if we neglect so great salvation !'

" Our conference was solemn ; we talked about revivals.
Mr. Woodhull preached in the evening.

" I would love to be at your tea-table this evening, and
then go with you to the house of prayer, on the evening of
this day sacred to the cause of missions. I long to feel
more, and to see signs of more feeling in others, on this
course. Oh, may God warm our hearts and hear our
prayers."

TO THE SAME.

"*July 8th*, 1822.

" I spent the whole day in my room. In the afternoon
wrote a good long letter to my dear aged parents. I have
received letters from my brother and sister both, since I saw
you : their families are in health. My sister, you know, is
the only professor of religion among them.* My parents
are as happy as they can be under the infirmities of age, and
in a new country, where their religious privileges are of necessity few. But God can provide for his people a well in
the wilderness as well as in the land of Canaan. The presence of God makes a heaven any where. In the chamber
or on the bed of sickness—yes, in the chamber and on the
bed of death, in the dungeon or on the scaffold, in society or
in solitude, at home or abroad, wherever we are in the empire of Jehovah, there is heaven to us if we are the children
of God. Oh, what a father is our heavenly Father! What
a gift is Jesus Christ! What a companion is the Holy Spirit, who dwells in the heart of believers! Let us be mind-

---

* His brother has since made a profession.

ful of our Christian privileges, and be grateful to the God in whom we live and breathe.

> 'May every hour be bliss divine,
> And every thought be heaven.' "

"*July* 25*th*, 1822.

———— " It is religion that gives stability to purpose and perpetuity to friendship, and stamps the seal of eternity upon the bond that unites congenial souls.

" It gives me pleasure to know that you enjoy the light of God's countenance. This will make you happy.— You may be called to pass through darkness, but you will feel the kind hand of your Redeemer leading you, and his voice saying, ' this is the way ;' and, ' fear not, it is I, be not afraid.' You may be greatly tried in the furnace of affliction, ' but one like unto the Son of God' will walk with you in the midst of the fire, that the flames shall not kindle upon you. God is every where, and he is your Father, and he will not be weary of hearing your cries ; he will not for-sake you ; he will guide you through life, and up to glory.

> ' Oh then let us praise him, let us bow at his feet,
> Oh give him the glory and his praises repeat.'

" We have had an interesting day. Mr. Goodell is in town, and this morning he addressed our Missionary Society. You know he is an accepted missionary for Western Asia, (Palestine.) He has lately visited the missionary stations among the Indians of the south-west, and he gave a most interesting account of them. After he closed his remarks, Dr. Rice made a few observations, and concluded with prayer. We expect Mr. G. to lecture for us this evening. I hope to be able to visit those missionary stations ; and while

I live, and wherever I live, my best energies shall be sacred to the cause of missions, the cause of Christ. Oh, that the spirit of Mills, and Martyn, and Newell, and Parsons, might animate every minister of the gospel, and every individual that is a friend to man and the Redeemer of man. How soon would the heralds of salvation be sent to every land, the Bible be read in every language, and the gospel-trumpet be sounded from pole to pole. Oh Lord, the work is thine; hasten it in its time. I trust you and I have much to do in this great cause. Let us be watching and praying for opportunities to be useful, and for grace to improve them when offered; and though we may not live to see the fulfilment of God's promises of mercy to Zion, and hear on earth the full chorus of praise from an emancipated, converted world, yet through grace we will look down from the top of the everlasting hills, and rejoice in the full accomplishment of a work in which we were permitted to labour on the earth."

TO THE SAME.

" Saturday evening, August 3d, 1822.

" I have been sitting alone by the light of the moon, (a little while,) and while I gazed I could not avoid the thought that perhaps your's is fixed too upon that bright orb. I was not in haste to check the thought, and only wished I could walk with you and talk of its brightness, and how it would grow dim before the rising sun; and how the sun, and moon, and all created glories, fade and disappear before the Sun of Righteousness.

" It is delightful to gaze upon the works of God in all their majesty and in all their minuteness—to see the touches of his finger upon the skirts of every cloud, his agency in every leaf that flutters in the wind, in every insect that floats in the air or creeps upon the earth, every planet that rolls in the heavens, every star that decorates our firmament, but that shines and radiates its effulgence in some far distant part of Jehovah's empire—the centre and the sun of a retinue of worlds. And then the littleness of man, with all his imagined consequence and towering expectations, forces itself upon the mind, and one can scarce repress the exclamation of the psalmist, ' Lord, what is man, that thou art mindful of him? and the son of man, that thou visitest him?'

" The week is almost gone; its cares have passed away, and some of its duties done and some undone. Brothers Breckenridge and Baird have been licensed—brother M'Farlane ordained. I feel thankful for any favourable symptoms in your mother's disease, and for all the goodness God is causing to pass before you."

TO THE SAME.

" *Princeton, August 7th,* 1822.

" Your letter was duly received this morning. I heard last evening that Dr. Richards was in town, and was at a loss at first to conjecture the cause, but presently concluded he must be a member of the committee of examination.

" It is quite needless for me to say I deeply sympathize with you in every sorrow, and in every painful apprehension of the issue of your dear mother's disease. It is known only to God, and blessed be his name that his ways are often hid by clouds and darkness from mortal vision; and while we lie still and submissive beneath the shadow of his throne, we can rejoice in that righteousness that does all things well, and all things in the tenderest manner for his children. How willing we should be to resign those that are dearest to us at our Saviour's call! He is a better friend to them than we can be. He knows better what they need than we can know, and will certainly do what is best for them. Oh, I know it is nature that struggles, but let us pray that God would give *grace* the victory, that he would subdue our wills and enable

us to submit cheerfully to his government, and to know that
he is God.

" I know that these ideas have been revolved often in your
mind, and doubtless you feel that Jesus Christ, the same yesterday, to-day and for ever, is the rock you must cling to in
every storm, the great pole-star that will guide you in the
darkest night, and the precious, heavenly friend that will
never fail you. No, death may rage and spread its ravages,
disease may blast our dearest earthly prospects, and bury in
one common grave all that can render life desirable. Yet
our Redeemer lives, and can make up every loss, and even
turn our mourning into joy that shall never end.

" With such truths before us, let us away for ever with
such thoughts as ' being alone and friendless in the world,'
and pray God to forgive the unbelief that would admit them
for a moment. I hope your dear mother will be restored,
and be enabled to praise God in the land of the living—to
live for the happiness of her family, and especially for the
glory of God. But if he is about to send her his final summons, may the language of her heart and our hearts be,
' Thy will be done.' And whether God has designed for
her a speedy departure, or a lingering disease, or a long life
of usefulness and happiness, this language equally becomes
us still."

TO MR. H. D., OF BALLSTON, N. Y.

" Princeton, August 17th, 1822.

" I am really concerned when I recollect that your last
kind letter, of the third of June, remains unanswered. But
my apology is short. I wished to answer it in a manner
suitable to the solemn intelligence it brought me, and therefore laid it by for time to execute the intention, and though
on ten occasions I have been as much disengaged as the
present, yet I have not had one hour suitable for answering

a letter of so dear a friend. Be not surprised at me, my brother, for I have at this moment more than half a dozen duties for the Seminary and for Presbytery that demand my earnest attention, and you are aware how illy we are pre-pared to do justice to our friends when the mind is jaded out with incessant application. Our friend Smith has often told me that the duties in the Seminary were very pressing, but the amount is greatly augmented since he was a member of the institution.

"By this time you have concluded how we are all em-ployed, and that I am making up the length of my silence by the length of my apology.

"But, my dear brother, your welfare for both worlds lies as near my heart as it ever did, and in the midst of all my hurry I can find time to pray for my friends, to pray for Zion. Yes, for Zion's sake I will not rest, in Zion's cause I will wear out my energies, for Zion's King I will lay down my life, and in Zion's everlasting triumphs I will hope to string a harp in heaven. There is nothing else worth living for. What are the few fleeting years of mortal life, but as they allow us to work for God and prepare for heaven? What is learning? what the dearest friends, but as they can help us to glorify God? As an immortal being, the salva-tion of my soul is to me the great concern. What is the whole universe besides? And if I am allowed to hope that my peace is made with God and my heaven secure, some of the principles upon which I build my hope of salvation will send forth an unextinguishable desire to promote God's glory in the salvation of others.

"Away with that religion that sends not abroad its ardent wishes and vigorous efforts for the extension of the Redeemer's kingdom. Without the spirit of Christ I am none of his. And what is the spirit of Christ? He came on a mission of mercy to this ruined world, and made sacrifices, and endured

suffering, which no human arithmetic can calculate, to purchase my salvation. And what, what have I done, what
can I do, ' for him that died to save my wretched soul ?'

" My brother, I know these are old thoughts with you, but
let me beg of you to ring them in the ears of God's people
wherever you find them. There are multitudes dying in
our land, and mighty multitudes in other lands, without hope
and without heaven ; and, with some individual exceptions,
our churches are asleep. Death is invading the missionary
and ministerial ranks, and who shall supply their places?
Our frontiers are extending their hands and directing their
cries to heaven, almost in despair of help from christendom.
While one part of our earth is illuminated with science and
salvation, another part is sunk in darkness."

TO MISS A. J., OF TRENTON, N. J.

" *August* 27*th*, 1822.

" All things continue as they were in Princeton. I have
not seen Miss S. ; brother Myers saw her at Dr. Miller's
last evening, when our singing brethren were invited to entertain the company.

" I rejoice that your uncle S. has visited you, and that he
speaks so favourably of your mother's situation as to think
that she is in no immediate danger. May God restore her,
and enable her at all times to have her house set in order,
and her lamp trimmed for her final departure.—Mrs. A. is
very anxious to visit you this week.

" Live near to God, he is a faithful friend—he sticketh
closer than a brother. May you all enjoy much of his
presence."   *   *   *   *

" It rejoices my heart to know that you are casting yourself into the arms of your heavenly Father. There you may
rest with confidence during every storm. There you may
fix your hope, and the convulsions of the world shall not

8

shake it. Your dear Redeemer will hear every prayer, hush every sigh, dry every tear, sooth every sorrow, make up every loss, support you in every trying hour. Thither then betake yourself, cling to his promises, trust in his goodness; he will not forsake you. Let the language of your heart be,

> ' Dear Father, if thy lifted rod
>   Resolve to scourge us here below,
> Still will I lean upon my God,
>   His arm will bear me safely through.'

" May God bless you all, and give you to feel much of his presence, support and guidance."

TO THE SAME.

" *Princeton, Sept. 20th,* 1822.

" I cannot resist the inclination to write though I have nothing new or interesting to communicate. My spirits sunk the day after I returned from Trenton—probably from having been kept up so long by exciting circumstances.

" I cannot realize the mournful scene that passed before our eyes while I was at Trenton.—It seems rather like the recollections of a distressing dream.—But it is sober, solemn reality. Your dear mother is gone! She sleeps the sleep of ages, and she sleeps in peace. No noise, no pain, interrupts her slumbers. She sleeps in Jesus. But it is only her dust that sleeps. Her immortal spirit lives, wakes, worships, soars and sings, in its Creator's, its Redeemer's presence. Yes, delightful thought, she is high in glory; the journey is ended, the conflict with sin and death is over; the victory is complete; the ties of earth are sundered; the swellings of Jordan are passed, and for the last week she has been learning more of happiness, of God, of glory, than she could have thought of for ages here below. You do not wish her back again. No; you love her better. Then let it be a part of the business of your life, while you cherish her memory, to recollect her pious counsel, to follow her example as she followed Christ.

" My heart has involuntarily dictated these thoughts before I was aware. You have them for what they are worth to yourself, sisters and friends.

" I hope you have much of God's presence that makes heaven of any place. The more you wish for communion with him, the more you will enjoy it.

" We are half through with our examination ; or rather I should say, I am. I shall probably finish to-morrow evening. We expect to be dismissed, as usual, on Monday evening. But as Mr. Hodge is to be inaugurated on Tuesday, and Dr. M'Auley is expected to preach on the occasion, I intend remaining here until Wednesday."

TO THE SAME.

" *Trenton, October* 3d, 1822.

" It would be needless to tell you how lonely and desolate Trenton* seems. I reached here on Monday evening.

" But such is the mutability of all things earthly. We cling to one spot of 'earth as though it possessed all the omnipotence of a charm that would last for ever. The slightest accident can dissolve the charm, and leave the spot as unlovely as the rest of creation.

> ' Earthly things
> Are but the transient pagents of an hour,
> And earthly joys are but a passing flower.'

" We need not, however, spend much time in expatiating on the nature of things beneath the skies, when we have our

---

* After the death of Mrs. Jackson the family went to Philadelphia.

inheritance above them. ⸰ Blessed be God we were made for immortality.

‘ And that the good man’s hope is fixed
Far, far beyond the surge of tempests, and the furious
Sweep of mortal desolation.   He beholds, unapprehensive,
The gigantic stride of rampant ruin,
And the unstable waves of dark vicissitude.
                        Even in death
His hope forsook him not, for it exists
Beyond the narrow verge of the cold sepulchre.’

“ Let the moments fly.   When I can feel that Christ and heaven are mine I will not regard their flight.   The days of our pilgrimage separate us from our Father’s house.   Let the days become hours, the hours moments, and let the moments be no more, so that God’s glory is secured and my work for eternity done.”

Sabbath evening, Oct. 6th, 1822.   In the hurry and arduous pursuits of another session, three months have passed insensibly by.   The mariner, hurried on by the gale, must make his observations to ascertain the distance he has run, and we mortals are carried on by a rapid current, but yet so steady, that we are often surprised when we look back to where we were a short time ago.   But though the summer is passed, and part of the autumn is already gone, they have not passed without making new impressions of God’s goodness on my mind.

And they have been replete with events altogether unlooked for and painful in the extreme.   I have been called to attend the death-bed of a friend.   Mrs. Rebecca Jackson has sickened and died, and gone home to glory.   Her family has been broken up in the short space of a few months.   But God does all things well; blessed be his name.   Every consolation, that religion can administer, has mingled with the cup of sorrow and allayed its bitterness. Though to live was Christ, yet for her it was pre-eminently gain to die. Oh, God, prepare her children to follow her when the duties of life shall be done. They are orphans indeed; but happy are those orphans whose God is the Lord. Wilt thou manage all the circumstances of their lives? May they live near to thee, and so be happy. Sanctify this dispensation, in all its bearings, to me. Oh, may I feel, more and more, the shortness of life; and what I find to do, may I do quickly.

"Father, whate'er of earthly bliss,
  Thy sovereign will denies;
Accepted at thy throne of grace,
  Let this petition rise.

"Give me a calm, a thankful heart,
  From every murmur free;
The blessings of thy grace impart,
  And let me live to thee.

"Let the sweet hope, that thou art mine,
  My life and death attend;
Thy presence through my journey shine,
  And crown my journey's end."

TO MISS A. J., OF PHILADELPHIA.

"*New York, Oct.* 11*th,* 1822.

"I did not intend to address you from this city, but I could not be released from Presbytery until yesterday, unless I went without accomplishing all my business. I was not at liberty early enough to take the evening boat.

"This day is set apart for those who fear God, as a day of special humiliation and prayer, that he would restore health to this afflicted city, and sanctify all his frowning dispensations, and pour out spiritual blessings. The day, however, will be but little regarded. The hum of business fills the air as on other days; the loud laugh of thoughtless mirth, the deep toned curses of infamy and crime are still heard in *this city*, that should be clad in sackcloth and repentance. There is much theoretical and practical infidelity that walks the earth and defies the heavens, but still Jehovah reigns, and has prepared a bottomless, eternal prison, for the despisers of his power and the rejecters of his mercy. 'Oh, that they were wise, that they understood this, that they would consider their latter end.'"

TO THE SAME.

(About the same date.)

" It is right for you to realize that you are an *orphan.* But you will not forget that God is the orphan's Father. It is right for you to realize that your dear parents are gone! But you will remember they are gone to glory. I must caution you, however, from indulging painful thoughts respecting your dear mother's illness. Rest assured, my dear A., every circumstance was ordered by the Lord. All second causes depend, both for their existence and their effect, upon his most righteous will; and, for any thing you can tell, those very circumstances which you regret, were ordered in mercy, in the place of others far more distressing. God knows what he has done. He loved your mother better than you could possibly love her. His was an everlasting love, and was capable of seeing just what was best for the object on which it was placed; and then, of bringing it about. Be not too anxious to desert this field of toil and conflict. Remember, the purest gold comes from the hottest furnace. The battle must be fought before the prize is awarded; and while you desire patiently to wait until your change come, let it be your constant aim to glorify God, and to tune your heart for those everlasting anthems which your father and mother are singing with all the redeemed from among men around God's throne."

TO THE SAME.

" *November* 18*th*, 1822.

" Yesterday was a delightful, and, I trust, profitable day for me. How sweet, in this wilderness of sin, to catch a ray of light from heaven; amid these clouds, and storms, and frosts, to be warmed, and melted down, by the bright sunbeams of a Saviour's love. These are some of the ' angel visits' of his mercy, that sweeten human life, relieve the toils of our journey, and strengthen us to renew the conflict with our spiritual foes.

" We might enjoy such seasons oftener, were we more faithful. But we are too content to live at a great distance from God. And yet he is pleased, sometimes, in matchless condescension, to surprise us by a refreshing breeze from the air of Paradise.

" Next Lord's day the Lord's supper will be administered in this place. Oh, for a heart prepared to meet the Master of the feast; to apprehend, and feed upon, Christ by faith.

" I rejoice that you enjoy the light of God's countenance; and find delight in meditating upon his holy word. By the assistance of the Holy Spirit, you may make your present sickness one of the most profitable periods of your life. While the ordinary business of life is suspended you may be employed in transacting business for eternity.

" It would be an old story to tell you I have much business on hand; but yet it is as true as ever. I should feel grateful to the preserver of my life, that I enjoy such excellent health. Oh, that it may be improved to some good purpose.

" No news to communicate.—I am very anxious to hear from my father and mother. It is now two years and two months since I saw them. They are aged and have constitutions shattered by disease and misfortunes, but I trust their inheritance is in heaven.

" To-morrow is the day appointed for the Sandwich missionaries to sail from New Haven. Oh, that the Lord of missions would give the winds and the waves charge concerning them. Make their voyage prosperous, and their lives useful."

TO THE SAME.

" *November* 21*st*, 1822.

" May you have grace to be reconciled to a protracted illness, if God, in his righteous providence, should so order it. We should always remember that God's *providence* is but the execution of his most holy *purposes;* and, as we hope that our salvation and eternal life are comprehended in those purposes, and the truth is revealed in God's word, that all things work for the good of those who love God, ' who are the called according to his purpose,' let us not shrink at any of the providences of God, however they may destroy the picture which our fancy may have sketched in its youthful visions, or cut down some nursling of our fond expectations. The more we look to God for patience and resignation the lighter will be the crosses we have to bear in our pilgrimage.

" May the presence of your Saviour be better than even vigorous health could be to you. May he mitigate every pain, relieve every anxiety, by occupying every thought.

" One of our brethren, Wm. G. K., from the city of Philadelphia, is quite ill with the bilious fever. His friends are expected to-day. His attack has been very severe. The disease is not yet at its height, so that he must probably be worse before he can be better, in the ordinary course of fevers. Oh, may God interpose in his behalf, and restore him to health and usefulness, and prevent death from making any breach among us.

" How important to be always ready. ' In the midst of
life we are in death.' May he prepare us for all his will and
service here, and for the joys of his kingdom hereafter."

TO THE SAME.

" *November* —, 1822.

" This day is very cold and stormy ; we scarcely go out
at all. Already the fields are covered with snow, which so
lately we saw covered with the beauty and verdure of summer. Oh, how rapid is the flow of time, and how it bears
upon its resistless tide the members of human society and
the monuments of human glory. How many wrecks of human hopes, and fragments of demolished grandeur, have
floated down the stream of time during the year that has
almost elapsed. Oh, what agitated wanderers should we be,
were it not for the Rock of Ages. There let us cling ; then
let the thunders roll, the tempest beat, the seasons revolve,
the world be convulsed, society be deprived of all its orna-
ments, and the grave be peopled with all that we hold dear.
Still, while we kneel at the grave of the last friend, and drop
our bitter tears alone, we will lean upon the arm of Jesus,
and rejoice that our Redeemer lives.

" Let us live nearer to God, strive more against the wickedness of our own hearts, endeavour to be more dead to the
world, more conformed to the image of our blessed Saviour,
so shall we be happy in sickness or health, life or death.

TO THE SAME.

" *November 25th*, 1822.

" Yesterday was really, to me, a precious day. Dr.
Alexander spoke at the table with freedom and effect. Generally, I do not approve of much speaking on such occasions. But the remarks of Dr. A. fell in with my train of
thinking and tone of feeling, and so were the more profit-

able. Oh, what a privilege to be again at the table of the
Lord. It is several months since I enjoyed the privilege
last. It was then in Dr. Ely's church, in May. To renew one's oath of allegiance to the Lord; to take and taste
the symbols of a Saviour's blood and body; to feel him present to melt and warm our hearts; to refresh our souls; to
make us humble by showing us our sins, and the fulness of
his salvation; oh, it is an unspeakable privilege.

"Saturday had been observed as a day of special humiliation and prayer; partly on account of the dangerous illness of our dear brother, who still lingers on the very borders of the grave, and partly as a day of preparation for the
services of the Sabbath. In the evening of the Sabbath,
Dr. Alexander preached most inimitably from these words
of our Saviour to the penitent thief on the cross, 'Verily
I say unto thee, this day shalt thou be with me in Paradise.'

" Indeed, I must say I do feel as if I had really begun again
in the Christian course; and with more vigour than I ever
felt before. But, oh, how impotent is man! How unable
to do anything aright! In fact, all that is done aright, God
does for us. We need the aid and agency of the Holy Spirit
to make any of our attempts either profitable or acceptable.
May we have that Spirit for a constant resident in our hearts.
Then, and not till then, shall we be consistent Christians.

" Brother K. is but just alive. His fever, though highly
bilious in its first attack, seems now to be quite typhus in
its character. Three physicians are in constant attendance,
and still have hope, because there is life, and for no other
reason. How it will terminate God only knows. At any
rate, it is a most solemn call of providence 'to be ready.'
It is not a year since brother Turner died. God seems to
have a controversy with us. Oh, may he teach us the
meaning of his providences, and quicken us all in duty, and
make us more diligent to do his will, and to prepare to meet
him than we have ever been before.

"I had a letter on the 19th, from brother Bishop; they had just embarked amid the sympathies and prayers of assembled thousands, on board the Thames. He has promised to write me again soon; probably from the Cape de Verd Islands."

TO THE SAME.

" November 26th, 1822.

"I received your letter last evening, and as brother Myers will accompany the body of our departed brother to the city, I send you a line by him. I was requested to stand as one of the committee of the brethren, to go down, but it was not in my power to leave the seminary, as I have an exercise to perform in the missionary society, on Monday next, if my life and health be spared.

"I know you are in God's hands, and under his kind care. Oh, for more faith to live near him under a constant sense of his presence, and agency, and parental care.

"Let us look to him that he would sanctify all his dealings, and wean us from the world. I met with the remark lately, in Cecil's Remains, ' That we should always record our thoughts in affliction, set up our marks, set up our Bethels, set up our Ebenezers, that we may recur to them in health; for then we are in other circumstances, and can never recover our sick-bed views.'

"May you be able to do so, and may this season of affliction be rendered one of the most profitable seasons of your life."

Dec. 1st, 1822. Last Sabbath I solemnly renewed my covenant obligations to be the Lord's, and again received the sacred symbols of his body and blood. I then, at his table, resolved to live nearer to him all my days, and by his grace assisting me, never to consider any of my powers and faculties my own, or to use them, but for his glory. But, alas! my resolutions are broken as soon as he leaves me. I can do nothing, absolutely nothing, without divine aid. Judgments will but harden me, ordinances will be barren; every service will be cold and frigid if God do not bless them.

Again the seminary has had a solemn call from eternity to prepare to die; to work while the day lasts, is the import of the summons to us all. One of our beloved brethren, Wm. G. Krebs, in the very morning of life, and in the bloom and vigour of health, was cut down in eight days. Deprived of his reason, most of the time of his illness, he said scarcely a word to inform us of the state of his mind. Turner exhorted us, in a most solemn and affecting manner, to live near to God, and to be active in our master's cause. His words were full of meaning, and he had his reason and speech till the last. But in the late visitation not a word was spoken; but the mute eloquence of a solemn death-bed scene seemed designed to enforce the same important lesson. Oh, how loud the call to be also ready; to work while the day lasts. May God impress every heart, and cause this affliction to work out fruits of righteousness. Lord, my spiritual enemies are stronger than I; undertake for me. Subdue my corruptions. Sanctify my heart, and enable me to follow hard after thee, and to enjoy much of thy presence, which is life; and thy loving-kindness, which is better than life.

TO THE SAME.

" December 2d, 1822.

" It is now nearly time for the monthly concert. The missionary society, in the seminary, has just adjourned. We have had some interesting intelligence, to-day, on the state of religion. Oh, that we could feel more anxious for the spread of the gospel ; for the salvation of sinners. This evening, I trust, though confined to a sick chamber, your soul will delight in God, and rise in ardent prayer for the spread of the gospel. Oh, may God pour out upon his supplicating Zion the spirit of prayer, and answer her cries for the coming of the set time to favour her."

TO THE SAME.
" Princeton, N. J. Dec. 12th, 1822.

" This has been a day of public prayer and thanksgiving, appointed by the governor of New Jersey. The day has been peculiarly solemn to me. It is just about a year since brother Myers and myself rode to Trenton, to attend the service on thanksgiving-day. Many changes we have seen since that day. But God has ordered them all. No event takes place without his permission. Oh, to feel it more and more, and to feel also that we are his, soul and body ; and to rejoice to have him do with us and by us as seemeth good in his sight."

TO THE SAME.
" December 20th, 1822.

" I have deferred writing until quite the last of the week, and even now I have nothing of special interest to communicate. The days of our lives which are least eventful are always marked by an uninterrupted series of mercies which gives opportunity to admire and adore. Though, alas, we too frequently become accustomed to our blessings, and then forget that they are the gifts of our heavenly Father. Hence the necessity of quickening our apprehensions by providences that seem afflictive and corrective, for none of the trials of God's people are of a penal nature.

" I rejoice that you view your present sickness as a salutary dispensation of your best, your almighty friend, designed to draw you nearer to himself, to facilitate the work of sanctification. If this is the effect, you will say of it, Happy sickness, sent in mercy, sanctified by grace, overruled for God's glory and my soul's good.

" The truths contained in the sacred Scriptures are well adapted to hush every thought that would rebel against his righteous government. Oh, to feel, in the midst of the most terrific storm, ' My Father is at the helm;' to feel, whilst smarting under the rod, ' My Father deals the blow ;' to feel, when clouds and darkness are round about him, that righteousness and judgment are the habitation of his throne; to feel, while on the rough sea of life, as we are dashed from billow to billow, ' Jesus is my pilot.'

" Heaven is the port where every believing voyager lands, and in the strength of Jesus I will mingle my praises with the tempest that ends my toils.

" I know not, my dear A., what God has in store for you in this world. Perhaps these trials are only preparatory to greater and more trying ones. But I do trust he has some-thing in reserve for you, that will in heaven show you cause to raise higher and higher your notes of thanksgiving and praise for eternity."

TO THE SAME.

" *December 25th*, 1822.

" May God perfect his begun goodness and restore you to perfect health, and enable you to come forth from this furnace like gold well refined, and hereafter to shine and reflect much of the loveliness of the Christian religion on earth ; and when all the will of your kind heavenly Father is done below, that you may shine in the kingdom of his glory, like the bright-ness of the firmament, or like a star for ever and ever !

" I have felt for some time that my proud heart must be softened and bowed by afflictions, and I have sometimes

thought that the illness of —————, and the temporary interruption of my own studies, are perhaps the commencement of
a series of chastisements designed by my heavenly Father
to bring me to a deeper sense of my dependence upon him,
to make me more spiritual, more dead to the world, more
entirely devoted to him, and thus the better prepared to glorify his name among men, and to preach the richness of his
salvation to others, when I am cut off from every other source
of hope and consolation myself. I am well aware, however,
that the book of providence is a mysterious volume, and is
most legible when read backwards, and I would by no means
wish to read my history were it in my power. Only

> ' Let the sweet hope that Christ is mine,
> Through all my life attend,
> His presence through my journey shine,
> And crown my journey's end'—

and I shall be happy, whatever may befall me in this ' vale
of tears.' It is important for me to learn effectually the lesson, ' Lean not on earth.' Let God be the portion of my
soul, ' my all-sufficient good,' and then I shall never be disappointed."

TO THE SAME.

" *December* 31*st*, 1822.

" There is something in the solemnity of the last day of
any particular period of time, especially of a year, that invites to contemplation, and brings to our thoughts the memory
of joys that are past, of friends that are now no more, and
that disposes us to hold converse with those whom our hearts
hold dear. There is much, doubtless, in the associations of
our ideas that gives interest to the close and the commencement of a year. In the days of our childhood, ' when all
was new and life was in its spring,' the thoughtless gaiety,

the festivities unalloyed by bitter disappointment, the youthful pleasures which marked the flight of time, all combine to
throw a charm around the ' grave of the year,' which the
experience of a few more years, and all the sad reality of
wo's wide empire, have now conspired to dissipate.

" We now associate the lapse of time with the career of
our immortal being, with the progress of our preparation for
the eternal world; and we find much cause for deep repentance in the review of our departed hours, and much cause
for thankfulness to God for the patience that has spared us,
and the goodness that has followed us, in the midst of our
ingratitude and sinfulness.

" We have been led in a way that we knew not, a way
scattered over with thorns, overhung with darkness, but led
by a Father's hand; and may we not humbly hope in the
way to glory?   Stripes have been administered, but they
were the stripes of a Father, who corrects his wayward children for their good, and sanctifies the smart.   Whatever
view we take of the past, whether of the mercies we have
received or of God's forbearance, of our temporal or spiritual
blessings, of our sorrows and afflictions, or of our joys, and
hopes, and consolations, we find cause for fresh gratitude
and new dedication of ourselves to God.   Is it not interesting
to stand on this seeming boundary between what was and
what is to be, and devote all to God, soul and body, time,
talents and influence, for both worlds?   Adoring him for the
supply of our wants, trusting him confidently for all that is
to come, imploring his pardoning mercy for the misspent
past of our lives, relying on his grace for the unknown future
of our being.   Oh, it is but a little while and every change
will be over, every tear will be dry ; time will be exchanged
for eternity, earth for heaven, if we are so happy as to be
the children of God.

" Ere this reaches you we will be in another year.   And

suppose we should not live to see its close; suppose, before half its months are numbered, we should either* or both of us be summoned away from these revolutions of time, and have tuned our voices to the melody of angels, strung our golden harps to the symphonies of heaven, and tried our unshackled energies in our Redeemer's praise, among higher intelligences who have never sinned. Oh yes, and suppose we shall have been greeted by some kindred spirits who were dear to us on earth, who were called before us to heaven, and who have been often sent on errands of love to guard our steps, to prevent our falling, to watch our repose, to warn us of danger,—who have watched with holy solicitude all the windings of our pilgrimage, and who now rejoice at our safe arrival, when our journey is ended and our victory complete. Oh, should we wish us back to earth again? When we look back upon the valley of death, and see it all luminous with glory, we shall wonder at the clouds and darkness that awed us as we entered it.

> ''Tis but a path that must be trod,
> If ever we would go to God.'

"Accept the compliments of the season, and may the grace and the presence of God make it to you emphatically *a happy new year.*"

TO MISS M. J., OF PHILADELPHIA.

"*Princeton, Dec. 20th,* 1822.

"I hope that the cares that devolve upon you this winter will not prevent your attending, more earnestly than ever, to that solemn work of preparation for a sick and dying bed, and an approaching day of judgment, which we all have in near prospect, whether now in sickness or health. I have

* To her it proved the last.

9*

little expectation that your sister will be able to leave her room this winter. But God will do all things in the best manner—to him let us commit her and ourselves.

"Death is always near, my dear M., and you have within a few months seen much to remind you of the importance of thorough preparation. Our friends contribute to our comfort while we are in this world, but when the dying hour arrives, they can only stand helpless and agonized spectators of our departing struggles. You have many dear friends, who long for your present and future happiness, but you are sufficiently sensible of the desirableness of having God for your friend. Other friends may fail us, death chills the hearts that were warm with affection, paralyzes the hands that were often stretched out for our comfort, closes the eyes' that beamed with tenderness for us, and consigns to the darkness, and dust, and putrefaction of the grave, the forms of those we fondly love. But, blessed be the God of the Bible, he is a friend that never fails. Oh, may he be yours, my dearest M., and then whatever catastrophe may dismember human society and convulse the world, you will be safe, safe amid groans and graves, safe amid the conflagration of all things, and certain of enjoying the society of all that was dearest to you on earth around God's throne of glory.

"I hope you will believe these wishes sincere, for I can assure you, my dear friend, they are dictated by a tender regard for your best interests, and the sincerest friendship."

January 1st, 1823. Already I have entered upon a new year. It is profitable to pause here and look back upon the past.

> " 'Tis greatly wise to talk with our past hours,
> And ask them what report they bore to heaven."

There is much to be grateful for and much to mourn over

in reviewing the past. Oh, to be deeply penitent for past transgressions and shortcomings, and to have more grace, and spirituality, and humility, and zeal, for the future. God knows the history of my immortal spirit, and the influence these passing periods exert upon my future prospects and eternal destiny. Oh, thou author of my mortal and immortal nature, enable me here, on this solemn boundary between the misspent past and all the unknown future of my being, to dedicate myself to thee. Thou art still the same, amid all the vicissitudes of time and the circling ages of eternity. Thou hast made me capable of loving, serving, and enjoying thee, and hast implanted in my soul a desire for this high and holy exercise, and wilt thou not by thy grace satisfy that desire? Use me in thy service here, and admit me to the enjoyment of thy presence hereafter, only for Christ's sake. Thy goodness I will record upon a review of the events of the past year, " amid changing scenes and dying friends." Thou hast followed me with thy tender mercies ; and oh, my God, whatever may be in reserve for me during the year to come, let me have a firm faith on thee and a sense of thy favour, and all will be eternally well.

TO MISS A. J., OF PHILADELPHIA.

" *Princeton, Jan. 6th,* 1823.

" I trust I can reciprocate, and respond to your expressions of gratitude to God for all his goodness, and hope I feel, and may always feel, the glow of ardent love and devout acknowledgment which your letter expresses (in view of returning health.) But you have learnt enough of your own heart to be certain that you will lose all these delightful exercises, and relapse again into lukewarmness and love of the world, without the special aid of the Holy Spirit. May he take up his abode in your soul, and then all will be well.

"I hope you are thinking and praying for the heathen to-day. This is a high day in Zion. May her King hear her cries, extend her borders, and give efficacy to every means adopted for the spreading of the gospel. Mr. T——, of the Mariner's church in New York, preached here last evening, and took up a collection for the benefit of seamen. He mentioned some affecting truths respecting the deplorable condition of that class of men—their profanity, profligacy, impiety, ignorance, intemperance, and these in connexion with the fact, which was his text, that the sea is to give up the dead that are in it, and they are to be judged every man according to their works. Christians should pray for them.

"I received a letter from Dr. M'Auley a few days since, in answer to one I had written him, inquiring whether I could have a mission for next vacation. He thinks it highly probable, though somewhat uncertain, as the society complains much for want of funds just now. 'But,' says he, 'get your license, and there is a glorious field for you somewhere. If I know you at all, you have no need to take any thought for the morrow. God will give you ground, and seed, and wages' (many souls.) He has just commenced his labours in New York."

February 23d. "My soul cleaveth unto the dust; quicken thou me according to thy word." This is my sad complaint, and this my constant prayer. Lord, hear me, and quicken me, and give me strength to rise. I have every day new mercies to acknowledge, new sins to confess. I have lately completed the twenty-sixth year of my life. Alas,

> "Much of my time has run to waste,
>   And I, perhaps, am near my home."

Oh God, may the work of sanctification advance with the progressive periods of my being, and every day may I grow

in grace, and have some success in the warfare with my inward foes. Oh, do thou, my dear Saviour, undertake for me
and perform the work, and take the glory which is thine for
ever. As the time draws near for me to enter upon the sacred and awful work of the gospel ministry, cause earth and
men, and the things of earth and all temporal things to sink
down in my estimation to their proper insignificance; and
may eternity, and God, and heaven, and the worth of souls,
and all the importance which three worlds can attach to human character and conduct, occupy my thoughts continually.
Oh, may I be sincerely desirous to be disposed of in the way,
whatever it may be, that shall best subserve the interests of
the Redeemer's kingdom. May I be willing to sacrifice my
private wishes and plans, the love of ease and retirement,
and every study, and whatever else the cause of the Lord
Jesus Christ may require. May the path of duty be plain,
and no matter how difficult, or dangerous, or disgraceful,
only grant me thy grace, the guidance of thy spirit, the light
of thy countenance, the supports of thine almighty arm, and
all will be well. Oh, bring down every high thought, every
lofty imagination. Deliver me from the ensnaring influence
of pride and popular opinion. Enable me to preach Christ
crucified in simplicity and godly sincerity, as one who feels
the worth of souls, and must give account to God for all the
motives with which he acts in his service.

Sabbath morning, March 9th. This is a delightful
morning—it looks like spring; and, blessed be God, it seems
something like spring-time with my soul. Oh God, may
the event prove that my long, long winter is past and gone.

> " Great Sun of Righteousness, arise—
>   Bless my dark soul with heavenly light."

Oh, grant me to-day something of the ardour, and the love,
and the purity, that animate the angels, and living creatures,

and the elders who worship around thy throne. What condescension it is in thee to notice the worship of sinners upon
the earth; yet so it is, and glory be to thy name for ever.

TO MISS A. J., OF PHILADELPHIA.

" *Princeton, March* 12*th*, 1823.

" I am pleased, my dear A., to find you distrusting your
own heart, and disposed to be watchful lest the creature gain
the supremacy over your heart's affections. It should make
us humble, and alarm us, when we find any thing occupying more of our thoughts than God, who preserves us, and
who is jealous of his honour. He will not share our hearts
with idols. If he has taken up his abode in our hearts, he
will crush the idols down, or he will blast it with his breath,
or remove it in mercy.

" It is all-important that we settle the question you pro-
pose on the subject of *evidences* of our adoption. I presume
you do not expect me to go over them for you, as you can
find them in God's word, whence I should draw them were
I to mention them. 1 John iii. 3, 7—14: Matt. v. 3: xvi. 24,
&c. &c.

" May God direct your inquiries, and grant you clear evidences that you are his, and that he is yours, the beloved of
your soul, all your salvation and all your desire—Jehovah,
your justifying righteousness, and Jehovah, your Redeemer."

April 13*th*, 1823. I have been endeavouring to dedicate
myself to God, and to examine again my motives in seeking
the holy ministry. I am sure there is much that is impure
in every thing I do, but I do humbly hope the ruling desire
of my soul to be the glory of God, though I feel conscious
of other things mingled in my mind and with my motives.
But oh, thou searcher of hearts, thou knowest me altogether,
and if thou hast not called me to serve thee in the gospel

ministry, I pray thee to set me aside. Suffer me not to run unsent. Carry me not up hence unless thou go with me. Oh, leave me not to myself, to my own strength and wisdom, and to my own wicked heart and sinful inclinations. Leave me not to the influence of worldly principles and worldly motives, but sanctify my heart and purify my motives, and guide me by thy counsel in every path of duty. I desire now to commit my way to the Lord. I desire to commit myself, soul and body, to the Lord. O, God the Father, for the sake of God the Son, do thou accept of me, and sanctify and save me by the powerful agency of God the Holy Spirit. Take me under thy peculiar care; lead me wherever I should go, and be on my right and left hand; defend me from every danger by land and by water. Assist me in every duty, and enable me to glorify thy most holy name, to recommend religion and to do good to souls. If it should please thee to arrest me by sickness and sudden death, let the covenant of grace be my security, and let me have a sweet sense of thy presence. And finally admit me, through Jesus Christ, my dear Saviour, into thy heavenly kingdom.

TO MR. H. D. OF BALLSTON, N. Y.

" *New York, April* 22d, 1823.

" I have waited to hear from you until I am discouraged. And have concluded to remind you that I have the inclination and the strength to urge my claim, not upon your purse, nor patience, but upon your time and attention. My health has been much as usual, for the last few months.

" I expect to leave this city this week, or the first of next, for the north. I hope to pass through Ballston on my return from the west in June. I expect to spend two or three weeks in Montreal, U. C. And from thence proceed up the St. Lawrence and the lake, as far as Gennesee river and

Rochester, to visit my parents once more, and return to Princeton to spend the summer. It is possible I may find a field for usefulness in Montreal that may induce me to return there in October next. I have been here about one week. I was licensed to preach the gospel on Friday last. I should like to have a long interview with you, and speak of the duties and the dangers of the gospel ministry. But I have only time to say, at present, I have had many misgivings. My heart has often sunk within me; but, ' through Christ strengthening, I can do all things.' "

" *Steamboat Phenix, Lake Champlain,*
" *April 29th*, 1823.

" You will perceive by the date of this what progress I am making in my journey. I have been disappointed several times, and misinformed, which has occasioned me some delay; but to detail it all would be uninteresting, and not worth using time or paper for.

" My health is quite good. I have just recovered from a severe cold, caught in New York, as usual. I spent the Sabbath in Waterford, where I only preached once, thinking it would not be prudent, on account of my cold. For this reason, also, I declined lecturing for Dr. M'Auley, on Wednesday last. This is to let you know that I am careful of my lungs when it is necessary.

" We have but few passengers, as the season for travelling has not commenced. The boat is a very pleasant one, and captain S̄. much of a gentleman. This lake seems like a kind of inactive or sluggish river, between the hills, or rather mountains, which present their steep and rugged, frowning and rocky bulwarks on each side, leaving often scarcely room for the management of the boat.

" I am now going on deck to see the remains of the celebrated fort Ticonderoga.

" The ruins of the old fortification are very interesting; and the grounds around them, which have so often swarmed with embattled hosts, who have long since mingled with the dust, even yet inspire sentiments of awe and melancholy.

" *Montreal, May 1st.* I have at last arrived at this place after a pleasant passage to St. Johns, and then rather a rough one to La Prairie ; from thence we came last evening, in an open boat, to this place. I had the pleasure of hearing the *Canadian Boat Song* in reality. It was interesting and beguiled much of the time in crossing the St. Lawrence.

" I had scarcely seated myself in the City Tavern, before several gentlemen called upon me, giving me a most cordial welcome. This morning others. They are much engaged. I do hope God will send them one to lead them and guide them, and to dispense to them his holy word and ordinances.

Of course I can say nothing of my feelings or prospects. My mind is perfectly at ease on the subject.

" I am now at Mr. B.'s. I shall probably remain with him. Montreal is rather more pleasant than I expected to find it; and the field that is open here for ministerial activity and usefulness is very wide, and seems to be ripe, judging from what I have heard.

" My cold is better. It is possible I may spend the whole of this month here, though at present I do not intend it."

———

In April, of this year, Mr. Sanford was licensed to preach the everlasting gospel, by the Presbytery of New York. Immediately after that important event, he went to Montreal in Lower Canada, and spent several weeks in preaching to the American Presbyterian Church in that city. In this first scene of his ministerial labours he won, to an uncommon degree, the affections of the interesting band of Christians who formed that church.   They were then destitute of a pastor, and, although Mr. Sanford spent but a few Sabbaths with them, they gave him a unanimous call to become their spiritual teacher.   It will be seen, from the following letters and extracts from his journal, that after having deliberated much on that call, and seeking, by consultation with judicious friends, and, above all, by prayer, for direction, he came to the conclusion that it was his duty to decline the acceptance of that call.   But although he did not feel it to be his duty to settle in Montreal, he never ceased to feel a very deep interest in that important city, as well as the important country in which it is situated.   He correctly appreciated the natural advantages of the Canadas, and deeply felt that they constitute a great field for the labours of faithful ministers of the gospel.

Montreal, May 11*th*, 1823. I have preached seven times since I was licensed, and I know not that any one is the better for it.   Oh, how impotent is man.   Paul or Apollos may labour in vain unless God give the blessing.   How should this reconcile me, unworthy, sinful me, to labour in faith and then to leave the event entirely with God.   O God, warm my heart and enkindle in my soul more love for sinners; more love for souls; more love for the kingdom of the Redeemer.   Wilt thou use me for thy glory in any way and at any time.   My life, my attainments, the talents thou hast given me; all, all I would devote to thee.

TO MISS A. J., OF PHILADELPHIA.

" *Ogdensburg, May* 23*d*, 1823.

"I left Montreal, as I expected, on the 19th inst.   I arrived here this morning, after various fatigues and perils, which I have no time to recount.   There is not a man here that I ever saw before; and not only am I a stranger in a strange land, but there is scarcely a possibility of my leaving the place unless I go back to Montreal. There are no stages from this village to any place. The roads, too, are very bad.

"I begin this letter calculating to continue it as I have time and inclination. And to send it, or deliver it myself, when convenient. I expect to preach here this evening, and to ride near seventy miles to-morrow.

"*Auburn, May* 28*th.* I have just arrived here; and, having taken tea, will proceed to give you some account of my journey since I wrote last, as you see above.

"I left Ogdensburg on Saturday last, and rode fifty miles, roads very bad. Staid all night at a place called the Great Bend. It is ten miles from Watertown. Found a fine, hospitable family. We had prayers in the evening, and I gave them some tracts. Rose at five and rode to Watertown. It was wet—I was completely drenched. Preached at Watertown twice. Rode to Brownville and attended a conference in the evening. Rode to Utica in two days (Monday and Tuesday.) Rode from Utica to Skeneatelas yesterday. Went to see my sister last evening. Returned from Skeneatelas to-day in time to take the stage for this place, (eight miles.) I leave this in the morning, at 3 o'clock, for Canandaigua (forty miles) where I expect to dine.

"*Manlius, June* 11*th.* I am nearly 150 miles on my way to New York. It is almost two months since I have heard a word from you. At Rochester I expected a letter.

"*Princeton, June* 26*th.* I have arrived here at last, and have just put my hand to this old sheet again; have concluded to fill it up and send it on, for I think it is yours by right.

"My health is good, and I am rejoiced to find myself in my own dear room again, enjoying something of that tran-

quillity and retirement for which the seminary is so celebrated.

I have conversed with both of the professors, and they
are at present of different opinions on the subject of my going to the north.   However, I hope to see them again in the
course of the day, and to find them agreed to advise me to
go.   Yes—to go to Montreal.   But I am not yet decided in
my own mind.   My heart must bleed in any decision.   I
cannot give the call from Montreal a negative without the
keenest regret.   I remember their anxiety.   I remember the
tears that glistened in so many eyes, when I told them I must
go.   I remember their entreaties that I would not forget
them.   And all this has been in a measure acted over in
Brooklyn.   I did hope to write this evening, and give a decided answer, but I cannot.   I shall write, however, and tell
them I am undecided.   Let our united prayers ascend to God
for his guidance and direction."

TO THE SAME.

"*Princeton, June 28th,* 1823.

"The remarks you may hear of Montreal or Brooklyn
I hope you will not regard.

"Whatever people may say upon the subject, my mind
has been most completely balanced.   It is still so.

"The professors still have different opinions on the subject, and say ' they can well imagine my mind should be in
great doubt and uncertainty, as to the path of duty,' and
this is actually the case.   And I can assure you, this moment,
I think it quite as likely that I shall decide to go to Brooklyn as to Montreal."

TO THE SAME.

"*July 2d,* 1823.

"You may be a little disappointed when I tell you,I have
concluded to go to Brooklyn.   After considering the subject

as deliberately and as solemnly as I am able; and after seeking divine guidance, and committing my way unto the Lord, I have come to the conclusion that, according to present circumstances and appearances, I may hope to do more, by God's blessing, for the church and the world by settling at Brooklyn, than by going to Montreal. Still, however, at this moment I would gladly go to Montreal, if there was any man who would exactly suit the people at Brooklyn.

"Should my hopes be disappointed, of being useful, I trust I shall have the confidence and comfort of feeling that it has *all* been ordered by the Lord.

" I do not expect to be ordained until October, probably about the middle of the month."

TO THE SAME.

" *Princeton,* ———

" To-day have I been seated at the table of our dying, risen Redeemer; and feeling disposed to speak of his goodness, to whom would I so gladly enter upon the interesting theme as to you?

" My mind was peculiarly exercised this morning with desires stronger than usual, to meet the Master of the feast at his own table: to see the King in his beauty: to have Jesus Christ make himself known to me in the breaking of bread. And I humbly trust, he heard and answered my prayer. I can surely say that I have never had so precious a communion-season in Princeton before.

" To go to the table of the Lord is the most solemn transaction a creature can perform this side eternity.

" The Lord's Supper commemorates an event, to the accomplishment of which all the providences of God for four thousand years had almost an exclusive reference; an event the most awful and stupendous that any world can ever witness. The God of nature suffering on a cross by the hands

10*

of his sinful creatures! And it exhibits an assembly of those creatures, sitting at a feast of their risen Lord, ransomed from eternal misery by the very blood they spilled, and professing their faith upon that once crucified, but now ascended Saviour, who is now seated upon his eternal throne of glory, which he had left, for a while, to become the *man of sorrows*, and redeem a race of rebels from the consequences of their rebellion. And, oh, the amazing love of Christ! the Babe of Bethlehem—the neglected carpenter's son—the houseless wanderer, who had not where to lay his head—the agonizing, supplicating sufferer of Gethsemane—the bleeding, dying victim of Calvary—the tenant of the rock of Joseph—the rising, conquering, and now reigning, interceding Redeemer. Oh, these are subjects for the anthems of eternity! These are themes for an everlasting song! The everlasting song of blood-bought sinners saved by grace divine!

" And the consideration that increases our wonder is, that with all our hopes of salvation, thus purchased, we can become so insensible and indifferent to a Saviour's love. That we can continue in sin! Oh, what a time to mourn over our sins, when we stand in sight of Calvary. Our love of sin, of the world, of self; our apathy, and coldness, and formality in the duties of religion; our conformity to the irreligious opinions and practices of society; our forgetfulness of God; our neglect of duty; our mockery in prayer; our idolatrous love of the creature; our want of zeal for the spread of the Gospel; our indifference to the misery of perishing millions—alas, for us, the long, humiliating catalogue rises, black and awful, before us! Oh, God of mercy, may it drive us to the Saviour, ' whose blood cleanseth from all sin.' Blessed, for ever blessed, be the name of our covenant-keeping God, ' that he so loved the world as to give his only begotten Son, that whosoever believeth on him should not perish, but have everlasting life.' Oh, let us go to him anew, if we have ever done it. And in a manner more solemn and unreserved dedicate ourselves to God. It is a work to be done in time, but it is for eternity. Oh, may God have mercy upon us, and establish us upon the Rock of ages."

TO THE SAME.

" *Princeton, July 19th,* 1823.

" I would have written to you yesterday, but a gentleman from Montreal called to see me, and spent the afternoon and evening, until near 10 o'clock, when he took the mail for New York.

" Before I gave the Montreal congregation a final answer, and while my mind was labouring, and distressed, and doubtful on the subject, I wrote to my friend, Jacob De W., Esq. As I had expressed myself doubtfully on the subject of coming among them they concluded it very improbable. Mr. De W. was selected by the congregation, and prevailed on to come immediately to the United States and see me, before I should decide, hoping that his efforts would secure a favourable decision. He was detained, however, nearly a week. Before he left, the final decision was received. However, as he had some other business in the United States, he came to New York on Tuesday last, and arrived here in the evening. He came, as he expressed himself, ' not to unsettle my mind, or to distress me, but to see me as a dear friend, whom he tenderly loved, and who, he had fondly, humbly, hoped, would be the means of leading him, and all that are dear to him, to Christ and to glory.' I can assure you, when he described the effect of my first letter upon the people, though it was by no means decided in its character, I felt as if my own heart would burst, and that I would give all the world, were it mine, could I see the path of duty leading me to Montreal.

"But for the present, I feel it my duty to go to Brooklyn. I say, for the *present*, because I feel satisfied as to present duty ; and that is all one should be anxious about. A long career in the gospel ministry has never entered into my fondest anticipations. The length of the race is a trifle, compared with the manner in which it is run. Oh, may God enable me, while I live, to live to his glory, and to be active in his service. And when (through strength derived from God) his work is done, whether it be done sooner or later, may I be prepared to enter into his heavenly kingdom.

TO THE SAME.

"My prayer is, that you may be useful in the church of Christ. There are many females (I mean wives of clergymen) who seem to content themselves with making their husbands happy. Now this is well, as far as it goes. But I could not be contented to have a wife a mere satellite. I would have her shine with her own light, in all the mild glory of female excellence, and with the reflected rays of the Sun of righteousness.

"The relation a female stands in to her husband, changes not her relation to the head of the church, and she is still to feel it her duty, as far as may be consistent with duties which arise out of the social relation, to exert herself for God and his cause; and indeed the glory of God should be the motive of every action.

"Let us keep it constantly before our minds that our steps are ordered by the Lord. He will dispose of us in his own time and for his own glory. Besides, it may be possible that he may never design us to enjoy much of each other's society.* We hold all our comforts at his pleasure. And

* How very prophetic!

he often frustrates the fondest schemes of his dearest children. We know not what is best for us."

Princeton, August 17*th*, 1823. By the absorbing tide of business, though sustained every moment by the hand of God, I have been hurried through several months to the present time. I have been led through various exercises and anxieties. My life has been preserved when it was in danger. My wants have been supplied. Every cup has been filled with blessing. Every hour has been marked by some kind token of the Almighty's care. " Blessed be the Lord God, the God of Israel, who only doeth wondrous things ; and blessed be his glorious name for ever and ever ; and let the whole earth be filled with his glory." I desire, with my own hand, to subscribe to the goodness of God. I am ungrateful and sinful, prone to wander from him. Unworthy of the least mercy, deserving of every frown and the fiercest displeasure, ruined and helpless, but still rebellious. Oh God, why am I spared, spared in the midst of so many provocations ; spared in the enjoyment of so many blessings, and privileges, and hopes ! I desire to be thine. I desire to accept of the offers of mercy, through Jesus Christ, and to know, by a more distinct and satisfactory experience, the richness and the suitableness of that salvation which it is my business to preach to others. I desire to be united to Jesus Christ by a living faith ; to be really in him, and thus free from condemnation. To feel the purifying influences of that spirit of adoption which dwells in the believer's soul ; to feel the power of sin growing weaker, and love to God and holiness growing stronger every day ; to be convinced more and more deeply of my native sinfulness and misery, and to cast myself upon Jesus Christ for wisdom, righteousness, sanctification and redemption.

This work, O God, thou alone canst perform. O wilt

thou work mightily in me and for me, **and** show me thy salvation and thy glory.

August 21*st.*   This day to be observed as a day of special humiliation and prayer.   I have been endeavouring to confess my sins, and humble myself before God; but, alas, there is so little sensibility, so little deep repentance, so much languor and coldness, so hard a heart, such vagrant feelings and thoughts, and such barrenness of soul as to make me apprehensive that I have never tasted the love of God.   I have endeavoured, however, to feel my sinfulness and help-lessness, and to give myself away to God my Saviour, to be saved in his way and upon the ground of his finished work and perfect righteousness.   My only hope is in the friend of sinners.   If I fail here I fail for ever.   O Jesus Jehovah, I am resolved to rely upon thee alone.   It is a faithful saying, that thou didst come into the world to save sinners.   O make me a subject of mercy and a trophy of thy rich grace.

Sabbath morning, Sept. 7*th.*   To-day I expect to go again to the Lord's table.   Oh Saviour of sinners, soften and sanctify my heart.   May I feel more humble, and come to thy throne of grace sensible that all my help must come from thee.   I would spread all my wants before thee.   I would dedicate myself to thee.   I would be thine, and thine for ever; draw me to thyself; bind me to thy throne; take possession of this soul of mine, oh Holy Spirit, and make it thy temple.

———

With the month of September Mr. Sanford ended his happy residence in the Theological Seminary at Princeton, and bid adieu to that beloved institution and its many privileges. On the 25th of that month he was married to Miss Anna Jackson, then of Philadelphia, but formerly of Trenton, N. J. Immediately after his marriage he went to Brooklyn, to take charge of the First Presbyterian Church in that city, to which he had received a call in the early part of the preceding summer. In that important and rapidly growing city he laboured with great faithfulness during more than five years. In this sphere his labours were eminently useful. His letters and journal will inform the reader through what overwhelming trials he was speedily called to pass. They will also show the progress which his own soul made in holiness, as well the success which attended his labours. It may not be improper to remark, that the mournful and almost instantaneous death of his wife was occasioned by a surgical operation. That her death produced a very deep, and lasting, and sanctified effect upon the heart of her bereaved husband, is evident from what he has written. She was a woman of eminent piety and loveliness, and possessed uncommon qualifications for the sphere into which she had but just entered when she was called away by death.

In the death of his excellent wife Mr. Sanford found great and merited sympathy in many Christian hearts, which hastened to offer their consoling tribute. Among the many letters which were addressed to him at this afflictive crisis, that of the Board of Trustees of his church, and those of the Rev. Drs. Romeyn, Miller, and Richards; that of Alexander Henry, Esq., as well as those of the Rev. Messrs. Hamner, Hall, Myers and Bishop, who had been his fellow students at the Theological Seminary at Princeton, may be mentioned as remarkably excellent. The last named of these young brethren and his wife, addressed to him a very dear letter from the Sandwich Islands, where they were labouring as missionaries. A few of these letters are here submitted to the reader.

"*Brooklyn, Dec.* 16*th,* 1823.

"DEAR SIR,

"The Board of Trustees, under a deep sense of the afflictive providence which has deprived their beloved pastor of a partner, and feeling as they do that the ties which subsist between man and wife are the most tender and the strongest that bind the human family together, the severance of them therefore cannot but be the most distressing. We will not presume to say what our feelings were at the heart-rending distress which you must have felt at so unexpected a disappointment of your temporal bliss. But, dear sir, permit us to say, we felt and do feel sincerely the distress which has fallen on our teacher, who, we trust, under providence, has come amongst us for our spiritual benefit.

"We beg leave to tender to you our warmest sympathies, and the assurance of our affection and condolence as individuals; and we are assured we are correct when we say, the affection the whole congregation feel towards you is almost unbounded.

"We have been directed by the Board of Trustees to express to you their desire, in their official capacity, to do all that is in their power for the advancement of your personal comfort and happiness; and if there be any thing in which they can give effect to this desire at the present time, they would be glad to receive an intimation of your wishes on the subject.

"In behalf of the Board of Trustees, we remain your sincere friends,

"ELKANAH DOOLITTLE, *Pres.*

"SILAS BUTLER, *Clerk.*"

"MY DEAR BROTHER,

"Permit me to mingle my tears with yours. You have indeed been called, at an early period, to suffering of the most acute kind and its consequence deep-and prostrating sorrow. May your covenant God support you with the consolations of that covenant, and cause you to *feel* that he is *your* God and Father in Christ Jesus his Son. I commend you to him and to his blessing on this occasion, knowing full well that if you are *his*, as I am persuaded, he will support and comfort you in this the hour of your affliction. The Lord God of his church be with you and bless you— enable you to carry out in your ministerial deportment the evidences of mediatorial fidelity to *his* own promises, who is *our* Jehovah, in righteousness and sanctification.

"Your sympathizing brother in the common salvation,

"J. B. ROMEYN."

"*Princeton, Dec.* 19*th*, 1823.

"MY DEAR SIR,

"I received, ten days ago, with unfeigned sympathy, the intelligence of the heavy bereavement with which it has pleased an infinitely wise and sovereign God to visit you. Be assured you have not been forgotten in those approaches to the throne of grace which my companion and myself are in the habit of jointly making; and I should have taken an opportunity of expressing to you our kind remembrance, had not a variety of circumstances, and among the rest a temporary interruption of health, prevented my enjoying a moment's leisure until this time.

"We little thought, eight weeks ago, when we saw you and your excellent companion going to New York together, that she would so soon take her flight to a better world. But it is all well—infinitely for the best. God has been pleased, indeed, in your case, to sever the tenderest ties that human nature knows—and, of course, to lay upon you one of the heaviest earthly calamities. But, oh how much mercy is mingled with the affliction! How seldom is it that surviving friends have so much evidence of the safe and happy departure of any one, as in the case of your beloved, and now, we doubt not, glorified partner! For this you have reason evermore to bless God, and to have his praise continually in your mouth. The Lord grant that while your heart is wrung with that anguish which such an event *ought*, in some respects, to produce, you may be enabled more than ever to rejoice in God your Saviour, and to praise him for the great mercies attending this dispensation! May He who has inflicted the stroke send the balm of consolation, and enable you to say, *It is good for me to be afflicted!*

" My dear young brother, perhaps the Lord, by thus early trying you in the furnace of affliction, intends to prepare you for a course of *peculiar devotedness to his cause*, and of *peculiar usefulness*. If so, will you not have reason for ever to praise him for it? If so, will not one of the most mysterious dispensations that has lately come to my knowledge, prove to be full of light, and mercy, and joy, in the end?

" I am unexpectedly cut short in my letter by an interruption, and have only time to add, again, the assurance of affectionate remembrance in our prayers, that the God of all grace may bless and comfort you.

" I am, my dear sir, with cordial sympathy, your friend and brother,

" SAMUEL MILLER.

" REV. MR. SANFORD."

" Auburn, Dec. 19*th,* 1823.

" MY DEAR YOUNG FRIEND,

" Your letter, conveying the mournful tidings of the sudden departure of your dear wife and our very dear friend, our beloved child I may say, has filled us with astonishment and grief. How marvellous are God's ways, even towards his own children, and often how dark and distressing. My dear sir, our hearts bleed with your heart under this sudden stroke, and with the hearts of the dear sisters. Poor things! how desolate are they made by this unexpected change, as well as you. Anna was mother, sister, all to them; they looked to her and depended upon her for every thing. I never saw such maternal care and tenderness on one part, and such affectionate confidence on the other, among sisters. But the tenderest relations, and the most distinguished virtues, present no barrier to the unwelcome tread of death. He marches through the thickest ranks, and lays our proudest hopes in the dust, just where and when he receives command. God however is upon the throne, and nothing, blessed be his name, falls out beyond or aside from his counsels. The darkest dispensations of his providence are all light to him, and to us they will one day appear as bright as the noontide sun. But what shall we do in the meantime, while clouds and darkness are round about him, and his paths are in the mighty deep? We can only bow at his feet, and say, *Righteous art thou, O Lord, when thou speakest, and clear when thou judgest.* This we know to be our duty, and that our happiness is connected with it; but often it is not easy to take this position, and to bring our hearts to this state of humble and cheerful acquiescence. Passion rebels, while reason says, be still. I have found, my dear brother, that in very trying conjunctures it was in vain to reason; that the tempest was too strong to be resisted by such feeble means; that Almighty grace alone could be resorted to as furnishing the adequate relief. Thanks to the God of all the earth that a way has been opened to his throne, and that *there*, in the name of our great advocate, we may come with all our wants and woes, with the kind assurance that we shall not be sent empty away. I need not tell you that in prayer you will find the truest support, and the only satisfactory pledge of a happy issue to this trial. You must not be surprised, if, while it is dark without, it is dark within also. When God hides his face in the external administration of his providence, it is not uncommon for him to withdraw the inward tokens of his favour. It was so in the case of Job, and often so with David, as the history of their trials clearly evinces. This indeed makes the cloud of affliction doubly dark, but by no means less salutary. It is especially calculated to bring sin to remembrance, and to lay us more effectually in the dust.

Your situation has greatly affected me, and continues to occupy my thoughts. After my feeble manner, I do not cease to remember you and the dear sisters in my prayers. Some good thing no doubt God intends to accomplish by this surprising visitation. Perhaps it is to bring some of the acquaintance and the relatives of the dear departed saint to the knowledge of the truth ; perhaps to make you a more holy man and a better minister. I pray God to sanctify it to us all, by keeping us more awake to our frailty, more active in his cause, and more perfectly ready for our last summons.

" We had anticipated much pleasure in seeing you and your dear friend next summer at Auburn ; but how little do we know what a day may bring forth. Where any of us shall be then is known only to him who holds our destiny in his hand. Still let me hope that I shall see you here before many months shall have past.   *   *   *

" Mrs. R. and my sons desire an affectionate remembrance

to you. They all tenderly sympathize with you in this great trial, and feel with myself that we have sustained a great loss.

"Very sincerely and affectionately yours,

"JAMES RICHARDS.

"REV. J. SANFORD."

"*Philadelphia, Dec.* 8*th*, 1823.

"REVEREND AND DEAR SIR,

"It is with a trembling hand and sympathizing heart I take up my pen. Nothing in nature could be more unexpected to me than the doleful intelligence your letter conveys. May the Lord grant his blessing to this heavy affliction. Often, my dear friend, I have thought of you and your dear companion. Every view I took of your prospects cheered my heart. Our beloved friend had a large share of my affections, indeed more like a *parental* than any other character, and I rejoiced in her prospects; moreover, I had believed that she had been effectually relieved from the painful local complaint. Think, then, my astonishment, when I learned the cause of her death was a surgical operation. The will of the Lord be done. I have, my dear friend, conveyed the dreadful intelligence to poor M., her sister, and the family in which they reside, with all the care and tenderness in my power; but cannot say that it has been received even with tolerable resignation. Indeed, poor M. is overwhelmed; till this moment she will hear nothing that is said. I trust, however, she will soon become more calm, and then it will be both the duty and the pleasure of Christian friends to endeavour to promote a sanctified use of the affliction.

"Heart-breaking as it must have been to you to communicate the facts, I am rejoiced to have them from yourself, and still more for the mercy that is extended to you. It does, my dear friend, rejoice my heart that you still trust in the Lord. May his right hand sustain you; may he open to you the riches of his grace; may you be made ever to rejoice. And why not, my dear sir, rejoice? Your Anna, much as she loved you, is infinitely more happy than she ever could be with you. Dark and mysterious as this dispensation is, ere long you will see infinite wisdom and mercy in it. I am unwilling to let a mail return without a line from me, but really I am not in a situation to write. You shall not be forgotten, my dear friend, nor will my attention to my dear children here be omitted. I wish, however, for your own sake, and their sake, you would come on as soon as you can.

" Very affectionately yours,

" ALEXANDER HENRY."

Brooklyn, Dec..7th, 1823. Alas! how short-sighted is man! How little did I suspect what God had in reserve for me when I wrote last in this journal. . How little did I apprehend that while this book was mislaid and no other record made for three months, events of such deep, everlasting and mournful consequences would take place. My marriage, ordination, and the death of my beloved wife!

Oh God, thou art on the throne. Thou turnest man to destruction. My dearest comforts are thy gifts, and thou hast a right to recall them. Thy will be done, O righteous God. Though my heart bleeds, it is thine holy hand that has inflicted the blow. O pour in the balm of Gilead. O sanctify me, pardon and support me till I have done and suffered all thy will, and then receive me to thy kingdom to behold thy glory, and there to meet my dear, dear Anna, from whom I have been so unexpectedly, so mournfully separated on earth. May we meet to praise thee together.

Oh God, my God, let me fly to thee for strength and comfort under this severe 'stroke which thou hast inflicted. Oh, how little did I think, when I made the last record of thy goodness, that such a furnace of affliction was preparing for me. But why should I weep? She is high in glory to-day, and is engaged in a nobler worship than she ever conceived below. Yet while I do weep and mourn I would not murmur. Oh God, I thank thee that I loved her and enjoyed her society so long. I thank thee for all the assurances her life has given that she was united by faith to the Saviour of sinners. I feel that I needed such a blow. However insensibly, I do feel that she was the idol of my heart; that in the enjoyment of one of thy best gifts I had, in a degree, forgotten the giver. I am sure there was a silent, secret alienation of heart from thee. Oh God, draw me to thyself. Show me thyself. May I feel the joys of thy salvation. I feel an alarming coldness and barrenness. My heart does not melt although it bleeds; and even while it bleeds I cannot realize that my dear, dear Anna is gone for ever. She is not here, but she seems to be absent but a little while, and that she will soon return. Oh God, may I feel that she is sleeping the sleep of ages beneath the cold clods of the valley. May I have that heartfelt reconciliation to the high decisions of thy will that shall enable me to say, "Sleep on, dear dust; the spirit that once animated thee is now in glory: I would not call it away from its glorious employment and the glories that surround it, if it were even in my power to do so."

Oh God, sanctify this tremendous blow to me, and make it the means of preparing me more effectually for the work to which thou hast called me, than her life, and company, and assistance could have done. I do believe it is for her good, and I pray that it may be for *my* good. She was in danger of loving me too much, and of making me her idol.

Besides, she had the seeds of a disorder that, in all probability, would have caused her great bodily suffering, and on these accounts it was good for her to go; and, as much as she loved me, much as her heart would have bled, had she anticipated such a separation, I believe that though now, from the heights of Zion, she may remember me on earth, and the painful circumstances in which she left me, it will give her no pain, it will not alloy the bliss of heaven, and that she would not for the world return to earth. Her work is done, her course is ended, her conflict is over, her victory over sin and death is complete, her harp is strung in glory, and she has already engaged in the everlasting songs of eternity.

Oh God, forbid that this providence should be in vain: may it be the means of bringing me more humbly to thy feet, and enabling me to serve thee with my whole heart. I have often prayed that

> "The dearest idol I have known,
> Whate'er that idol be,"

might be torn from thy throne, that I might worship only thee. But how little did I suppose that my wife was that idol! How little did I think that the dear partner of my joys and sorrows, the dear friend I looked upon as one of God's most distinguished gifts, as one of the tokens of his love to me, was, in any way, a hinderance to me, or that she was occupying the place in my affections which belonged to her Saviour. It would have made her heart bleed to think so. I believe she would rather have died. But she was not called upon to make the painful decision. She was not made acquainted with the painful truth. I do not think she was at all conscious of the approach of death. I do believe she found herself in eternity, welcomed by the Saviour she loved, to the joys of Paradise, before she was conscious of having left her body, and pain, and disease, and sin behind.

I do believe, O my God, that this providence is what I should rejoice in, could I see the whole case in all its causes and consequences. I know that it is right. I desire to *feel* more heart-submission; not the mere submission of necessity to a thing which I cannot control, or to a decision which I cannot reverse, but the submission of filial affection that rejoices to know a father's will, and feels that it is best. Oh God, grant me this filial submission. O let not this affecting call of thy providence be unheard or unheeded. But may I learn what it is designed to teach me. May I repent of the sins of heart and life, for which it is a severe but righteous chastisement. May I arise, and in the strength of the Lord, go about the work in which it admonishes me to be up and doing and to be faithful. Oh may I give all diligence to prepare for that eternity which is so near. May her dear orphan sisters be supported and directed to the orphan's father. O may they now at last lean upon thine arm, when their last earthly prop is broken down. God of mercy pity them, pardon them, sanctify them, and prepare them, when their race is run, to follow her to glory.

May this church and congregation hear the voice from the grave and from eternity, that calls most affectingly to them to improve the time, to prepare to die, to be reconciled to God.

December 9. And, oh my God, from the very grave of my dear departed wife, may I set out to serve thee. Oh forgive my past unfaithfulness, unbelief and sluggishness: forgive my inordinate love of the creature and my forgetfulness of thee. O heal the aching, bleeding wound in my heart by the comforts of thy salvation. I desire to bid earthly things a last farewell. I desire to live alone for God. I desire to choose thee for the portion of my soul. To draw my joys and consolations from the heavens. To serve the Lord with all my powers, and love him with all my soul. May this be the business of my days. Oh God, may I have a livelier sense of thy presence. May I not be disappointed of thy favour. I desire to rely upon thy mercy, and to live by faith upon the Son of God in the faithful performance of every duty.

———

Towards the close of this year Mr. Sanford received a second call to the American Presbyterian Church and Society in Montreal. This call was accompanied with many pressing letters from some of the most influential men in that congregation, earnestly entreating his acceptance of it. Among the gentlemen who wrote to him on this occasion, were Messrs. De Witt, Bigelow, H. Gates and the Rev. Mr. Purkis. These letters attest the very deep affection which was cherished for Mr. Sanford, in that city, and the high opinion which was entertained of his qualifications as a minister of Jesus Christ. But after mature and prayerful deliberation, he felt it to be his duty to continue in the field of labour upon which he had just entered.

———

January 4th, 1824. *Sabbath evening.* After a day of laborious exertion, O my God, my supporter, I would commit all my duties, my preaching, prayers, with my soul and body to thy mercy and grace, to be purified by the blood of Jesus, and to be blest. O God, sanctify me, forgive me for dwelling so much upon the dying scenes and mouldering dust of my dear, departed, glorified wife. O God, sanctify me ; may I be ready to follow her, but not be impatient. May I serve thee faithfully and successfully while I live. Oh bless the people of my charge. Though I speak to them in great simplicity, that all may understand, yet they will not without thy blessing. Bless the word and ordinances.

Awaken sinners to a sense of their awful danger while out of Christ; and may they be converted unto God. Prosper thy cause every where. Much good seed has been sown to-day.

January 25th. Once more I have been allowed to speak in thy name, O God. Wilt thou own thy word, however feebly spoken. I have been dwelling on the glorious truth, that there is " no condemnation to those who are in Christ Jesus." May thy people learn to appreciate their spiritual privileges, and to honour him with soul and body, who has freed them from the curse of the law.

May sinners seek such a union to Jesus Christ as shall entitle them to the strong consolations of those who have fled for refuge to lay hold on the hope set before them in the gospel. Oh God, may I have more of that faith in the Saviour which I recommend to others. May I understand the plan of salvation better, and love it more and more. May I be more weaned from the world, and never again place my affections upon it. May I be excited by the sudden death of my dear, dear wife, to be always at work, and to be always ready for the summons that shall soon call me home.

February 6, 1824. This day I enter upon the twenty-eighth year of my life. God only knows when, or in what circumstances, I shall end it. The last year of my life has been more eventful than all the rest. It is to-day two months since my dear, dear Anna, my life's loved companion, breathed her last. Oh death, thou art indeed a conqueror commissioned to destroy. Oh my God, support me under the heavy hand of thy righteous chastisements. Be pleased to sanctify the stroke that has cloven down my earthly stay and comforter; and left me in desolate grief to toil through life's pilgrimage. May I lean upon thine arm. May thy presence more than make amends for the absence of my dearest earthly friend; and by the application of the blood of Jesus, may I be prepared to follow her to that world of unmingled peace, and purity, and holiness, and joy, where, I trust, she is now celebrating the wisdom of thy providence, the wonders of thy love, and the riches of thy grace.

Sabbath, March 6th. Three months, to-day, since the dear wife of my bosom fell asleep in Jesus. Her dear dust is mingling with its kindred dust, but it shall rise again. It shall be raised incorruptible; it shall be fashioned into a glorious body to lodge and accommodate the spirit that once inhabited it, and, together, freed from every imperfection, they shall dwell for ever in the house not made with hands.

Oh happy Anna! I can sometimes rejoice that you are at rest in glory. When I think of my loss my heart bleeds afresh; but when I recollect what your gain is, what your blessedness is, I am satisfied to spend my days on earth in sadness, deprived of your dear enlivening society, and to toil on alone in the narrow, rugged, thorny path that leads to the hill of Zion. What tribulations and conflicts you have been spared; how much sorrow would have agitated that dear bosom; how many tears would have gushed from those eyes of tenderness and affection; how many nights of sleep-less anguish and pain; how many struggles with sin and Satan have you been spared! How much your " dear, dear husband" might have hindered you in your heaven-ward course by engrossing so much of your time and your affections; and how much he might have suffered in spirit by continuing to love you too, too fondly, by allowing you to occupy a place in his heart's affections which no creature ought to fill. O my God and Father, sanctify me wholly, and guide me in every duty, and sustain me in every con-flict, and finally receive me to thyself.

Sabbath evening, March 14th. Another sacred day is gone. Another week of my life is gone. I am nearer to eternity by so many days. My dear Anna has been another week in glory. O God, my heart and my thoughts continue to follow her thither. May I be growing in grace and ripening for glory. Guide me, O thou great Jehovah. Assist me in deciding the question now before me, in such a way as will be for thy glory. O God, I desire to know thy will, and I think I desire and feel ready and willing to do it. O guide me; suffer me not to wander from the path of duty. Bless both congregations; may they be supplied with the faithful preaching of the gospel.

April 11th. Last Sabbath we had a precious season, and much to encourage us, at the Lord's table; but how soon do we lose good impressions. On Wednesday evening, the service was unusually solemn; but to-day the weather has been so unfavourable that very few have attended the courts of the Lord, and I know not whether any seriousness remains after all our recent solemnities. But, O God, the cause is thine; the work is thine, the subjects and instruments are all thine. Thy people shall be willing in a day of thy power. Come, and let sinners be awakened in the midst of us. Lord, revive thy work. May I be more engaged. May I feel more for souls. O forgive all my feelings which are still so prone to murmur at the mysterious dispensations of thy providence. I would not, for the world, forget my dear, departed Anna, but I desire to cherish the warm remembrance of her love and her piety, with complete resignation as to the time and the manner of her removal. It was arranged by thy wisdom, and I desire to be still and submissive.

Sabbath evening, May 23d. Had it been for thy glory, O my God, I had still enjoyed the society of my dear departed wife, and had it in my power to review, with her, the duties and enjoyments of the day that is just closed, and converse on the subject of our common salvation, and sing thy praises, and bow the knee in prayer. But it has pleased thee to remove her. O sanctify the loss. May I turn away from earthly things and think more of heavenly things, of communion with God ; and hold more converse with myself. O Lord, make me a better Christian and a better minister of Jesus Christ, by this awful stroke of thy providence. I desire to finish my work, to do and suffer all thy will concerning me, to be made holy, and then to be away to thine own heavenly kingdom, and there, among the ranks of blood-washed sinners, and with my much loved Anna, to adore and praise thee even for this severe stroke of thy providence, which I think I can never cease to mourn over while I live. O God forgive and sanctify me, support me, and finally bring me home. Be pleased to follow with thy blessing my humble efforts to dispense thy truth to-day. O suffer not my unworthiness, and weakness, and ignorance to prevent a blessing on saints and sinners.

TO MR. H. D. OF BALLSTON, N. Y.

"*Steamboat, Aug. 27th, 1824.*

"I left Ballston last evening, not without great regret that I could not see you. Since last I met you the hand of the Lord has been heavy upon me, and my heart still bleeds with the wound, and mourns over the desolation it has left behind it. The revolution of eight months, and almost nine, has left me if possible more awfully sensible of the nature and the sad reality of my loss, than I have ever been before. But I know who hath done it. I do wish to bow to his mysterious, righteous will, to do and suffer all he assigns me ; by it to be prepared for meeting my departed wife, and saints, and angels, and then to be away."

Saturday, Sept. 25th. This is the anniversary of my marriage. It is one year since I was permitted to consummate one of the purest, fondest of earthly friendships, and to become the happy husband of my beloved Anna. Ah, on that day that joined our hands, how little did I think of being so soon called to close her eyes. That within not more than three-fourths of the first year after our union, my dear wife would be sleeping the sleep of ages! It was a righteous providence that dashed my earthly hopes to the dust, and I desire to be very humble under the hand of the Lord. But, oh God, let light, peace, and heavenly joy be poured into my desolated heart. I do not pray to have the wound immediately healed: no, let it bleed, let my heart break and melt; but let the love of Jesus warm it; let the love of God fill it; let heavenly joys and glories attract it; let spiritual duties occupy my attention and my best energies; let me do something to glorify God while I remain on earth; let me have bright evidence of adoption into the family of God; more clear and convincing evidence of an interest in Jesus; an unshaken confidence in the promises of God, deeper hatred of sin in all its forms, and sweeter tokens of the indwelling of the Holy Ghost, an earnest of the joys above. Grant it, O Lord of my salvation, for the sake of Jesus Christ.

TO MR. H. D., OF BALLSTON, N. Y.

"*Brooklyn, Oct. 11th,* 1824.

"I received your kind letter in the regular course of the mail, and was glad to hear of your safe return. I hope you were all benefited by the journey, and that you found your excursion (what I seldom find one to be) spiritually profitable, and that you are now endeavouring, with new resolutions and deeper sense of your weakness, to live for God and to God. Oh, press toward the mark, for the prize of your high calling in Christ Jesus.

"'It might, my dear brother, have afforded me a momentary though melancholy satisfaction, to have recounted God's
dealings with me since I had the pleasure of bowing with
you before the throne of grace. God has bestowed many
rich blessings upon me. But such is the greatness of my
ingratitude, that I am continually forgetting God's mercies,
under the absorbing, withering, tremendous stroke that has
desolated my heart of all that gave life its charms. I feel
at this moment as if my earthly prospects and hopes were
dashed for ever. Time wears away the first transports of
grief, and of convulsive, sleepless, and almost tearless agony
—but it heals not the wound, it calls not the affections home
that love to cling around the grave, where the fond companion of one's bosom sleeps the sleep of ages; it repairs
not the awful desolations which the hand of death has made.

" It is one of my heart's warmest and most constant wishes,
that seems to gain strength with every passing month, *to do
the work my Master has assigned me*—to prepare for his
kingdom, and then to be away.

" Excuse me for saying so much of myself and my feelings. I have felt that I was writing to a friend.

" I have nothing in particular to communicate respecting
the state of religion in my congregation. Indeed, I dare not
tell what I hope for; but this I may say, I believe we have
some who are ' waiting for the consolation of Israel.' There
is more attention than usual in several congregations in the
city. ' Oh Lord, revive thy work.' ."

Sabbath evening, Oct. 17*th.* This day completes one
year of my ministry. Alas, how unfaithful! That God
has been so near to me by his afflicting providence, and that
I have had so little of his gracious presence! Lord, forgive
all my unfaithfulness, prevent the injury of all my errors.
Bless the word of life that I have preached. Suffer not my
imperfections to prevent thy blessing; but, Lord, bless thy

word and ordinances, the means of thine own appointment. May I feel more for souls, more for God's glory. Enable me at all times to address sinners of every class as those who are soon to be in eternity, and for whom I have to render an awful account if they perish through my neglect. Grant me wisdom from above, which is profitable to direct both how to understand and how to divide to others the word of God. May I not shrink nor be disheartened at difficulties and discouragements, but committing my way to the Lord, and relying on his guidance and his blessing, may I go forward in every duty. Oh, may I live near to thee by meditation, and constant, fervent prayer, and enjoy more of the light of thy countenance and the joys of thy salvation.

November 28*th*. Oh, God of providence, it is not quite one year since thy righteous hand dashed my earthly prospects. Twelve months ago this evening, my dear Anna sat by my side, and we reviewed the duties, the delights, the imperfections of the day. She had been detained by indisposition from the sanctuary, but her last exhortation to me as I went out to perform my duties was, " *Be faithful.*" Oh. God, bless her exhortations and her example, and may I profit by her fall. Sanctify, "Oh thou who driest the mourner's tear," sanctify the severe providence.

Sabbath, February 6*th*, 1825. Another anniversary of my birth. Another year of my life gone for ever, a year of sorrow it has indeed been to me. I pursue my solitary path, thinking perhaps too much "of joys departed never to return," and too little, much too little, of joys in future prospect, bright and glorious, never to expire. Oh, my unbelieving, rebellious heart, how much it rejects the consolations which the gospel offers. Saviour of sinners, apply thy blood, cleanse me from all sin, assist me in every duty, support me under every trial, prepare me for heaven. May my future life be spent more for thy glory.

Tuesday evening, 22d. Have just heard of the death of my former pastor, the Rev. Dr. Romeyn, who died suddenly this morning, after a short, illness. Oh how loud and affecting the call, " Whatsoever, thy hand findeth to do, do it with all thy might."

Thursday, 24th. Attended Dr. Romeyn's funeral. Oh that I may profit by the warning, and be also ready. May I work while it is day, as the night cometh when no man can work.

Sabbath, 27th. Day stormy and unfavourable, church thin—all things looked cold and dreary.

28th. As usual, visited the sick. Met a few inquirers in the evening.

March 1st. Spent the day in parochial visiting; found some things interesting, especially this afternoon. This evening, at ten o'clock, visited a sick woman in a very happy state of mind. Oh that on my death bed I may be as calm and confident, upon clear, scriptural grounds.

Saturday, 5th. An unpleasant day; heart cold, mind melancholy and bewildered; little comfort in prayer, and little success in study.

6th. Felt unfit and unworthy to stand as God's ambassador to a congregation of sinners. Preached with a degree of feeling and tenderness from Balaam's wish, " Let me die," &c.—P. M. Brother Nettleton from Rev. xxii. 17: " And whosoever will, let," &c.—In the evening, from " The Son of Man came to seek and save that which was lost." May the Lord bless his word and revive his work.

7th. Visited the sick this morning. Bible class at two P. M. Prayer meeting of the Board of Missions at four. Missionary Society of Brooklyn at seven. Lord, hear the prayers of thy Zion for her prosperity and the extension of her borders. May thy kingdom come, O King of kings.

Wednesday, 9th. Visited a careless sinner, who is draw-

ing near to eternity. Oh the hardening, blinding, stupify-
ing nature of sin! Unable to lecture in the evening on account of a severe cold; spoke a little on the supreme love
which Christ requires, and the earnestness with which sinners should seek his mercy.

April 3d. Disappointed to-day in my expectation of
commemorating the Lord's Supper. Morning very stormy
—postponed the service. Had a good time in preaching to
a thin house, on seeking first the kingdom of God, &c. But
not so much freedom this afternoon: Rom. iii. 23, " For all
have sinned," &c.

April 10*th.* Lord's Supper celebrated; a precious season,
solemn and silent. Oh, that good may be done—that sinners may be awakened, saints encouraged and strengthened.

June 30*th.* Have felt very feeble and languid for several
weeks, so as to have little comfort in any duty. But the
Lord has been gracious; some few sinners have been added,
I hope, to the Lord, and some others are anxious for their
souls. Some are about to name Christ before the world.
Lord, search and try them. Felt much freedom last night
in prayer for a revival, and in addressing the people from
Ps. lxxx. 14, " Return, we beseech thee, O God of Hosts:
look down from heaven, and behold and visit this vine."
May the Lord revive us, and grant us all the blessings of
his grace.

Friday evening. Preached a preparatory lecture on
hungering and thirsting after righteousness, and the blessings
of it.

Sabbath, July 3*d.* Though very weak, and scarcely able
to go through with the exercises, preached from Solomon's
Song ii. 10—13: " Rise, my love, my fair one come away."
Urged Christians to the duty of activity and faithfulness in
God's service, from their particularly favourable circum-
stances and blessings. Was assisted at the table by Dr.

M'Auley, very opportunely and ably. May the Lord reward him, and bless the whole solemnity. Oh to feel more spiritual life—to work as for eternity, now so near!

August 16*th.* Returned after an absence of several weeks. My health but little improved. Lord, strengthen me for thy service. May I live and labour like a dying man commissioned to publish salvation to dying men. Oh Lord, revive thy work.

August 21*st.* Preached this afternoon from 2 Cor. iv. 3: " But if our gospel be hid," &c., with much feeling and comfort. In the morning, from 2 Cor. iv. 13: " We also believe, and therefore speak." Had but little freedom. Felt very deeply the importance of the subject before service, but as on similar occasions before, my thoughts and utterance confined and inadequate. The Lord bless his own word, however feebly delivered.

28*th.* To-day resumed the consideration of the moral law: preached all day from the third commandment, with tolerable freedom and comfort. But more in some desultory remarks in the evening on Christ as an advocate, and the importance of the cause we have to commit to him.

Wednesday evening. Lectured with some degree of feeling on Ps. ciii. 11, 12. O Lord, teach me the greatness of thy mercy, and may I know by sweet experience that it is great, and high, and glorious, as the arch of heaven.

Sept. 4*th.* Preached to-day on the fourth commandment, on the subject of its permanent authority, as appears from the situation and authority of the text. The general tenour of sacred scripture in relation to it. The circumstances of the original institution, Gen. ii. 3. From its indispensable importance to human society, and families, and individuals.

25*th.* This day I have completed the discourses on the fourth commandment, by attempting to show how the Sabbath is to be improved in God's service.

This day completes two years since I was married. My heart still bleeds. O, God, bind it up. I am not so much in danger of forgetting this desolating stroke, as of misimproving it. Oh may it be the means of weaning me more completely from this world, and of quickening me in preparation for eternity. Oh that the language of my heart might be, " Whom have I in heaven but thee, and there is none that I desire on earth but thee." May I be more faithful in my duties, more engaged in prayer for myself and my dear congregation, and may thy Spirit be sent down upon us to revive us. Follow the services of this day with thy special blessing.

October 2d, 1825. This has been another day of high spiritual privileges—a sacramental sabbath. I attempted this morning to show the meaning of Rom. x. 10. Remarked at the table on the erecting a spiritual monument in honour of Jesus Christ, and on the use of the sacramental supper to the faith of Christians. Presented subjects of the best kind for contemplation—God, eternity, heaven, hell— to teach the insignificance of the world, and that this is not our rest; and that our Lord will come again in grandeur and great glory. This evening presented the subject of Simeon's embracing the infant Redeemer, as the foundation of some practical remarks on the importance, the nature, and the effects of looking to Christ. Oh God, accept of all my feeble and polluted services; forgive all my coldness, ignorance and unfaithfulness; accept also of my sinful self, cleanse me with the blood of sprinkling, and fit me for nobler services above.

October 9th. To-day endeavoured to present the duty of children to obey and honour their parents, and of all who have living parents to honour and comfort them, and be grateful for their kindnesses. Oh that for myself I could do more to repay my dear mother and father for their days and nights of anxiety and toil for me. My God, bless them with the richest of thy blessings, even life for evermore. The congregation really appears solemn and very attentive. Oh, may they be doers of the word, and not hearers only, deceiving themselves. In the evening a peculiar stillness seemed to mark the whole assembly, when I was discoursing on the importance of the present moment of time as the starting point in a career of glory or of wo! Oh God, come and revive us, and bless thy word—make thy truth effectual.

Monday, 10*th*. I feel an indescribable languor upon my frame, and depression of spirit. Oh how little have I done for God—how much of my time has run to waste. How little do I feel for the condition of sinners, compared with what I ought to feel. How low my attainments in holiness. God of mercy and grace, quicken me in every duty, and suffer not my unworthiness to prevent thy blessing. Oh Lord, revive thy work in the congregation, and especially in my own soul.

October 16*th*. This day completes the second year of my ministry in this place. Here have I laboured two years for the glory of God, the good of souls—with what fidelity, and zeal, and prayer, and singleness of heart, oh God, thou knowest. I have reason to blush and be humbled before thee, that I have been so unfaithful—that I have done so little of what I should do, and so little as I should do it. The world, and probably my congregation, do, on the whole, approve my ministry, yet I have reason to fear that the church will give me credit for more, much more than I deserve. The success with which thou hast blessed my labours is not owing to my faithfulness or purity of motive, but it is to be ascribed to thee alone. Thou dost employ the most unworthy instruments to perform thy work, and I would fly to thee, oh my Saviour, for forgiveness for all my sins, and for the purification of all my services. I do delight in thy service;

I do rejoice to tell sinners of the grace and glory of the gospel, and to see them repent and turn to thee. Oh may I have more zeal, and love, and faith, and be enabled to be more diligent in business and fervent in spirit in all that remains of my mortal career, and at last be called home to glory.

January 1st, 1826. A new year has already commenced and the last has fled for ever, and borne with it the record of my life. What awaits me in the present year I know not—but one thing I desire to know, that the Lord Jesus Christ is mine—O let me but be sure of this and I will smile at the rapidity of the flight of time.

Sabbath evening, 8th. The Lord's supper, which was postponed last Sabbath, has been celebrated to-day, and I hope it has been a profitable season to many souls. I preached a second sermon on Luke, xxiv. 26, but felt astonishingly cold in meditating on the sufferings of Christ. I ascribe it, in part, to indisposition, but more to an alarming and distressing degree of spiritual barrenness and deadness. O God, revive thy work in my soul. Forbid that after preaching to others I should myself be cast away. Create within me a clean heart, O God, and renew a right spirit within me.

> " The rocks can rend, the earth can quake,
> The sea can roar, the mountains shake;
> Of feeling all things show some sign,
> But this unfeeling heart of mine.
>
> " To hear the sorrow thou hast felt,
> Dear Lord, an adamant would melt;
> But I can read each moving line,
> And nothing melt this heart of mine."

Felt more animated, this afternoon, in administering the holy supper; received fourteen persons on examination, and eleven by certificate. O that they may all walk worthy of the vocation wherewith they are called, and belong to the invisible family of the Redeemer. Lord, watch over the sheep of thy pasture and the lambs of thy flock.

February 5th. To-day I have been once more permitted to publish God's message from Mal. iii. 10, and John, vi. 44, and to apply them both in an exhortation with some degree of freedom this evening; but oh how little feeling! Alas, my barrenness. I tell others of their danger, and duty, and unfaithfulness, when I only describe, in the latter, my own history! Oh God, if I have ever been convicted by the Spirit of God and drawn to Jesus Christ, may I have more sensible tokens of his love. But this I cannot expect while I am so unfaithful and cold in my religious duties. If I am yet unregenerate, oh God, may I become truly and alarmingly sensible of my state and danger, lest after preaching to others I be cast off for ever myself.

I think my own unfaithfulness is a sufficient reason why God does not bless my congregation with a revival.

Monday, Feb. 6th. This day is the twenty-ninth anniversary of my birth. Retired last night exhausted by the services of the day, and was very restless in the night, though I feel mercifully refreshed this morning, and have, as usual, been visiting some of the sick in the congregation. But, beside my usual pastoral duties, I have to begin a *new year* to-day. Oh how the past has fled! How little done for God; how little for eternity! How little have I lived and laboured like a dying man. How little have I ever done for the years of my life that have gone by. The half of a long life—and my life may not be long—and then it is almost spent. Oh that I may begin to redeem time, as the benighted traveller mends his pace as evening advances. Lord I would devote myself to thee. I would feel more spiritual life. I do not enjoy the world, but I fear my disrelish is ever occasioned by the stroke of God's providence that has cloven down my comforts and withered the tenderest sensibilities of my heart, and carried them down into the very grave.

Sabbath evening, 12th. This day I have been preaching of the rich, worldling, both parts of the day, with some degree of feeling. Feel somewhat tender in prayer this evening, in view of the awful duties of my sacred office. Oh to have the spirit of it, and to be faithful in it. May the Lord bless the message of his *truth.* O may every worldling in the congregation be brought to feel his danger and fear his doom ; and do thou speak to them this night, not to summon them to eternity, but to call them to repentance, convince them of sin, and lead them to Jesus Christ.

February 26th. I wish to have enough of the gospel in every sermon to lead the sinner to the Saviour. Last Sabbath preached on the incompatibility of the love of the world and the love of God. 1 John, ii. 15. " If any man," &c. In the afternoon, from Zech. xiii. 1. O precious truth ! The day has dawned, the prediction is fulfilled, the fountain is opened " for sin" to take away its guilt, " for uncleanness" to remove its pollution.

To-day I have been showing the case of the young ruler, Matt. xix.—as an example of the influence of the love of the world and the consequence of wanting love to God. O fearful price he pays for the enjoyments of the world. This afternoon spoke of the cities of refuge and the law that relates to them as illustrating the guilt, danger and remedy of sinners. This evening have been speaking of the suitableness of the law to prepare man for the gospel ; and that if so amiable and moral a man as the young ruler was lost, because he had no love to God, what should those think who are, perhaps, less moral, &c. Oh God, do thou own thine own truth and bless it as dispensed to-day. May my whole

13

soul be bathed in the blood of Jesus, and may much more of his Spirit rest upon me at all times and in all duties.

Tuesday, 28*th*.   Heard to-day of the death of the Rev. Dr. Woodhull.   This is a season of unusual mortality.   I am conversant every day with sickness and death.   Now the infirm old man, whose existence was a burden to himself and to those around him, on account of the loathsomeness of his disease.   Now a wife and mother, in the morning of life.   Now an infant whose eyes have just opened upon the world.   And now the minister of Jesus, in the vigour of his days—all this within one week.   Such, O death, are thy ravages!   O God, give me a just sense of the solemnity of my circumstances, and the importance of my duties as a man and as a minister.

March 7*th*.   This evening attended Mr. S. in his last moments.   He expressed a firm hope in the divine mercy, through Jesus Christ, and has, during the day, been anxious to depart.   Has given some comfortable evidence, during the last week, that his heart has been renewed. Has spoken repeatedly of the preciousness of Jesus, and of loathing himself on account of his sins.   But, alas, how little, how little dependence should we place on such appearances in a man of health, unless attended by a holy life.   All things are in God's hands, and it is righteous and wise in him to allow those who have not served him in health to leave the world without those triumphant evidences and assurances with which he sometimes blesses his tried and experienced followers.   May none take occasion, from this providence, to delay the work of preparation for eternity till the hour of death.

TO MR. H. D., OF BALLSTON, N. Y.

" Brooklyn, March 9th, 1826.

" Yours of the 13th ult. was duly received. I had long looked for a line from you. I have heard, in general, of the course of events in B., but nothing of my friend D. I had hoped, however, that you were pursuing the march of your pilgrimage to glory, with a firm, and more accelerated speed, feeling the attraction that binds body and soul to the earth sensibly diminishing, and the flame of the love of Jesus rising higher, and brighter, and purer, to waft your soul upward towards his throne. May the Lord speed you on your way, and fit you and all that are most dear to you, for the society and the songs of heaven.   *   *   *
    *   *   *   *   *

" I have nothing to say of the state of religion here that is interesting. My congregation is becoming quite large enough, and the demands upon my time quite oppressive. My health is good at present, though it has been a season of much sickness and mortality, in the midst of us, and, indeed, throughout the country."

March 26*th.* To-day have been reviewing the subject of the creation, to show that it is *very good,* and this afternoon from Rom. i. 18, have been striving to impress upon the minds of the people, and my own, that God hates sin, and has given many expressions of his hatred of it. Visited a dying woman in the interval of public worship, who has since expired. Thus the work of God goes on. I have reason to bless him that I felt somewhat tender in my services to-day, and strong desires to have the message of God blessed. Send thy blessing, O God, and then the word will be effectual.

"When thy good Spirit deigns to breathe,
  Life spreads through all these realms of death;
  Dry bones attend thy powerful voice,
  They move, they waken, they rejoice."

Sabbath evening, April —, 18*2*6, 11 *o'clock, P. M.
Auburn, N. Y.* I have thought, as the stage is to go at
12, it is not best to retire, but to wait and be in readiness for
the summons.

Now, O my soul, learn a lesson of the greatest importance. Did I expect the coming of the Son of Man at " midnight," am I ready? Should the cry be made to me at
midnight, " Behold, the Bridegroom cometh, *go ye out to
meet him,*" is my *lamp lighted, furnished, trimmed?* Oh
God, may I henceforth make it my great concern to be prepared for the hour of my final " *departure,*" that so, when
the period arrives, I may feel no more alarm than I now
feel, when I am called to pursue my journey ; but that I may
have the humble, holy hope and joy of a sinner saved by
grace, who is just entering through the gates into the celestial city.

April 30*th.* This is the second Sabbath since my return
from a journey. I came home with desires to be more faithful in my private and official duties; but, alas, a great degree of deadness prevails; and I have reason to fear that I
have none of the right spirit of preaching. I am sure that
God sometimes makes use of wicked men to accomplish his
work ; but none can calculate upon his blessing here or
hereafter, but those who are full of the Holy Ghost and of
faith ; and I am sure this is not my condition. I think,
sometimes, that I do truly and ardently desire the salvation
of sinners, and the prosperity of the cause of Christ; not
for the credit and reputation of being a successful minister,
but that his name may be glorified. But these desires are
too cold and transient.

I have been preaching this morning on the history of the fall of man. This afternoon on the subject contained in Luke, xiv. 31, 32 ; and this evening, in the lecture room, on the grand test of Christian character, which consists in loving Christ more than any thing else. Have felt some degree of freedom and solemnity. Oh God, search and try me and thy people, and revive us.

May 14*th.* Our interesting anniversaries have just been celebrated, and to-day three of my brethren, from different sections of the country, have supplied my pulpit. It is truly gratifying to see the union of so many hands and hearts in the benevolent enterprises of the day, and to exchange feelings and sentiments and sympathies with the ministers of Jesus Christ of different denominations. Oh may this union of hearts be more complete, and this system of Christian exertion be more extended and more efficient.

21*st.* To-day have completed my discourses on the fall of man, by considering its effects upon the human family. Alas, how sad is the condition, and how dreadful is the character of human nature! Soul and body under sentence of death ; and both destined to an eternity of misery, unless rescued in time by the sovereign grace of God !

> "My God, I feel this dreadful seene,
> My bowels yearn o'er dying men,
> And fain my pity would reclaim
> And snatch the firebrand from the flame.
> But feeble my compassion proves,
> And can but weep, where most it loves."

May 22*d.* To-day I have heard of the sudden death of my dear father. I cannot realize it. Only a few weeks ago I left him in health, and with the big tear in his eye, while I wished him, for the future, to be free from the oppressive weight of worldly cares, and to spend the evening of his life in religious duties and enjoyments. But he is gone, and I was not with him to make any suggestion from the word of God, that might refresh and strengthen him for the last conflict, and to remind him of the precious promises of Jesus, suited to a dying hour. But I do believe that he loved the Saviour, and conscientiously endeavoured to perform his duties to God and man; and that his hopes for eternity have long been fixed on the " Rock of Ages ;" and so I am confident, that Christ was near him. He might not have been aware of his approaching dissolution, but I believe he was safe in the hands of a covenant-keeping God, and that he is now in glory. The storms of life have often beat upon him, but they are over. His aged frame, so often wearied by the hardest toil of husbandry, is now at rest. He had a treasure in heaven, and is now enjoying it. O may God, the widow's God, support, and bless, and sanctify my aged mother under this most desolating stroke ; and may brothers and sister, and their companions and children, be everlastingly benefited by this solemn providence.

June 8th., I have just returned from visiting my mother. I left her very feeble, though, probably, convalescent. The shock was almost too much for her feeble frame to bear; but I hope that the God of the widow will sustain her. She bears the stroke like a Christian, though her grief is most deep, and awful, and heart rending. O God, compose her mind by thine own power and grace, and let her find the promises of thy word, and the blessedness of thy presence able to console and comfort her. When those who have walked on so many years, and who have reached the evening of life together, are suddenly separated, it seems to be attended by more than ordinary sorrow. May he who can dry the mourner's tear, and who understands the widow's woes, be ever with her.

I left the following inscription for the small, neat stone that is to mark the spot where my father's ashes repose.

"In memory of Mr. Joseph Sanford, who ' fell asleep' on the 14th of May, 1826, aged 63 years, 10 months, 5 days.

> ' The trump shall sound, the dead shall rise,
> From the cold grave the slumb'rers spring,
> The saints, with joy, shall mount the skies,
> To hail the coming Judge—their King.' "

June 11*th*. Preached to-day from the 21st verse of Rom. v. Oh that the glorious subject of the reign of grace might warm my heart, and may I be one of its certain trophies.

P. M. Mr. Waterbury, from Hebrews. "How shall we escape," &c. We both addressed the people in the evening, when the audience appeared to be particularly solemn. Lord may there be a great shaking in this valley of dry bones.

SEAMEN.

" To give them the gospel is like giving it to the winds of heaven, to carry round the world.

"Ah, they are indeed like the winds of heaven ; and as they fly round the world, under God, it depends upon you to say, whether they shall resemble a moral pestilence, that shall spread contagion and death in its course ; or like the breezes of Paradise, to revive, and cheer, and bless the nations.

" The sailor is eminently the son of song; amidst whistling winds, and pelting storms, and yawning waves, he pours forth his wild notes in defiance of the tempest. But teach him the *songs of Zion*, and while he yokes the winds to his car, and rides upon the mountain waves, his notes shall be heard and approved, amid the thunders of the ocean, by him who directs the storm and makes the clouds his chariot."

June 25th. To-day had the assistance of a dear brother who gave us an interesting discourse on *letting our light shine.* O may God reward him, and make his superior talents eminently useful to the church of Christ. Save him from his own sinful heart, and from the idolatry and applauses of his friends. May all ministers of Jesus keep behind the cross; and while they glory in the cross, may they be able to add, " by whom the world is crucified unto me and I unto the world." I preached this afternoon, though oppressed with severe indisposition, from Gen. v. 24, on *the history of Enoch;* but was too unwell to enter into it and enjoy it myself, and of course did not make it very interesting to others. O God, give me Enoch's faith that embraced the distant promise, and enable me to walk with God, and to obtain some comfortable evidence that God has accepted me and will accept my poor, meagre services, on account of Christ alone.

July 2d. Unable to preach—sacramental service postponed—

> "Lord, what a feeble piece
> Is this our mortal frame."

May I learn to improve health better when I enjoy it.

RELIGIOUS INSTRUCTION.

" One of the solemn considerations which give so much importance to religious instruction is, that it exerts an influence for eternity. The influence will be felt while being lasts. The principles of truth, which are implanted in the mind, can never die, can never be annihilated. The good seed will remain. It will be warmed into life and usefulness by the Spirit of God, and grow into an immortal tree of righteousness, the planting of the Lord."

July 9th. Communion service. Morning, preached on the jubilee. Sacrament in the afternoon. I felt too feeble to enjoy it, and the exercise rather too much for my strength. O God, prepare me for that service where the worshippers shall never grow weary.

July 30th. History of Noah the subject of one discourse, and Heb. xii. 14, the other; the latter in the morning. Oh Saviour of sinners, own thine own word and bless it. Felt in somewhat of a comfortable frame to-day, but desire more light, love, faith and every grace.

August 13th. This day presented the solemn truth that none of us *liveth to himself.* O God, may I live indeed to thee. Much of my time has run to waste. Enable me to redeem the time. To improve it more diligently for God and for eternity. May the influence of Christians be holy and heavenly.

27th. To-day considered the calling of Abraham. May I really forsake all for God. Believe and obey him, however trying the circumstances.

September 3d. Preached this morning from Ps. lxxiii. 14, and this afternoon on the character of Melchisedec. This evening spoke on the subject of the 17th Ps. "What sinners value, I resign," &c., in connexion with the morning subject. O God, revive thy work.

17th. To-day have been considering the destruction of Sodom. Lord, may all who heard, learn the awful lesson, and take warning and not venture, like Lot, to sacrifice spiritual for temporal advantages; nor, like his wife, dare to disobey his commandments; nor, like the guilty inhabitants of Sodom, reject the last message of mercy, and suffer the vengeance of eternal fire.

This evening urged the sentiment, that we are on a steady march to the grave. O God, in whom all our hope is to be fixed, be pleased to awaken sinners here; and may they live like those who expect to die, and who really believe that after death comes the day of judgment.

October 1st. To-day preached from Luke, xxiv. 26, last clause. Considered two particulars of Christ's exaltation, his resurrection and ascension; and administered the sacrament in the afternoon, half past three o'clock. Had but little comfort, but felt really desirous to serve Christ better and to love him more. O Lord, revive thy work; revive my own soul. May Christ be more precious to my own soul, so that I may have better evidence of being really a disciple, and of growing in grace and holiness. Addressed communicants, previously to the celebration of the supper, on the importance of inquiring "*Lord, is it I?*"

November 5th. Concluded the subject of the commanded offering of Isaac, as a burnt sacrifice, and preached this afternoon from Mal. iv. 2. "But unto you that fear my name shall the Sun of Righteousness arise," &c. Improved and applied this subject this evening in an exhortation. Some may suppose I perform an excess of public duty; and it is indeed a heavy draft on my strength. But I do feel anxious for the souls of my congregation. O to feel more so, and continually! To be more faithful, not only in preaching to them, but in praying for them.

December 6th, 1826. The third anniversary of the death of my beloved Anna. Another year has she been in the presence of Jesus, and like him, in some humble measure. I do not wish her back again, though I seem to need her as the companion of my pilgrimage. But God, my Father, knows best, and he has given his unalterable decision. He took her from me when I just began to appreciate her worth, and to realize her usefulness as the wife of a minister of Jesus. But I am conscious that my heart loved her too fondly. It had already begun to lose sight of God. The creature was engrossing and absorbing its affections. The

Lord saw it, and in dreadful, mysterious mercy to us both, called her home to heaven. Father, not my will, but thine be done.

December 7th. The day appointed for public prayer and thanksgiving. Have been preaching from Ps. xcvii. **1.** " The Lord reigneth, let the earth rejoice."

This doctrine certainly affords a ground of joy to the earth and its inhabitants, as all the mercies we receive flow to us as specimens of the goodness with which he is supplying the wants of the subjects of his government. It affords refuge for the mind under the ills of life. And even my bleeding heart may find a balm of consolation in this interesting truth. It was a sovereign God who dashed my hopes; and on this day, which commemorates the wreck and ruin of all that gave life its loveliness, I will bow in silent submission at his awful throne. And may I feel what the psalmist expresses, and to which my understanding responds: " Righteousness and judgment are the habitation of his throne."

Sabbath evening, Dec. 10th. To-day have resumed the subject, Ps. xcvii. **1.** And have applied the expression to Jesus Christ in his mediatorial character. Have considered the nature and extent of his kingdom. Its subjects; revenue; blessings. Its prime minister, the Holy Ghost. The retinue of the Prince. His laws. The privileges of his subjects. And this may justify the joy of earth and its inhabitants.

Evening, in lecture room, spoke of the " chief end of man." Follow with thy blessing, O God, the services of the day. Bless thine own word, and accomplish thine own work, in thine own way and time.

January, 1827. We are already in another year. The past is indeed gone for ever. How many of its hours have passed without improvement. How many sins committed.

How many duties neglected or carelessly performed. Lord, with the new year, may I begin anew for God. Renewing the act by which I have professed to surrender myself to God, may I regard soul and body as consecrated to the Lord.; as not my own, and not to be used or employed but for his glory.

February 6*th.* This is the first day of my thirtieth year. O God, I am a monument of thy rich mercy. Why am I not a monument of thy righteous wrath? I have completed twenty-nine years of my mortal pilgrimage. Alas, they have been so many years of " wanderings." Oh how far I have strayed from God. O God, I would thank thee for any evidence that when my wanderings are ended I shall be safely conducted through Jordan and enter the promised land—that land, of which Canaan was such a lively emblem.

May I, in imitation of my divine master, who entered upon his public work, when " he began to be about thirty years of age," feel that I have a work to perform, and feel straitened till it be accomplished ; and may I enter with such holy zeal upon the duties of my sacred office, that it shall seem like the beginning of my course.

> "Teach me the measure of my days,
> Thou Maker of my frame,"

so that I may apply my heart unto wisdom. That I may work while the day lasts, and prepare for the night that is approaching, and the day that is to follow it. " Great day, for which all other days were made."

March 25*th.* To-day finished a series of sermons on the divine origin and authority of sacred Scriptures, by summing up the several subjects of discussion. This evening made an appeal (to myself solemn) on the subject of the insensi-

bility of sinners; their danger and duty requiring them to
awake and call upon God.

April 17th. The fourth anniversary of my licensure to
preach the gospel. For four whole years, with very little
interruptions, I have been engaged in this interesting work;
with what faithfulness, and with what success, the judgment
day will disclose! May the Lord prepare me for that day,
and cleanse me with the blood of Jesus Christ.

TO MR. H. D., OF BALLSTON, N. Y.

" *Brooklyn, July 2d,* 1827.

" Mr. S. gave me reason to expect a call from him this
morning, previous to his leaving the village, and I take this
opportunity to send you a line, though I have nothing of
special interest to communicate, except the goodness and
mercy of God, which are exercised continually.

" Our religious assemblies are well attended; but that is
all, and is to be connected with the tremendous fact, that
the word of God is always ' a savour of life unto life, or of
death unto death.'

" Our house of worship is so nearly full that unless we
can take measures for enlarging it, I shall consider my
sphere of usefulness too narrow to be satisfactory. I saw
your brother in Philadelphia, at the General Assembly,
though I had no opportunity of conversing with him.

" I am expecting to spend a few weeks at the springs, in
the course of this month, and will try to give you a call.
My health suffered a little this summer from a slight attack
of pleurisy in Philadelphia, but my general health, through
the last winter and spring, has been good.

" I have heard that Mr. Henry was expected to go to Ogdensburg, but Mr. S. said, yesterday, he thought not. I
hope you will not be left again without a pastor. Make my
best regard to P., and I should add, Christian regards to all

14

who inquire. I am informed that many of my acquaintances have died. Death is doing his work, and is on his way. Oh to live continually with our lamps trimmed, and burning, and ready to obey the summons of the Son of Man."

October 16*th.* The fourth anniversary of my ordination and installation as the pastor of this church and congregation. Alas, that the visible success of my ministry has been so small. The congregation has increased, and are under the necessity of providing more extensive accommodations. But how little life and spirituality among us, in proportion to our duties and hopes! I am sure my own soul is deplorably barren. My spirits flag—heart fails—hands fail. Eternal Spirit, improve my animal and moral vigour, and fill my soul with the love of God.

December 6*th.* Ah, this is also an anniversary, sad indeed to me. And why cannot I hail the return of the day which emancipated my life's loved companion from earth and sin, and introduced her to the perfection and bliss of heaven? I will enter it as a day of thanksgiving on the calendar of time. A wife in glory!

TO MR. H. D. OF BALLSTON, N. Y.

"*Brooklyn, Dec.* 26*th*, 1827.

" I have been long intending to write you, to say I do wish you would come to Brooklyn; I mean, to live and do good, to serve your generation, and to finish your course.

" This is a place of much importance, and it is rapidly increasing; and there is much for active, intelligent Christians to do, and but few to do it. You need not embark in business, which will exhaust your time or strength, nor consume or risk your capital. My object is not to invite you into the whirlpool of mercantile speculation, to make a fortune, but in'o the very centre of religious influence in our

land, to promote the Máster's glory. Every man has influence, and every good man should endeavour to make his
precious time and his influence bear upon the greatest amount
of human minds. We should try to do good on the largest
possible scale. I have much to say on this subject, but have
not time to-day to write it. But I do sincerely wish you
would come and see, and ask, ' Lord, what wilt thou have
me to do?'

" It is months since I began to think on this subject, and
to pray over it. I would not write to you at first, for I was
afraid to trust my first feelings and impressions. But at
last I have felt it my duty to write, and leave the event with
God.

" I wish you could spend the first Sabbath in January
with us. It will, by the leave of divine providence, be our
communion Sabbath; and there is no friend on earth whose
presence I think would gratify me more."

" A gleam of light breaks through the darkness, and revives the guilty soul of man. Let me stand a monument of
thy grace on earth, and bring me a trophy of thy victory in
heaven. When this clog of earth that weighs down my soul
shall be shook off in the dust, and my imprisoned spirit dis-
entangled from its clay, let the wings of love direct my flight
to the heaven where thou art.

" Whilst I spend the moments of existence allotted me in
this world, though distant from earthly friends, may I not be
distant from thee; but with thee ever find my joy and hope.
From the never-failing fountain of divine consolation may all
my wants be supplied. May I find consolation at all times
in the word ' Jesus,' the dearest, greatest, and sweetest name
that heaven and earth afford. Join me in mystic union to
thyself, that I may be separated from the pollutions of the
world, and follow the Lamb of God whithersoever he may

lead me. From the tabernacles of thy grace on earth, may my soul mount up to the tabernacles of glory in heaven. Oh that with tears I might bedew those deadly nail-prints, that tell at once my crime and my forgiveness. Lord, help me to enter into the ark of safety; let pardoning love fasten the door against an accusing conscience and a condemning law; let thy faithfulness and truth be as a brazen wall around me, that none of my fears may break through, none of my sins destroy me."

MAN IS A SINNER.

"Look upon the being God has made in his own image and for his own glory. He walks erect, his face is set towards the heavens; he is capable of knowing God, he is capable of endless progression in knowledge. He can explain the laws which bind the world and elements together; he can measure, and number, and name the orbs of heaven. He is the lord of this world, and made to be heir to a crown and a kingdom on high. Is he not worthy of the Being from whose hands he came, worthy of the heaven for which his Creator made him?

"But look again.—In all the rounds of life he never thinks of God, he never thinks of heaven. Earth, earth is his home and portion—mammon, mammon is the idol to which he bows; to gratify the appetites of the body is his aim; and he walks abroad as seemingly unconscious of the immortal principle in his bosom as though he was kindred, in every part of his nature, to the brutal tribes around him.

"His heaven-directed visage bends to the earth; the aspirings of his immortal spirit are checked, degraded, extinguished. Is he not fallen? 'Has not the gold become dim?' Has he not suffered some awful shipwreck in the voyage of his being?"

THINGS WHICH ARE SEEN ARE TEMPORAL.

" I may refer you to your own experience, to your observation, to your most vivid and painful recollections, for the
evidence of this. Have you not heard, and seen, and felt,
that all below is transient. Is there nothing within you that
responds to this affecting sentiment? Did you never feel, in
the midst of all your worldly possessions and prosperity,
that it was all vanity, all fading and unsubstantial? Or, if
so just a conviction was never forced upon your mind in the
day of prosperity, have you felt it in the day of adversity?
Has some worldly loss or disappointment taught you these
interesting lessons? When you saw your darling child upon
a dying bed, tossing in agonies which it was not in the power
of man to mitigate or relieve, and perhaps crying in vain to
you for help, did you not then feel the nothingness of earth?
When you saw the husband or the wife of your bosom torn
away by the strong and resistless hand of death, and saw
the grave close upon your mutual hopes, and returned to
your desolated dwelling, and had time to feel the anguish of
an aching and bleeding heart, did you not conclude that the
world was incapable of blessing you? Have you never seri-
ously considered how short is the longest probable term of
your earthly existence, and how much shorter than this your
life may possibly be? How certain is the event of your dissolution, and how solemn the consequences of that event!
How little the whole world will avail you in your final conflict with the king of terrors! How your soul, with all its
capacities for suffering or enjoyment, is to outlive all the objects upon which it is accustomed to depend for its happiness!
You have surely seen the circumstances of those around you
changed by sickness and misfortunes—you have seen one
calamity follow another in a most fearful succession. Sometimes a circle of friends gives life its principal attraction,

and every blessing of nature and of providence is more than doubled in their participation and in their society. But death invades this circle of kindred spirits, and its first and loveliest members fall beneath his stroke, and break the charm that bound the survivors to the world.

> ' For who would not follow when friendships decay,
> And from life's shining circle the gems drop away;
> When-true hearts lie withered and fond ones have flown,
> O who would inhabit this bleak world alone"

Earthly possessions are as uncertain and as transient as earthly friendships. You may be in affluence to-day, and surrounded by every comfort and luxury that wealth can procure or heart desire, but to-morrow a revolution of the wheel of providence may bring you down while it exalts another. Nay, events may be already in train, without your knowledge or agency, which shall reduce you to poverty and to want. The imprudence or dishonesty of another, or some of the elements of destruction, may entirely sweep away your possessions and your hopes. You may boast perhaps of an unsullied reputation, but what security have you that you shall escape the blasting breath of slander? But yours may be a character that can defy the shafts of calumny; and you may occupy, what few attain, the envied eminence where superior talents, and tried and acknowledged patriotism and philanthropy, and even popular applause, can place you, and fame may blow her trumpet, and swell her loudest, longest blast; but alas, how soon she wreathes the melancholy cypress for the brow of her favourite sons!

" You have seen the beloved and revered chief magistrate of this most important section of the Union, from the very summit of his greatness, and in the very noon of his usefulness and his fame, cut down by the stroke of death, without the warning of a moment! The statesman of unrivalled talents, the best representation of his country's greatness, the pride and boast of his native state, the acknowledged patriot and philanthropist, the efficient patron of science and benevolence, the public benefactor, the high minded and virtuous citizen, the exemplary husband and father, has fallen before the universal conqueror, and is in the dust! One week ago, who that had not learned a noble ambition from the Bible would not have coveted the talents and the fame of Clinton? But this bright western star has set. His fame may live in the recollections of ages, and will be even identified with the glory of his noble state. But what is this to Clinton now—and what are the splendours of his public career? What the success of his projects of internal improvement? What the merited tribute which his political friends and foes are eager to pay to his memory? What a proof of the vanity of earth!

"If the fall of such a man, which is an awful public calamity, and which clothes a whole community in mourning, might be the means of leading men of all classes to improve life, his death would produce effects more valuable than all his public services."

January 1st, 1828. This day we enter on a new year. I would begin anew for God, adoring him for the past, and trusting him for the future. Oh that I may feel more and more deeply that important sentiment which I have endeavoured to impress upon the minds of the Sabbath-school children this morning, "That the way to be happy is to be holy," and that with more zeal for God and more love for holiness, I may enter upon the duties of the new year. The mercies of God have been still abundantly continued. Oh that they may not be lost upon me, so as to leave me only a "cumberer of the ground." I have been prevented by indisposition from entering my pulpit one Sabbath only in the year, though I have been absent three other Sabbaths on business. But of the other forty-eight Sabbaths what have been the benefits? The last great day will disclose. I would labour for God more faithfully and prayerfully. My church and congregation are both increasing—the attendance upon the means of grace encouraging; but why are the special influences of the Holy Spirit withheld? Lord, thou knowest.

February 6*th*. This day I enter upon my thirty-first year. I can scarcely realize that so many years are numbered and gone for ever. They are indeed gone, and yet I have a solemn relation to them. They are not gone as the clouds that curtained my infant sky, or the flowers that strewed my infant path. Oh it is a solemn truth, that upon every moment of my existence God has enstamped accountability. May I ever feel it and act under its influence, and thus act for eternity. I cannot expect to see thirty years more this side of the grave. It is more than probable that within that period I shall be in my eternal state of bliss or wo! I would daily review life in reference to the great end for which it is given, and inquire to what purpose have I lived? What good have I been the means or the instrument of accomplishing? How have I glorified God in heart and life? And should I pass suddenly to my last account, what could I expect at the hands of the righteous sovereign of the world? My only hope is in Christ Jesus, the friend of sinners—he is precious to my soul. Oh may he become more and more so, and may I serve him more faithfully.

March 2*d*. A sudden death of one of the members of the church, and one who I believe received her first religious impressions under my ministry. Her illness was very short and distressing, unable to collect her thoughts until about two hours before her departure. But during that season, as far as the severity of her disease would permit, she express-

ed a most gratifying sense of the presence and the preciousness of Jesus, and desired him to hasten the wheels of his
chariot to come and take her. " She thought she was willing and ready to die." Endeavoured to improve this solemn
providence this morning, by considering the exhortation and
the argument of our Lord, Matt. xxiv. 44: " Be ye also
ready," &c. O God, may this afflictive event be improved by
us. May the church feel it and awake. May this call from
eternity be heard and never forgotten. Three weeks ago our
dear sister joined with us in the songs and services of the
sanctuary—to-day we trust she worships in the upper temple,
and mingles her voice in a nobler choir and in sweeter melodies! Jesus, Master, come and comfort us with thy presence and spirit.

TO HIS MOTHER.

" *Brooklyn, Feb. 19th, 1828.*

" I have postponed writing to you much longer than I intended. But I hope you have been satisfied that I have had
nothing special to communicate, and that my official duties
have occupied my whole time. Indeed, a clergyman who
will faithfully perform his duties, can have no time to spare.
I have usually three services on the Lord's day, two Bible
classes on Monday, a lecture in the church on Wednesday
evening, and a church prayer meeting on Friday evening,
which I am always to attend. Besides, the sick are to be
visited, and all the congregation as often as practicable, and
all the members of the church according to their circumstances and wants. And then every minister, more than
any other person, requires time to attend to his own soul's
interests and to the improvement of his mind. Thus you
see, my dear mother, how my time is disposed of, though I
have been so long silent.

" I hope you receive the New York Observer regularly, and from that you will learn all the religious intelligence of the day—and much of it will rejoice your heart. The kingdom of our Lord is advancing, and you, my dear mother, by your prayers may do much to speed its progress.

" Mr. H. was in Brooklyn a few weeks ago; he expects to visit Galway in April, and says he shall by all means try to see you. His wife is in a feeble state of health. His son, that was insane, is now restored. His eldest daughter has a school in this village, and I think will make a profession of religion at our next communion."

April 13*th.* To-day our earthly temple is closed for the purpose of an enlargement; while my health is such as to render it unsafe for me to go out in the storm of snow and hail that has been falling all day. Who would have thought five years ago that this infant congregation, which was then scarcely organized, would so soon require more extensive accommodations. God has indeed blessed my ministry far beyond what I could have expected. Some I hope have been born from above, and have become heirs of glory, through my unworthy instrumentality in dispensing the good seed of the word. A church of more than three hundred members has been collected, besides thirty or forty who have been called away by providence and by death. I have reason to be amazed and humbled at what God hath wrought, though the special influences of the Holy Spirit have been withdrawn. May the Lord take care of his flock while they are now to be for several weeks dispersed; may we at length meet in our enlarged sanctuary; and may the windows of heaven be opened, and may God pour out blessings so that there shall not be room enough to receive them.

THE SAFETY OF GOD'S ISRAEL.

" ' The Lord will preserve thee from all evil.' There is but one idea more awful than the atheistical opinion that there is no God, and that is, *to have this God for our enemy!* These words were addressed to a peculiar people, and this is important in the outset to prevent all mistake. The psalmist seems to have had a primary reference to the nation that went up to Jerusalem to worship. ' I will lift up mine eyes unto the hills,' &c. The Israelites looked with much delight to Mount Zion, where was the house of God, and all the visible tokens and symbols of his presence, where he was wont to hear their prayers. God saves his people from all evil, that is, from every thing which would not work for their good ; from every thing that would destroy them ; from the ruinous evil of sin into which they have fallen·

" 1. *He saves them from dangerous, soul-destroying errors.* Men are in great danger of this. Draw the line between truth and error where you will, *some errors* are damning. External advantages and cultivated minds are not secure against this.

" 2. *He saves his people from falling under condemnation.* They are justified, but Christ constantly applies his blood.

" 3. *He saves his people from apostacy.* The righteous are ' scarcely saved;' they come very near being lost ; they are prone to fall, often tempted, often straying, but he saves them. Think of the safety and happiness of such. Think of the love of God in Christ Jesus towards sinners. Unlike the love of men, it sees nothing lovely in its object.

" Dismiss your fears then, Christian—doubting, trembling Christian. You are safe. All is well. Be grateful for such a mercy."

June 15*th.* This day entered our house for worship, with its enlarged accommodations. Preached all day from Ex. xx. 24. " In all places where I record my name I will come unto thee and bless thee." Considered the presence and the blessing promised. O God, grant them both in mercy, and take possession of our sacred edifice.

> " Enter with all thy glorious train,
> Thy Spirit and thy word:
> All that the ark did once contain,
> Could no such grace afford."

The congregation appears to have enlarged with the building. Open our eyes to behold wondrous things out of thy law. Open our hearts to receive thy grace; and open our lips to speak forth thy praise.

TO HIS MOTHER.

" *Brooklyn, August* 7*th,* 1828.

" I have just received a letter from Mrs. Howe, informing me you are in Brutus. I hope you received the letter I wrote by Mr. K. I should have visited you in July, if you had staid in Galway; but the opportunity of going with Mr. K. was too good to neglect. I am glad you embraced it. Mrs. H. did not mention how you endured the journey; but I concluded it did not injure you, or she would have mentioned it. It is true, my dear mother, I would feel better satisfied could you feel contented to live in Galway, because I could see you oftener, and you could have greater religious privileges. But if you prefer, on the whole, to live in C. you have my entire approbation. I wish you, by all means, to do that which will make you most comfortable.

" If I can leave Brooklyn this fall, I will try to go out to C. to see you, in the course of September or October. But it is extremely difficult for me to be absent from my congregation long enough for such a journey. I am anxious to see brother E., to know what are his prospects, &c. My health, this summer, has been better than usual; and my labours are such as to require all my time and strength. Mention my respects to all friends. It is doubtful whether I shall be able to stop in B., should I go to the west. It would require one whole day; and my time is precious, and not my own. May the blessing of the Lord descend upon you, and his presence cheer and fill your desolated heart."

August 24. Detained from the house of God to-day by indisposition. Taken ill last evening, and too much enfeebled to-day even to attend the preaching which, by the kind providence of God, my congregation are favoured with. " Lord, what a feeble piece," &c. A few hours' sickness prostrates this frail tabernacle, and bends it towards its native dust. O to live with an assured confidence of a building of God, ready to receive me when this earthly house is dissolved; and to work in the vineyard of the Lord every day, as though I expected to be laid aside to-morrow.

——

In the month of September, of this year, Mr. Sanford received a call from the Second Presbyterian Church, in the city of Philadelphia, to become their pastor. This call was given with almost entire unanimity. This large and important church had become vacant by the resignation of the Rev. Dr. Janeway, who had been appointed Professor of Theology in the Western Theological Seminary, which was then about to be opened, at Alleghenytown, near Pittsburg. That a call from such a church—one of the most respectable in the United States—which embraced a large number of men of distinguished usefulness, and which had been blessed with a succession of able pastors—should be considered with great attention by Mr. Sanford, is what all would be ready to pronounce an obvious and imperative duty.

This call was long and prayerfully considered by Mr. Sanford. The advice of the best and most judicious friends was sought. He consulted such men as the Rev. Drs. Green, Miller, Alexander and M'Auley. From them he obtained most appropriate counsel. All of these excellent fathers and brethren in the church expressed to him the great happiness which it would give them to see him settled in that church, if he should find it to be his duty to accept the call.

On the other hand, his large and beloved church in Brooklyn, was greatly opposed to his leaving them. And what served to increase the perplexity of his situation, was a *third, unanimous* call from the American Presbyterian Church in Montreal. The unanimity of this call, after two previons failures, the interesting state of that church and congregation, and the prospect of great usefulness, not only in that important city, but also in the entire province, were reasons for serious and just consideration of this important call. Indeed it would not be possible for any one to read the letters which Mr. Sanford received, on this subject, from Messrs. De Witt, Dickinson, and Bigelow, on the part of the church in Montreal, without being struck both with the importance of that post and of the high and long-cherished opinion which that people entertained of Mr. Sanford's eminent qualifications for that place. It does not comport with the object of this small work to give that correspondence, but it may not be improper to insert, here, two letters which Mr. Sanford received, in relation to this call. The first is from the Rev. Mr. Hoyt; and the second is from the Rev. Dr. Nott, President of Union College.

" Montreal, Jan. 19*th,* 1829.

" REV. AND DEAR SIR,

" Though a stranger, yet you will permit me to address you on a subject in which my own feelings are deeply interested. I refer to your anticipated removal to this city. I have been supplying the American Presbyterian Church, in this place, for a few weeks past; and I have had a fair opportunity of observing, on the spot, what, I have no doubt, are facts relative to the importance of this post. And, for what I have here witnessed, and for the knowledge I had previously acquired, I have no hesitation in expressing my firm belief that Montreal presents one of the most prominent and inviting fields of evangelical labour in North America. I cannot conceive how, by any impartial and enlightened mind, it can be viewed otherwise. Were this city only to be taken into account such would be the fact. But it is not. This whole district of country is materially affected, and will be thus affected, by the moral atmosphere inhaled in Montreal. The light of eternity only can disclose the amount of good which, under God, an able, judicious, humble, devoted minister of the gospel may here effect.

" I am persuaded that brother Christmas will always rejoice in view of his connexion with this people and region. But I have no doubt that Mr. Bigelow has presented before you, fairly and fully, the imperious claims of this part of the heritage of Zion.

" What I want to say, brother, is that you are the man for Montreal. Yes, the very man to come and labour in this vast field, already ripe for the harvest.

" I know that you have the esteem, and confidence, and affection, to as great an extent as any man should have, of those who have invited you to come. Their eyes are fixed upon you with intense anxiety. If they are disappointed the shock will be no ordinary one. It will be very difficult

for them to be fully united in any other man.   And there is
a fair prospect of the society being at once, and to a considerable extent, enlarged, should you come.

   " I have no interest in this subject, only what regards the
general prosperity of the church.   I leave here to-morrow
morning.   As I have an opportunity of sending directly to
New York, I have been constrained to drop you a line on
this subject.   I pray that the Great Head of the church will
be with you, and guide you to such a result as shall be most
for his glory and your eternal well being.   In haste,

" Yours affectionately,

" OTTO S. HOYT."

" DEAR SIR,

   " Nothing but a sense of duty could induce me to address
you on a subject that seems, by a decision you have already
made, to have been put at rest.   But circumstances have
come to my knowledge, that lead me to apprehend that the
contemplated church in Montreal will either expire or go
into the hands of dangerous errorists, unless measures are
taken to prevent this.   That those measures involve your
removal to that place ; and that there has been a change of
circumstances and a development of facts, since you were
there, that not only justify, but call for your solemn and deliberate review of the whole case.   And to induce you to do
this is the sole object of this letter.   The facts and circumstances alluded to, will be presented from another source.   I
am aware that you are pleasantly settled, and that an address of this sort may appear like an intrusion on your peace,
and on the peace of your society.   I respect both ; but neither are to be put in competition with the great and extensive
interests of the Redeemer's kingdom.   God, in his providence, has opened a door for the Presbyterian Church to
make a lodgement in that land, not only of want but of de-

lusion. If that lodgement is made, other posts may soon be taken possession of. A Presbytery may soon be formed there—from this, other Presbyteries may arise—so that, in a single generation, the Bible Society, the Missionary Socie- ty, and the Sunday School Society, together with all our other moral machinery, may be extended over a country, which will not only be redeemed itself, but, in the end, react and pour its contributions into that treasury consecrated to the conversion of the world. To my mind, the object has an importance that would justify the taking of any pastor from any church in the United States, that might be deemed peculiarly fitted therefor. And the continued attachment of the congregation *there*—their continuing to hope against hope, seems to be an indication of Providence, with respect to the individual so fitted. If the friends of vital piety will not take possession of this field, the enemies will; and agents of error and of evil will occupy the region, which, we might have oc- cupied; and generations pass away before another oppor- tunity, equally favourable, will offer for adding this province to the kingdom of Jesus Christ. I am aware that you will be pressed by friends, whom it will be painful to deny, to de- cline the reconsideration of this subject. But you will call to mind that you are not the master of your own labours; and that the question is one that respects the present and the future interests of the Saviour's kingdom. It is a question, to be sure, on which, when the whole circumstances are be- fore you, you must judge; and must not, and ought not, to be governed by the opinion of others. All that I wish to do, is, to bespeak your prayerful and solemn reconsideration of the whole case—the present situation, the future pros- pects of Canada—and see whether the prospect of useful- ness and range of action, *there*, be not far, and decidedly greater than that of the place you at present occupy. See, also, whether the evil of refusal be not likely to be far greater

15*

in extent, and lasting in duration, to that province, than any probable evil that can befall your present charge in consequence of your resignation thereof.

"It may be that I am in error—that the time has not come to plant the gospel in that land, so long overshadowed with darkness. Be this as it may, a door is opened to make the attempt. Success would be glorious; and it would be glorious too, even to fail in such an undertaking. I will not add more; perhaps I have already said too much. I do not wish to prejudge your judgment; but merely to urge you to reconsider and review the whole case, and decide according to the light which God, in his providence, may afford you.

"Wishing you the guidance of his Spirit, I am, in very great haste, and with esteem,

"Your's sincerely,

"ELIPH. NOTT."

———

Notwithstanding the powerful appeal which was made in behalf of Montreal, Mr. Sanford, after long, and anxious, and prayerful deliberation, decided in favour of Philadelphia. At first his Presbytery were opposed to his removal; but, upon consideration of the subject, they yielded to what he believed to be the call of duty, and of the Great Head of the Church.

The following extracts from his journal and letters will show with what spirit he considered this call, and finally went to his new field of labour, where much usefulness and many trials awaited him; and where, in less than three years, he ended his days on earth.

———

October 1st. This day received notice of a call from the Second Presbyterian Church of Philadelphia, to become their pastor.

May the Lord give me wisdom to discern, and grace to perform, my duty. May I be enabled to decide this important question in the light of eternity. Lord, what wouldst thou have me to do? Lord, direct my paths and make my duty plain.

October 19*th*. This day completes five years of my ministry. Preached this afternoon from Eph. iii. 8, and endeavoured to call the attention of my congregation to the inquiry, What have been the results of my ministry with them, as individuals; and whether, if they should be called to-night, to their final account, they would bless or curse God, through eternity, for the message of his mercy!

Oh God, the future is all unknown to me. " Guide me, oh thou great Jehovah." Enable me to take such views of the subject that now occupies my mind, that I may judge impartially, and in the fear of God, and in fear of nothing else. I would acknowledge thee in all my ways; wilt thou direct my paths. I would not confer with flesh and blood. I desire to know what the will of the Lord is, and what the interests of Zion require.

November 2*d*. Preached this morning from Heb. iv. 1, and called my congregation to consider the fact, " that a promise of entering into rest is actually made to us;" that many fall short of it. Christ has taught it, and our own observation justifies his teaching on this subject. Urged the apostle's exhortation upon all. This afternoon spoke with tolerable freedom and comfort, from Ps. xxxiv. 15 : " The eyes of the Lord," &c. Oh that I may desire, more than all things else, to secure God's approbation; and that I may act as in his presence, and avail myself of the blessed privilege of spreading out all my wants before him whose ear is ever open. Truly I need this at this time especially. How shall I dispose of this call from Philadelphia? " Lord, what wouldst thou have me to do?"

On the 6th of November, of this year, Mr. Sanford was united in marriage with Miss Margaret H. Boardman, of Albany ; a young lady of devoted piety, and of whom he justly speaks, in his journal, as " a friend, congenial, sympathizing and suitable to be the companion of a minister of Jesus Christ." After their marriage they visited Rochester and several other places in that part of the state of New York, and returned to Brooklyn towards the end of the month.

December 4th. Reached Brooklyn, after many delays, fatigues and perils. This is the day of public prayer and thanksgiving. O who has greater cause for thankfulness than I?

December 25th. To-day Presbytery met to consider the call from Philadelphia. Though the thought of separation from my dear congregation is painful, I do feel that God calls me to make the sacrifice. I gave this answer. The business postponed until to-morrow.

26th. The commissioners have been heard. My brethren all think I ought not to remove. I am sure they have not examined the subject as I have done. They decide as I expected. They adjourn till Tuesday next, to give me time to consider their advice. O may the Lord guide me under these accumulating responsibilities. May he give me wisdom from above. Lord, I would commit my way unto thee. Do thou direct my path.

Tuesday morning, Dec. 30th. To-day the question must be finally settled, and I do feel that I must follow my own convictions of duty, though against the opinion and advice of my dear brethren. Oh God, in thy sight, I wish to act for eternity. Let me have the presence of thy Holy Spirit to-day. Suffer me not to mistake my duty. I would commit my way to thee. O my God, direct my paths. May I not misinterpret thy providence and mistake thy will. Nor make a decision which I shall hereafter regret. Thou art the King of Zion: rule then in every heart, and in mine to-day. May I perceive and perform my duty, and leave consequences in thy hands.

January 4th, 1829. To-day administered the Lord's supper to this dear church, which I am so soon to leave. The day very cold, snowy and unfavourable—but few of the church attended. The season, however, was solemn. May it' be profitable. Never can I expect to meet this whole church, to which I have so often dispensed the word and sacraments, till we meet in judgment. O may we meet to bless God for the relation which we have sustained.

January 11th. To-day have taken leave of my congregation. Preached this morning from Ps. lxxxvii. 3. "Glorious things are spoken of thee, O city of God." Spoke of the extension, prosperity, perpetuity and coming glory of the church of God. May we all become citizens of Zion, and meet in heaven. Preached this afternoon from the words of Paul, in his farewell address to the Corinthians, 2 Cor. xiii. 11. "Finally, brethren," &c. Had difficulty in commanding my feelings so far as to be capable of utterance; but the Lord assisted me. Oh may these familiar exhortations be improved to the good of many souls. Into thy hands, my dear Lord and Master, I have resigned my charge of this people. Many, many imperfections have marred my services; and yet, I hope I have laboured in sincerity and truth. I have my unfaithfulness to deplore in thy sight; but I trust I am clear of their blood. O bless this people. Send them a pastor whose ministrations thou wilt own and bless; and build up this people, and dwell among them continually. And do thou take me under thy gracious care and guidance. I have desired to act for the love of Jesus, the good of souls, the prosperity of Zion, and the glory of Zion's King. May I now renew my covenant engagements to be thine; and do

thou employ me in the place and under the circumstances
where I can do most for the kingdom of Jesus, and ripen
most rapidly for the services and the society of the church
triumphant. May I have clearer evidences of my love to
God and his love to me. May all my graces be in progress
and in exercise, and the work of sanctification be evidently
advancing. Prepare me for all that awaits me, of joy or
sorrow, prosperity or adversity, sickness or health. And
may I run with patience the race set before me, with my
faith and hope fixed on Jesus.

The following extracts are given from the excellent vale-
dictory discourse which Mr. Sanford delivered to his dear
people on this affecting occasion. It is replete with the best
advice, and is worthy of a careful perusal by all.

"My dear hearers: This day my official labours among
you are to close. After a deliberate, and prayerful, and
certainly painful attention to all the recent indications of the
providence of God, I have judged that the Head of the church
requires my removal to another part of his vineyard.

"For upwards of five years I have been with you at all
seasons, in sickness, in health, in joy, and in sorrow; in
prosperity and in adversity. I have wished to be instant in
season and out of season, to declare the whole counsel of
God according to my best judgment of your capacities and
wants: to keep back nothing that would be profitable to you,
for fear of losing your confidence, or wounding your feelings;
to teach you publicly, and, as far as practicable, from house
to house; and to present to you, in a manner that should
not offend the most cultivated mind, while it aimed to become
intelligible to the humblest capacity, all the fulness of the
blessing of the gospel of peace. And I wish to take you all
to record this day, that while I am conscious of great weak-

ness and imperfection in the performance of my duties, I feel pure from the blood of your souls.

" Perhaps I owe it to you, as well as to myself, to state publicly to all, what I have often said privately to many, that it would have been unspeakably gratifying to my feelings, and would have been most accordant with my sincere and ardent attachment to this church and congregation, and with my deliberate preference of this place to any with which I am acquainted, and with my personal and professional comfort, to have finished my ministerial course in the place where I commenced it. It would have been most grateful to every affection of my heart, to have led this dear flock in the way of holiness and heaven ; to have been the honoured instrument of training them for glory ; to have attended those who might be called home before me, on the bed of death, and to the verge of heaven ; to have slept the sleep of ages among their sepulchres ; to have risen with them when the judgment trumpet shall wake the dead ; and to have entered with them into the joys of our common Lord ! But such a course, though it would be agreeable to the wishes you have so unanimously expressed ; agreeably to the opinions and advice of many of my most valued brethren and friends ; and most compatible, as all have acknowledged, with my personal ease and enjoyment ; most gratifying to those feelings of exalted Christian friendship, which several years of pastoral intercourse are so well calculated to form, and fix, and strengthen, and refine—my own solemn convictions of duty have not permitted me to pursue. I yield, therefore, and make the sacrifice which involves my feelings as well as your feelings and wishes, not, I trust, your friendship ; and I should be unworthy of your confidence as a minister of Jesus Christ, if I could refuse to make it.

" But the sacrifice is made, I humbly hope and trust, for the *love of Jesus*, for the *good of souls*, for the *prosperity of*

Zion, and for the *glory of Zion's King*. It is in the belief
that such high considerations as these have turned the scale,
and ought to turn it, that by the blessing of God I may hope
to be more extensively useful to the church of Christ, that I
have regarded the divine will as indicated by the providence
of God, and that will, as far as we can satisfactorily ascertain it, ought to outweigh a world that would oppose it.

"My brethren have permitted me to follow my own views
of duty, and this day concludes my ministerial services.

"And now, before we separate, could I present the substance of all the truth which has been here delivered in the
course of my ministry—all the array of motives and arguments by which I have endeavoured to show you your condition and your duty, and to lead you to Jesus and to glory, in
a few sentences that should be lucid with the light of eternity,
and impressive as the voice and authority of God, and that
should fasten conviction upon your hearts, and make you
wise unto salvation, how gladly would I do it! But it cannot be, and I have only to ask your attention to a few familiar
words of affectionate exhortation, such as the Apostle Paul
addressed to the church of Corinth, when he closed his last
epistle to them : ' Be perfect, be of good comfort, be of one
mind, live in peace, and the God of love and peace shall be
with you.'

"1. One of the first objects of the gospel ministry is the
perfection of the saints. The word signifies to *compact,
settle, mature,* and *complete.* Thus it is used by the apostle:
' And he gave some apostles, and prophets, and evangelists,
and some pastors and teachers, for the *perfecting* of the
saints, for the work of the ministry, for the edifying of the
body of Christ.' Eph. iv. 11, 12. And again in the epistle
to the Hebrews, xiii. 20, 21: ' Now the God of peace,
that brought again from the dead our Lord Jesus Christ,
make you perfect in every good work to do his will,'

&c. Many of you have only entered upon your Christian course, and are only babes and children in the knowledge of God, and the duties of religion. ·'I have fed you with milk, and not with meat, for hitherto ye were not able to bear it; neither yet now are ye able.' You are attending to the very alphabet of the language of Canaan; to the rudiments of the science of salvation. And this exhortation is that you should grow in grace, and in the knowledge of God. The knowledge of God is the foundation of all the graces, and is to be attained by an attentive examination of the sacred Scriptures, and the teaching of the Holy Spirit. Make yourselves well acquainted with the evidences of the divine authority and origin of the Bible, and then study its contents, and become familiar with its precepts, its promises, its history, its biography. Strive to learn well the first principles of the doctrines of grace, and then to pass on to the more deep, and difficult, and sublime communications of the will of God. The simple milk of the word is suited to the condition and wants of the infant believer; but the inspired volume contains aliment for the disciple of greatest age, and largest attainments in the school of Jesus Christ. The wayfaring man, though comparatively a fool, may here learn his duty; and the man of the loftiest intellect may find room enough for the exercise of his most cultivated powers. God's truth is the appointed means of your spiritual progress and prosperity, and it is to furnish you with your principles, and rules, and motives of action. ' The more you study the word of God, under the influence of the Spirit that inspired it, the more you will see of your guilt and misery by nature ·and by practice; the more you will see of the loveliness and the richness of the grace of the gospel; the more you will learn of the character of God, as it is most completely and gloriously manifested in the cross of Jesus; the more you will crucify the flesh with its affections and lusts; the more you will glorify God by your lives and conversation; the more rapidly will you make your preparation for the perfect and perpetual society and services of the upper world.

"And it may well be remembered, as a consideration that should at once humble and animate you, that after all your efforts and advantages, it is but a little you ever learn of God below. Though the dispensation of shadows has expired; though all its glory has passed away, like the mists of the morning before the brightness of noon, yet even now, under the gospel dispensation, you see but '*through a glass darkly,*' and under the most favourable circumstances, with your field of observation widened, and your vision strengthened by God's completed Revelation, you will '*know but in part.*' But the brightest light you here enjoy, is only the twilight of what you may anticipate. 'When that which is in part shall be done away, and that which is perfect is come;' when your faculties are completely emancipated from the influence and the imperfections of sin, and you come to take your places among the disciples of a higher school, the perfections of Jehovah's character, and the operations of his hand, shall spread out their ample pages, and invite your investigation; and there shall be heights, and depths, and lengths, and breadths of his wisdom, and goodness, and righteousness, and grace, and glory, that shall exercise, and elevate, and delight your immortal and untiring energies through everlasting ages.

"But the apostle's exhortation includes progress and perfection in *grace*, as well as knowledge. The child of God is compared to a tree of the Lord's planting, standing by rivers of water, whose leaf never withers, whose fruit never fails. The Holy Spirit dwells in his heart, and the fruits of the Spirit are manifest in his life. These are 'love, joy, peace, long suffering, gentleness, goodness, faith, meekness, temperance.' Gal. v. 22, 23.

· " Every disciple of Christ is required to ' abound in fruits of righteousness, which are by Jesus Christ unto the praise and glory of God.' Christ is the author and finisher of his faith, and faith may be regarded as the parent of the graces. The existence of these fruits of the Spirit will be an unequivocal evidence of the soundness of your religion, and the safety of your condition. By these you will glorify God, and by their growth and prosperity you will evince your progress towards the perfection of your Christian character, and your preparation for the world of glory.

" Your progress in knowledge and grace will incline you *to persevere in every good word and work,* which is the other branch of your Christian perfection. This was the apostle's prayer for the Hebrews, that they might be perfect in every good work to do the will of God. Heb. xiii. 21. You will be anxious to learn how you can most successfully and efficiently glorify God ; you will make the cause of God your own, and think nothing too good or too dear to sacrifice in promoting it ; you will regard yourselves as servants, and strive to do the work of your Master—as soldiers, · and feel that earth is a field of battle, and that heaven is the home of your repose ; and however humble your circumstances or obscure your condition, while you can cast a mite into God's treasury, or offer a prayer at his mercy seat, you will not cease to strive for the coming of his kingdom, and the complete establishment of the empire of truth and righteousness throughout the world.

" When the members of the church, in their individual capacities, comply with the apostle's exhortation, then will the church itself, in its organized capacity, as a branch of the family of God, (1 Pet. v. 10.) be compacted, and settled, and established, and thus matured and perfected in the faith and obedience of the gospel.

" 2. But the Corinthians were exhorted to ' *be of good comfort.*'

" I should do great injustice to the very numerous and gratifying expressions of affection, I have so long and so lately heard, were I to doubt that many souls are sorrowful in the prospect of our separation. I have anticipated, my hearers, and I have *felt* the anguish it is to cost; I have already told you that my feelings and strong affections all inclined me to ' *pray to be excused,*' when I began to believe the Lord was calling me away. I have prayed over this subject, and have wept over it, and have tried to examine it in the light of eternity, in the fear of God, and in no other fear. And I trust I am not mistaken, when I say, *the love of Christ constrains me.* That love, my Christian friends, is the principle of the exhortation I would now address you. Comfort yourselves in God your Saviour. He abides with his church for ever, by the person and influence of the Holy Spirit. He manifests his presence and dispenses his grace in the ordinances of his house and service. Your souls are the witnesses of his love and mercy. Let your faith renew its hold on the cross of Jesus. Live at the mercy seat of God. Believe and obey the responses of the sacred oracle, and the light of God's countenance shall shine upon you, and the spirit of consolation shall make your hearts his perpetual abode.

" 3. ' *Be of one mind,*' or mind the same thing. Let the glory of God and the good of Zion be the object of your common anxieties and efforts. This you will all profess, and I hope all will strive to pursue it. A good degree of unity has hitherto prevailed. Strive to keep the unity of the spirit in the bond of peace, and this will be easily done if you have in view your common interest and prosperity.

" I wish to urge this duty in relation to the choice of your future pastor, which I most earnestly hope may be made as speedily as possible. If the church needs a man of peculiar qualifications, and such a man can be found, let that be the man of your choice, though your own taste may not be exactly gratified. Say not in the spirit of unaccommodating partiality, I am for Paul, and I for Apollos, and I for Peter, but *be all for Christ*, and unite in such measures as promise most for his glory, and the prosperity of the church.

" 4. ' *Live in peace.*' This will be the determination of all who really love our Lord and Saviour. There may be, and there always will be, some diversity of opinion in this world of ignorance and error. But still you may live in uninterrupted harmony. Having the same grand objects in view, though you may differ in opinion as to the best methods of attaining them, yet there will be no unfriendly interference or opposition that will interrupt each other's peace, or retard each other's progress, or check the growth of the church and congregation.

" When the professed friends of Jesus Christ evince a litigious and contentious spirit, the very reverse of that forbearance and forgiveness which the gospel teaches, they do an injury to the cause of religion which they never can repair ; and bring a stain upon it, which all their tears of repentance can never wash away. Labour then, my dear hearers, and pray for the peace of Jerusalem, they shall prosper that love thee. Peace be within thy walls, and prosperity within thy palaces. For my brethren and companions' sakes, I will now say, peace be within thee. Psalm cxxii. 6, 8.

" 5. When the preceding directions are complied with, you may take the encouragement which the promise or the prophetic declaration of the text is so well calculated to afford, ' *And the God of love and peace shall be with you.*' This will secure your happiness and best prosperity. ' God is love,' and it is the amazing revelation of himself as such, to a world of sinners, that constitutes the glory of the gospel ; and it is his love that caused the proclamation of peace to be made among a race of rebels, when the prince of peace be-

came incarnate for their salvation. It is his love that carries
forward the plan of mercy in our world, by which peace is
produced between man and his Maker, as well as man and
his fellow man. . It is the love of God that subdues the sinner to the obedience of the gospel, and teaches him to love
God with all his heart, and his neighbour as himself, and
thus through Christ to fulfil the law of God.   And it is love
that has promised the blessed comforter to continue with the
church for ever.

" It is the presence of the God of love and peace that you
now especially need, and which I would urge you most earnestly to supplicate.

" I fondly hope and believe that the Head of the church
has rich blessings in store for you.

" For several years the incorruptible seed has been sown
among you, and it is according to God's frequent mode of
operation to appoint another to come and reap of the harvest.

" Whoever is the favoured instrument, by whose agency
the harvest of souls is to be gathered in, no one will rejoice
more sincerely, my hearers, than your late pastor. If you
can enjoy a ' time of refreshing from the presence of the
Lord,' such as God gives in answer to the prayers of his
people, and such as he is now affording to many of the
churches, you will see the grace and the glory of the gospel,
as you have never seen them before, and regard it as a new
and most glorious era in the history of this congregation.

" If the God of love and peace will come and dwell among
you, he will guide you through all the wanderings of the
wilderness, and feed you with the heavenly manna, and
refresh you from the river of life, and conduct you onward from grace to grace, till grace shall be exchanged for
glory.

" I am unwilling to close this discourse, without a few
suggestions to several classes of persons in this assembly.

" My affections and anxieties are first directed to the *members of this communion.* My dear Christian brethren and sisters, you are aware of your high character and profession, and of the duties incumbent on those who name the name of Jesus. You are here the living representatives of the church of God. The world will form its opinion of religion from your lives and conversation. If you strive to exemplify all its power and loveliness at all times, and under all circumstances, God will be glorified, and his truth be honoured. You are *living epistles,* to be known and read of all men, and let me exhort you to beware of misrepresenting the gospel of God our Saviour. Let it be evident from the whole course of your lives, that you verily believe the truth you profess respecting the sinner's danger, and never allow your friends who are out of Christ, to find in your calmness and apathy and unconcern respecting their salvation, an excuse for their impenitence, and an argument for disbelieving the messengers and the word of Jesus Christ, which warn them of the impending wrath of heaven, and beseech them, without delay, to become reconciled to God. Strive to be blameless and harmless, and to prove yourselves the sons of God, without rebuke, in the midst of a crooked and perverse nation, among whom ye shine as lights in the world; holding forth the word of life, that I may rejoice in the day of Christ, that I have not run in vain, neither laboured in vain. Phil. ii. 12, 16.

" *To the young communicants,* I may say with the apostle, ' Ye are my joy and crown.' You have but entered on your Christian course, and have yet to learn that the path is often rough and thorny. I would most affectionately exhort you to settle it as a principle of action, that you must enjoy some tender sense of the presence of Jesus every day, and progress in the knowledge of God, and in the grace of the gospel.

" ' I have no greater joy than to hear that my children walk in the truth.' ' Only let your conversation be, as it becometh the gospel of Christ; that whether I come and see you, or be absent, I may hear of your affairs, that ye stand fast in one spirit, with one mind, striving together for the faith of the gospel.' ' Be thou faithful unto death, and the Lord, the Righteous Judge, will give thee a crown of life.'

" To sinners in this assembly, who have hitherto refused the calls and offers of the gospel, what shall I say? How can I say farewell? When I bid adieu to those who love the Saviour, I hope to meet them at his right hand, in the day of judgment, if not before. But when I take my leave of you, I tremble. Oh my friends, you know how gladly I would have led you to the Saviour. I have honestly believed the truth I have so often addressed to you, that you are all lost by nature, and the children of wrath—actually under condemnation; that Jesus Christ has come into the world to save sinners; that if you will believe in him, and accept of him, he will save you; but that if you refuse and reject him, he will cast you off for ever!

" Must I appear as a swift witness against you, when we meet you at the bar of God? Must a ministry of five years, which many have improved to their everlasting joy, be only cast into the scale of your condemnation? Must the doctrine of Christ crucified, which will swell on the air of heaven in the loftiest, sweetest songs of the saints redeemed, be heard mingled with the eternal wailings of your damnation? And now I exhort you to believe and obey the gospel. Behold, now is the accepted time; behold, now is the day of salvation.

" To those who conduct the music of this congregation, and who perform a service so important and acceptable in the worship of God, I will mention not only the pleasure I have felt, to observe your zeal and success in this delightful exercise, but the pain it has occasioned to see the choir divided and broken up, when the table of the Lord is spread, and so many of you stand at a distance, when the friends of Jesus approach to commemorate his dying love. Will any of you be satisfied to sing the songs of Zion here, and to have no part in the anthems of eternity? Shall those powers God has given, and which are so practised and employed in the melodies of earth, be lost and unattuned to the melodies of heaven? Will you aid and edify the worshippers of Jesus here in the sanctuary, when they are preparing for their future joys, and then be shut out at last when the Church of the First Born shall assemble, and the everlasting song shall begin? May God forbid it, and by his grace prevent it. May you all feel the love of Jesus inspiring your notes of praise, and enabling you to sing with the spirit and with the understanding, making melody in your hearts as well as with your voices, unto the Lord; and then may you hope to see his face, and to sing around his throne; ' To reach that blissful station, and to give him nobler praise.'

" I desire on this occasion, to return, thanks for the uniform courtesy and kindness with which I have been received among you. For the punctuality and the liberality with which you have fulfilled your engagement for my worldly maintenance. For the readiness and tenderness with which you have rejoiced with me in my joys, and mourned with me in my sorrows. For all the indulgence and attention with which you have listened to my ministry. O that that ministry, notwithstanding all its imperfections, may be more abundantly blessed to you. May you so remember it, and so improve it, that when it is reviewed in the light of eternity, you may bless God for ever, that you have enjoyed it.

" And now, my dear hearers, I must say, farewell. ' Be perfect, be of good comfort, be of one mind, live in peace;

and the God of love and peace be with you.' To him I resign my charge. He is able to keep you from falling, and
to present you faultless before the presence of his glory,
with exceeding joy. To his paternal, and providential, and
gracious care I commit you, while I bid *you* all an affectionate—Farewell."

January 21st. Installed pastor of the Second Presbyterian Church of Philadelphia. The constitution of this new
relation involves, of course, new responsibilities. It is to
influence the immortal destiny of multitudes. May the Lord
give me wisdom, and strength, and grace to perform my
duties so as to glorify his name, and to promote the salvation of immortal souls.

TO MRS. S.

" *Philadelphia, Jan. 21st,* 1829.

" By the kind care of our heavenly Father, I arrived
here last evening, after 10 o'clock, in health and safety.
The roads were bad. I came in the steamboat to Amboy.

" Mr. H.'s family are well. They were much disappointed that you did not come with me.

" The installation is expected to take place this evening.
The door appears to be wide and open. May the Lord
come and aid me in labouring for him.

" I learn that the last days of Dr. Chester* were peculiarly calm, peaceful and happy. The last night before he
died he slept soundly and sweetly. He awoke much refreshed, spoke much in words of consolation and hope ; and died
at 5 o'clock. His death has been expected for weeks, and
every mind was made up for the event, to him so joyful and
glorious !

* Mrs. Sanford was a member of his church.

     ' 'Tis done—and now he's happy,
And the glad soul has not a wish uncrowned.'

" Mrs. Chester is quite well, and bears her bereavement with great calmness and resignation. The Lord will sustain her. How loud the admonition, my dear wife, to live for God and for heaven. The night cometh; let us work while the day lasts, and as if every day might be the last.

  " It is uncertain on what day I may reach Brooklyn; probably Tuesday next. As yet I have not met the session, congregation, nor the Presbytery.

" Make your arrangements so as to be ready to leave Brooklyn in a few days after my return. Unless the roads should improve, we had better take two days to come here. Perhaps the boats may be running on the Delaware, which will make the journey easier.

" Love to all friends—and may the light of God's countenance rest upon your soul; and the sweet sense of his presence make you completely happy."

TO THE SAME.

" *Philadelphia, Jan.* 22*d*, 1829.

" I wished to write you by the mail, to-day, but could not, with any satisfaction, for want of time; and, as I have nothing very special to communicate, I thought better to wait for the mail to-morrow.

" Last evening I was installed pastor of the Second Presbyterian Church in this city. The house was quite crowded. Services solemn and interesting. And oh, what consequences depend on this connexion! The pastoral relation here formed, will be remembered both in heaven and hell! May God grant the wisdom and grace necessary for the faithful and successful performance of every duty. May we both be enabled to adorn our profession and our station.

Many inquiries, of the most gratifying character, are made
after you every day. And I believe we shall be received by
the whole congregation with open arms. I am persuaded,
that, when you come here, and see this affectionate people,
your fears and anxieties will be dissipated in a moment.
The causes of anxiety have appeared to you like so many
mountains; but they will become mere molehills, when you
come nearer and see them as they really are. I hope you
will seek daily, and earnestly, the qualifications and strength
necessary for you. I do believe you will soon find yourself
as much at home, and among as kind and generous friends
as in Brooklyn.

"I am much pleased with all I hear and see of this congregation; and believe that my prospects for usefulness,
and comfort too, are flattering. All hearts are in the hands
of God."

January 25*th.* Endeavoured to exhibit the apostle's
commission, Matt. xxviii. 19, 20, and to urge the exhortation of the apostle to the Thessalonians, 2, iii. 1. May the
Lord give us all the spirit of prayer, that shall be prevalent
for his blessing to attend his word.

February 15*th.* Quite unwell, but preached all day from
Luke, xii. 8, 9, and attended a prayer meeting in the lecture
room in the evening.

19*th.* Mrs. S. worse—expectorates blood. My preparatory service performed by Mr. How. My Lord fulfil thy
promise: "My grace is sufficient for thee."

21*st.* Attended the prayer meeting. Announced to the
church the postponement of our communion, in consequence
of the alarming illness of Mrs. S. Had a solemn season.

O my God, teach me to pray as my dear Redeemer did
in the night of his agony. "*Father, if it be possible, let*

this cup pass from me; nevertheless, not my will, but thine be done."

March 8*th.* Lord's supper administered. Congregation appeared solemn. May God add his blessing, and give a new impulse to his cause in the midst of us. Lord, may I commit my mortal and immortal all into thy hands and be at peace, and wait with silent submission to the decisions of thy most holy will.

25th. What claims to gratitude and love for all the mercies of my heavenly Father, and especially for such enconraging prospects of the recovery of my dear wife.

April. 8th. This evening addressed my congregation from John viii. 36. "If the Son shall make you free," &c. Oh that I may be made free from the condemnation, pollution and misery of sin; and know, by sweet experience, the whole amount of gospel liberty.

TO MRS. S.

" *Philadelphia, April* 15*th,* 1829.

" Under the care of a kind providence I reached the city this evening before 7 o'clock ; called at Mr. H.'s, and took a cup of coffee ; learned that the Rev. Mr. R. was engaged to lecture for me, and feeling fatigued, concluded to come home instead of going to the lecture room.

" I should like to know how you are now situated, and how you feel ; presume you are on board the Constitution, on your passage for Albany. May the Lord have you in his holy keeping, and comfort you with his perpetual presence. I desire to commit you into the hands of Jesus, and leave you there, believing, that in his keeping you will be safe."

17

TO THE SAME.

"*April* 17*th*, 1829.

" Nothing has occurred of any special interest, but the daily recurrence of the blessings of our covenant God and Father, "new every morning and fresh every evening." Oh that they may draw our hearts nearer to him, and fix our thoughts more upon him. Let us aim at more spirituality; this will be the safest way to obtain more peace and joy.

" I was interrupted, while writing the last sentence, by a call from Mr. R.; his family are well, I presume, as I inquired in general, and respecting Mrs. C. in particular."

TO THE SAME.

"*April* 20*th*, 1829.

" The hour of our appointment* was in some measure interrupted this morning, still I had a few moments of sweet communion with God, and I hope we may both enjoy more of his presence.

" The services were, I hope, solemn and profitable yesterday. I preached, in the morning, from the exhortation of Joshua: ' Choose ye this day whom ye will serve;' and in the afternoon presented the resolution, ' As for me and my house, we will serve the Lord.' Evening exercises as usual —may God add his blessing.

" I have commenced visiting; and have visited, in all, upwards of forty families. Expect to attend the meeting of Presbytery, this week, at Frankford."

May 24*th.* All the pleasures, privileges, and distractions

* A prayer-meeting, composed of pastors, in Philadelphia, which Mr. S. attended.

of the General Assembly. May they all be improved. Sermons delivered to-day by three clergymen to the congregation. O Lord, bless thy word and work.

June 21*st.* Sacramental Sabbath. Once more we have been " showing" the Lord's death; may we bear it about with us, and thus make the life of Jesus manifest in our lives continually.

TO THE REV. J. M.

" *September* 14*th*, 1829.

" I could not make arrangements to see you this summer. I wished to visit my aged mother, but while on my summer excursion I found so much to do in Montreal, officially, for a congregation which I am deeply interested in, that I felt constrained to relinquish a visit to my only surviving parent in Clarendon.

" On my return through Lake Champlain I saw your brother Peter on the wharf, at Plattsburg, for one moment. He was there on account of the dangerous sickness of your mother. He feared she would not recover: he has doubtless written you, and the result will be arranged by a wisdom that never errs. May we always *feel* it, and learn to improve all the changes and sorrows of life to the glory of God, and to our own spiritual and eternal advantage.

" Mrs. S. has been greatly benefited by our journey to Quebec, and unites with me in affectionate regards. I observe Henry's Commentary is now completed. If you are not yet supplied with a copy I can furnish you with one, which can be forwarded as you direct. Allow me to hear from you soon, and tell me your plans and prospects."

TO THE SAME.

"*October* 13*th*, 1829.

" I am a little surprised that I hear nothing from you respecting Henry's Commentary, or any thing else. I know there are many ways in which you may have been prevented, but the length of time since I have heard a word from you gives me some uneasiness; and the subjects of my letters, too, have been such as to make your silence the more mysterious.

" I have just received a line from my brother Edwin, informing me that my mother is dangerously sick. Will you inquire of Dr. Elliott, who probably attends her, how she is, and write me immediately? My letters to my brother are always delayed, or lie long in the office.

" I feel anxious to learn from you if any thing has been done for the Biblical Repertory. We must sustain it, or we may as well give up the Presbyterian cause at once. There is a prospect of obtaining Dr. R., eventually, as the sole editor of the work, though this is not for the public at present. In the mean time we may, and ought, to do something to extend the circulation of it.   *   *

　　　*　　　*　　　*　　　*　　　*

" I may see you this fall. It will depend, under God, upon my mother's health. Should she not be better, I shall come, if the Lord will."

Syracuse, N. Y., Oct. 25*th*, 1829. Arrived at a late hour last evening, much to my regret and disappointment; but have had some refreshing rest, and do hope to enjoy a profitable Sabbath, far from my ordinary labours, and far away from all my heart holds dear, except Jesus the beloved of my soul! I do rejoice that he is omnipresent. Blessed Saviour, may I feel thy presence to-day. The loneliness of a stranger's feelings and circumstances are favourable to religions duties, and tend to lead the mind to its only source of permanent enjoyment. In the circle of our friends, and our ordinary duties, there are other things to divert and distract the mind; and, alas, how frequently do they draw the thoughts from God. O may this day be rendered memorable by the manifested presence of the God I love.

Tuesday, 27th. Reached Clarendon and found my mother convalescent. Blessed be God that she is yet an inhabitant of this world. Her sickness has been very severe and alarming.

Wednesday, 28th. Left my brother's. Lectured for Mr. M. at Brockport, in the evening, and urged a little company of sinners "to strive to enter in at the strait gate," &c. Meeting solemn. May the Lord bless his word, his cause and his people.

29th. Took the boat for Rochester. Friends well. Nearly one year ago detained here several days, by the illness of my dear wife. Since then how many mercies? O for more gratitude.

TO MRS. S.

" *Packet-boat, near Utica, Oct.* 24th, 1829.

" We are now near Utica, and I take a few moments to tell you I am well. I reached Schenectady in time for the boat, and had the pleasure to find a pious captain, and very agreeable Christian company. I never had a more pleasant passage on the canal. We had worship last evening, and the due acknowledgment of God's care and goodness at our meals.

" It is a sweet privilege to devote these moments to you while all the rest of the passengers are on deck or on shore; and sweeter still to devote you anew to the hands and the care of a covenant-keeping God, whose tender mercies are over all his works, and who exercises a paternal care over the least and humblest of his children."

TO THE SAME.

" *Syracuse, Oct.* 25*th,* 1829.

"This holy morning finds me far away from the scenes and services, and the friends, and the peculiar privileges, and joys, and sorrows of ministerial life. But, blessed be God, we live not far from his presence and his throne.

"We reached this place at a late hour in consequence of some unexpected delays. But I have been mercifully refreshed by sleep, and feel that it is the Sabbath of the Lord. Some truly plaintive and touching airs were played by the boatmen, who were getting under weigh at an early hour; and, notwithstanding my grief that this day is here so dreadfully violated, I did enjoy the thrilling notes of the bugle, as they brought home to my mind some of the most tender and impressive sentiments which I used to sing with my sister in the days of other years, before the providence of God had separated us from the scenes of our childhood for ever, and from the society of each other.

"It is now the hour for public worship, and I expect to hear Mr. A., the brother of the one who travelled with us last fall. May we both be fed by the provisions of God's house this day.

" *Sabbath evening.* I have heard Mr. A. twice. In the morning, on the divinity of our Lord; and in the afternoon, his object was to show why the church regards Christ as the 'chief among ten thousands, and the one altogether lovely.' "

November 1*st. Sabbath, Auburn.* Dr. P. preached. I assisted in the administration of the Lord's supper, in the afternoon. How good to be thus refreshed in one's pilgrimage. Occupied a room in which I have several times spent a Sabbath. How wise to recall the events of life, and look back to the past and forward to the future. Strengthen me, Lord, for every duty, every trial, every change.

2d. Left at an early hour for Utica, where we arrived at too late an hour for the monthly concert. Hear the cries of thy supplicating church. Send forth thy light and truth to fill the whole earth.

3d. Left early in the canal-boat for Schenectady. How different the company and conversation from what we had on the other line. Pamphlets in favour of Sabbath-mails and amusements circulated.

Reached Schenectady the next morning and took the stage for Albany, where we arrived at 12 o'clock. Found my dear wife well, and the family preparing for a marriage service in the evening. Company large and gay. Performed the service at 8 o'clock, and soon after retired with a clerical brother to another room, and had a pleasant and profitable interview.

5th. Left for New York.

6th. Visited a few Brooklyn friends. Dear is the scene of my first ministerial labours and trials. The scene of my first domestic joys and sorrows.

7th. Left for Philadelphia. The day stormy. But the Lord preserved us, and we arrived in safety.

January 1st, 1830. Another year is gone. May thy grace, O God, be given in measures and forms suited to my situation. Much of my life is passed, and, alas, I have done but little for eternity. Oh may I redeem the time and improve it for God and for souls.

4th. Monthly concert for prayer. Send down thy Spirit, O God, to bless thy word, to prosper thy cause, and to enlighten the nations. May the representatives of the great republican family, in Congress assembled, be disposed to legislate in the fear of God. May wisdom from above guide them; may no sectional jealousy, no political or personal animosity prevent the enactment of such laws as thou wilt approve and bless. May they individually and officially sanctify thy holy Sabbath, and instead of legalizing its public profanation, may they repeal every statute which is inconsistent with the law of God and the dictates of every enlightened conscience, and thus promote their own and their country's interests, by preserving the day of sacred rest and the institutions of religion from unhallowed invasion. And in legislating for the people of these United States, may they remember that the rich and the poor, the bond and the free, the wise and ignorant, the weak and powerful, the red man and the white man, are all by nature free and equal, and have equal claims to the protection of those who have the keeping of the nation's faith and the nation's fame, and who, under God, have charge of the nation's destiny. May all our rulers and all our people be guided in the way of righteousness which is the only way of permanent national prosperity.

TO THE REV. J. M.

"*January* 13*th,* 1830.

" Accept for yourself and your dear companion the compliments of the season. May the Lord afford you his presence, and then the new year will be a happy one, and you will be making evident preparations for a state of happiness which circling years and ages shall never wear away.

" But while I have daily occasion, and, I hope, desire to bless God for his unspeakable gift, I have also reason to thank him daily for many other blessings, of a temporal nature, which that gift procures.

" I received a letter a few days since from brother G.

Mrs. G. is in delicate health. Brother G. is not satisfied where he is, and wishes, as soon as his engagement expires, to recede farther from the North Pole, and to come this side of the Green Mountains.

" Dr. M'Auley has entered on his official labours with very gratifying prospects. May the Lord prosper him, and make him a blessing to this city of moral death and deadness.

" May the blessing of Abraham, which comes on the Gentiles through Jesus Christ, be your present and eternal portion."

24th. Sabbath. Confined at home by sickness. O Lord, how frail is man! Impress this lesson on my heart. Aid me and direct me in the way of holiness, and of arduous and faithful duty ; and give me such measures of success as may best promote thy glory and the good of Zion here. Teach me how to preach and how to live, so that Jesus may be honoured and sinners saved. Bless the congregation to which I am called to minister ; may the message delivered to-day be more abundantly blessed than mine would have been ; and may I desire to have thy cause prosper, though that prosperity should sink me into insignificance, and even into mortal infamy. But if it might please thee, bless thy word as administered by me, and let me seek thy salvation.

February 6th. This day is the anniversary of my birth. The time flies as on eagles' wings, as the archer's arrow, as the swift ships, as the weaver's shuttle ; and whither am I borne by these winged moments of a brief and fugitive existence? Well may I cry out at this terrific career of mortal things. Read this morning at family worship 90th psalm ; Hope my heart responded to the prayer, " So teach us to number our days, that we may apply our hearts unto wisdom." May I be brought now to understand and answer the interesting question, upon which, I have been meditating as the theme of an address to my congregation : " Lord, what wilt thou have me to do?"

March 7th. Again under the necessity of remaining at home in consequence of a severe cold. I think I feel an increasing solicitude for Zion. O thou King of Zion, feed the flame of love in my heart, and make it more intense and consuming. O Lord, revive thy work in the midst of us, and leave us not to incurable deadness and declension. Take away all our iniquities, and receive us graciously, prosper thine own cause, and glorify thy name.

March 18th. Day of special humiliation and prayer. I rejoice in the appointment of a season for sorrow and supplication. Oh grant me true humility of heart and deep repentance. Enable me to look to Christ, and mourn over all my transgressions. As a sinner, as a husband, as a minister of Jesus Christ; aid me in the exercises of this day, and accept and bless me. '

Accept, great Head of the church, the services in which thy people have been engaged this morning. May they learn to esteem others better than themselves. Oh may we be brought, by thy Spirit, into the place and the state in which thou wilt meet us in mercy. I would dedicate myself anew to God. How often have I attempted it—how often have I failed—broken my most solemn engagements! Lord, bind my thoughts and affections to thy throne, and may all my heart and all my days be thine alone.

Preparatory lecture this evening on the examination of those who would worthily approach the Lord's table, as to knowledge, faith and life. Leading aim to honour Christ. Alas, Lord, how deficient even while I point out the path of duty. May I understand the service which is expected of me as a minister of Jesus. Bestow divine assistance in performing it, so that thy name may be glorified, thy people edified, thy cause promoted. But oh, may my soul be refreshed, may a holy impulse be felt, may I act more in the view of eternity. Saviour of sinners, I do desire to fly to thee for quickening grace. Sprinkle me with thy blood. Grant me such divine teachings that I can lead others in the way of holiness. " Oh for a closer walk with God." May thy presence be continually felt. Oh take not thy Holy Spirit from me, though I have often grieved him. May there be more piety in my intercourse with my ministerial brethren. Enable me to be more watchful over myself in this particular.

21st. Administered the Lord's supper. Preached in the morning from Song of Solomon ii. 4: " He brought me," &c. Endeavoured to show how the sovereign grace of God is exercised in bringing sinners to taste the delights of communion with him in his word and ordinances, and the rich provisions of his house on which he feasts them.

Had a solemn day at the table; urged the necessity of professing the name of Christ. Oh may we renew our formal and sincere dedication to God. May we renew our strength by waiting on him.

24th. Lectured this evening on Matt. iii. 16, in hope of enabling professors to ascertain their characters. How important that we should judge of the tree by its fruit, and not by its location, height, size, age, or any other circumstance. Lord, grant me grace to do this in my own case, and may I abound in fruits of righteousness.

TO THE REV. J. M.

" *March 6th,* 1830.

" Yours of the 26th of January was duly received on the 2d of February. And I have waited thus long, in the hope of saying something definite respecting a loan for your congregation. I do not see any prospect of effecting it, unless one of my favourite enterprises succeeds. Every year there

are thousands of dollars given for building churches, and
many of the applications descend to be turned civilly out of
doors. I wish the friends and patrons of church building to
organize and act upon the principle of loaning, giving only
at discretion, and in cases of peculiar urgency. The benefits
of such a system would be incalculable in general to all the
parties. I have some hope of succeeding in this, though like
others I am often defeated, perhaps mercifully, in my plans
for doing good. If we succeed, your loan can easily be
effected; if not, you might perhaps personally negotiate it.

"Mrs. S. is in tolerable health, desires her affectionate
remembrance to Mrs. M., and would be happy to see her
with you in May, should the Lord spare us. My mother
also is well, and much more contented than I dared to expect.

"This is a desolate part of Zion, my dear brother, and
what God intends to do with his churches here, and with
ours in particular, I know not. I cannot but hope he will
sift, and winnow, and otherwise purify it, and visit us in
mercy. We have the spiritual desolations of many generations. May the Lord repair them. We have resolved on a
day of special humiliation and prayer. May the Holy Spirit
come in the midst of us, and bring us down to the state and
in the place in which he will meet us with a blessing.,

"We have lately and silently organized a 'Presbyterian
Tract Society,' to furnish such Tracts as our churches need,
and as the American Tract Society cannot supply. The
measure will doubtless be censured, but I hope it will be so
far patronised as to secure a supply of Tracts on the Constitution and Discipline of the Church, Duty of Ruling Elders
and Deacons, &c., by the meeting of the Assembly in May.

"*March 8th.* My letter was not finished in time for the
mail on Saturday. I was unable to preach yesterday in
consequence of a cold and hoarseness. Last night we had

a fine thunder shower, and the fog that has hovered over us is gone, and all the snow with it.

> ' As yet the trembling year is unconfirm'd,
> And winter oft at eve resumes the breeze.'

" Love to Mrs. M. and Anna."*

April 1*st.* Verily, the time is short. Oh how swiftly time flies away. Divine Redeemer, fill me with thy love; make me,

1. More attentive and devout in reading the sacred scriptures.
2. More constant, fervent, and prevalent in prayer.
3. More particular in confession of sin.
4. More watchful over my thoughts.
5. More circumspect in all my deportment.
6. More spiritual in ministerial intercourse.
7. More faithful and tender in official duties.
8. More economical of my time.

> " Then shall I love thy gospel more,
> And ne'er forget thy word;
> When I have felt its quickening power
> To draw me near the Lord."

TO MR. L., OF BROOKLYN.

[An answer to Mr. L.'s letter, which was addressed to Mr. Sanford immediately after his conversion.]

> " *Philadelphia, April* 30*th,* 1830.

" Your favour of the 26th came duly to hand, and no one can understand the emotions of gratitude and joy it produced

---

* A little daughter of the Rev. Mr. M., who bore the name of Anna Sanford, (in memory of Mr. S.'s first wife,) who also is now deceased.

without knowing all the friendship and affection of a brother's heart, and all the intense solicitude, the sleepless anxiety, the tender concern, and the solemn responsibility of the minister and the pastor. I do rejoice with you and your dear companion, for all the goodness and the mercy with which the Lord has visited your soul. I desire to unite with you here, and hereafter, in ascribing to him all the glory. My heart responds an earnest '*Amen*' to the prayer that you ' may be a sincere, devout, and humble Christian,' and that you may be enabled to testify your love to Jesus by keeping his commandments; and that you may glorify God, who has called you out of darkness into his marvellous light, by exemplifying the power and loveliness of the gospel of Christ, in a life of consistent and sincere obedience.

" It would be a most grateful exercise to comply with your request, by addressing you ' a long letter' on the great duties of the Christian life, which, I trust, you have just commenced. Indeed, my dear brother, I have many things to say to you, but I cannot say them now. I have much fraternal counsel to give you, which I could not well communicate in one letter, though it should prove ' a long one.' But I will endeavour to comply with the spirit of your request, by sending you often in short letters, at such times as my pressing official duties will permit, and which may, by the blessing of God, afford you some useful hints respecting your Christian course.

" You have already, I trust, learned something of the duty of ' looking to Jesus.' It was in this way you first found peace and comfort to your troubled spirit. You found him a loving, life-giving Saviour. And now were I to tell you on my responsibility to God, and for eternity, what is your first duty as a Christian, I would say, ' look to Jesus;' what the last duty, ' look to Jesus;' what the main duty, it would be the same. 'As ye have received Christ Jesus the Lord, so walk ye in him,' is an apostle's direction.

"If the hope you now cherish should grow dim, and darkness and doubt should surround you, 'look to Jesus'—he is the sun of righteousness, and all that is cheering and illuminating must come from him. If your faith, in this season of its infant exercise, should seem to fail, and your fears should rush in upon your soul again, and the dreadful apprehension should arise that all the past has been but a fond delusion, and that it cannot be possible you are a Christian, 'look to Jesus,' the author and the finisher of faith, and cry unto him, 'Lord, I believe, help thou my unbelief.' And suffer not the adversary of souls to tempt you to question the veracity of God, or to distrust his grace.

"Your heart is now tenderly impressed with a sense of the goodness of God, so that you want a thousand tongues to praise him. It melts with penitence when you think how your sins have pierced the Saviour; and how long you have rejected his mercy and resisted his spirit. It overflows with gratitude, when you think of the love that would assume your guilt and take your chains. But should you ever feel it otherwise—should you find your heart still hard and insensible—should you have occasion to bewail your ingratitude and impenitence—should you feel the load of guilt again upon your conscience, and enough to sink you down for ever —should you lose the sweet sense of God's presence and favour, and be tempted to give up all for lost, 'look to Jesus;' look to him for a renewed sense of pardon, for penitence, for gratitude, for peace, for all that is necessary to enable you to live to him here, and qualify you for his presence above. Keep your eye steadily upon Jesus, and your vision shall improve, your grace flourish, your example shine to the glory of God and the good of men, and you shall rise at last to see him as he is, without a cloud, or glass, or doubt, for ever.

"My dear wife unites with me in an affectionate and grateful remembrance to Mrs. L. and Mrs. S.; indeed, to all Brooklyn friends beloved in the Lord. It will give me much pleasure to hear from you at your convenience, and to write you as often as my other duties permit, and without ceasing to mention you in my prayers."

May 2d. Unable to attend the house of God. Pulpit supplied in the morning, church closed in the afternoon. Oh how important to have one's work always done, or ready to be left. How little I expected to be prevented from performing my ordinary services. But may the Lord feed his own flock, and carry on his own cause. Another month has passed away, and brought on the season of Zion's festivals. May my soul be filled with more love for God and for souls.

9th. Lord, what wilt thou have me to do? Presented this inquiry to my congregation, as a theme for our mutual consideration. May I thus submit my all to the control and direction of the holy will and wise direction of God. Found my cold so oppressive that I could not go on with the subject in the afternoon.

TO MRS. S.

"Princeton, May 14*th,* 1830.

"I arrived here a little after eleven this morning. The weather was fine, the country delightful. The examination had been in progress some time. I dined to-day at Dr. M.'s, and now write according to promise, to set your mind at rest.

"May the presence of Jesus bless and comfort you. It is that, my dear wife, more than any thing else, that can make you happy. Let your most ardent aspirations rise to him.

Endeavour to make his service more and more the business of your life, and he will provide for every want. I feel condemned that worldly cares are allowed to exert such an influence upon my mind. I wish it were otherwise, and that I had more firmness of faith—that my soul might be stayed on God, and my mind thus kept in perfect peace. May you enjoy such a peace, and then you can perform the work of life with comfort and success. Love to all, and supplications for the presence of God to rest upon you."

17th. Monday. In my address to the students of the Seminary at Princeton, urged the importance of more piety. O God, make the schools of the prophets more eminently holy.

20th. General Assembly opened. O thou King of Zion, preside in the Assembly, pervade it with thy presence, direct all its deliberations and its decisions for thy glory and Zion's prosperity.

26th. This day observed as a season of special prayer by the Assembly. May the throne of God be peculiarly accessible, and the cries of thy children reach the ears of the divine Majesty, and prevail for the best of blessings.

June 27th. Lord's supper having been postponed for one week, was this day celebrated. Preparatory exercises on renewing covenant with God. Sermon, Luke ii. 14, considered the good will of God at the very foundation of the plan of mercy. Had a comfortable season. God's presence was felt. O Lord, revive us all.

" *May 26th,* 1830,

" Your favour of the 11th instant was duly received, and relieved my mind from a long suspense, in which your silence had left me. I rejoice to hear that Mrs. M. is better. May the Lord in mercy spare her to you, your children, and the church. My dear brother, I desire to feel more and

18*

more how feeble our hold is on life, and all life's dearest comforts, and to live daily for heaven.

" The Assembly. is now in session.   Little has been done yet.   Yesterday was the anniversary of the American Sunday-School Union.   One resolution contemplates planting a Sunday-school in every district in the valley of the Mississippi, where there is a population willing to patronise it, within two years, in reliance upon divine aid.   A. Tappan, of New York, and S. Allen, of this city, have offered each four thousand dollars towards the accomplishment of this object.

" To-day the Assembly engages in special devotional exercises ; to-morrow business will begin in earnest.

" We are in usual health.   I want more gratitude for my many mercies, and grace to be more faithful in the service of God. ᛫ Mrs. S. and my mother unite in affectionate regards to Mrs. M. and yourself. May the Head of the church bless your labours, my dear brother."

July 5th.   Yesterday presented the claims of the American Colonization Society. to my congregation, and made some mention of our duties in relation to the coloured population of our country.   In the afternoon met the children of the congregation for catechetical instruction.   O God of Zion, look on this lovely flock, and take these dear immortals under thy immediate care, and train them for thyself.   To-day the sons of freedom celebrate their independence.   Forbid that they should remain the slaves of Satan, wear his chains and perform his drudgery.   To-day the church of God raises the voice of her supplications for blessings upon a world lying in wickedness.   Oh may many prayers rise unto God for the preservation of our country's liberties.   May the influences of the Holy Spirit descend upon us as a people and a nation, and may we become a people whose God is Jehovah.

TO MRS. S.

" *Atsion, July* 30*th*, 1830.

" We have just arrived, after a very pleasant ride, and find this interesting family in good health. My head has not suffered from the ride; and I do hope my visit, which must be short, will be useful to me. The driver returns this afternoon, and by him I send this line, simply to tell you that we have arrived in safety. Surely God is loading us with his benefits, and calling upon us to love and serve him more.

" The young ladies, S., E. and A., send their love, and desire me to thank you for your letter."

August 1*st.* In the country, quite disabled by the unusually oppressive heat of the summer. Preached in a small house of worship. May the Lord bless the exercise, and make the day profitable to me and to my congregation, at home, who will have one sermon in my absence. O how important to work while the day lasts.

3*d.* Returned and found my dear wife and family in comfortable health. Bless the Lord, O my soul. May I begin with new zeal to serve him. Holy Spirit, take possession of my heart.

22*d.* Preached, to-day, from Ps. xxvii. 4. " One thing have I desired of the Lord," &c. Had been unable to write or even think much, on the subject, in consequence of a nervous affection of the head; but the Lord assisted me. Have been injured by too close attention to the Psalms and Hymns, which have been committed to me to prepare for the press.* I hope they may aid the devotions and promote

---

* Mr. Sanford was a member of the committee appointed for that subject.

the sanctification of the people of God long after I shall have joined the worshippers above.

August 29*th.* Urged, to-day, the duty of repentance and the encouragement, Ez. xviii. 30. Why will sinners refuse to forsake their sins and come to Christ? They need not die. Christ is willing to save them; and if they will turn unto God, and *set their hearts to seek him,* as they set them on worldly enterprises, they will find him and he will bless them.

September 5*th.* Oppressed with a cold which rendered preaching extremely difficult, yet was enabled to preach onee, to carry on the series of subjects on hand, from John viii. 21. "Ye shall seek me, and shall die in your sins." This awful prediction has been fulfilled in relation to the Hebrews. God's curse is threatened, Deut. xxviii.; and if we change the future tense to the past, the chapter will give us the history of the execution of it. It is not less true of the hearers of the gospel. O may I attend to this awful subject, both as a sinner and a minister. Alas, how much deadness in religion; how much am I absorbed in worldly cares. "My soul lies cleaving to the dust." O Lord, revive me, give me life divine. In this season of domestic solicitude help me to fix my mind more on God, and may my fondest expectations be from him.

Sept. 6*th.* My dear wife a joyful, grateful mother; and her unworthy, and, alas, too ungrateful husband, a father. Will the Lord grant us grace to praise and glorify him. O to fulfil our new duties in his fear. May our child be spared to be a blessing, and may its spared life be made a blessing to us and to the world. Lord, we would bring up this child for thee, and thee alone. The Lord has dealt in great mercy with us, and more than realized our fondest hopes.

8*th.* My dear wife and babe apparently doing well. Bless the Lord, O my soul. Rainy this evening, changed the evening lecture to a prayer meeting. Feel it good to look to Christ and cast every care on him.

12th. Preached this morning on quenching the Spirit, and followed up the subject in the evening. Rev. Mr. S. kindly aided me in the afternoon. O that we may enjoy the Spirit's presence in the church and congregation.

My dear M. is better. O may the very shaking of the rod prove sufficient, by thy grace, to bring us nearer to the cross. Preached a preparatory lecture this evening, 1 Pet. i. 16. O may we, as a church, strive for more evident attainments in holiness, and may all thy providences and ordinances be blessed and improved to this end.

19th. Sabbath. Sacramental occasion. Preached this morning from Luke xxiv. 26, the last of a series of sacramental discourses, on the necessity and nature of the sufferings of Christ, and on his exaltation. Lord's supper. Had some enjoyment. Felt Christ's nearness and preciousness. O to be more devoted to him and his cause.

26th. Sabbath. Preached from Heb. ii. 3. "How shall we escape if we neglect so great salvation?" Met the children in the afternoon, and held the usual exercises in the evening. Bless thy word, O God, and revive thy work.

October 3d. Sick with a cold, and detained from the house of God. The Rev. Mr. How supplied the pulpit. Lord restore me, if thou hast work for me to do. Revive the drooping graces of my soul.

6th. Still unable to go out on the evening of my lecture. May the supply, providentially sent, be blessed to the people. May the recollections of this day of the month warm my heart with gratitude.

10th. Attended the sanctuary ; but afraid to trust myself in the public exercises of so large a house and congregation. Have high hopes of resuming my official duties this week : cough abated, though still troublesome. Lord, give me strength and zeal to labour for thee and for souls. How much of my life is already gone! How little have I aecomplished for God and for eternity!

13*th*. Lecture this evening on Hab. iii. 2. "O Lord, revive," &e. Considered the import of the prophet's prayer; what is involved in a willingness to offer it; and the result that may be expected from such an exercise. May we all desire it. O Lord, revive us.

TO HIS BROTHER, ON THE DEATH OF HIS OLDEST DAUGHTER.

"*Philadelphia, Oct.* 20*th,* 1830.

"The death of a child, at such an age, will have a tendency to lead to serious reflection on the course pursued, on government and education.

"It should lead you, the parents of your children, to inquire what you are now doing to bring up your children for eternity and heaven.

"I have often written you on this subject; and, perhaps, you may sometimes feel as if I thought too much about your children. But, in the course of my official duties, I see instances in which parents wholly neglect the souls of their children, and treat them like animals merely. And I see other instances where parents are training up their offspring in the fear of the Lord.

Oh that you and your wife may so improve the providence that has called you to mourn, that you may be more faithful to your surviving children. My wife and child, as well as our dear mother, are now in a comfortable state of health.

TO THE SAME.

"*New York, April* 13*th,* 1830.

"None can be either comfortable or happy, until they give their hearts to God, and endeavour to make his service and his glory the great end and object of their lives. We must make religion our chief business. We must study the word of God, and pray over it, for instruction. Every day we must forsake all sin, and turn to God, and he will own and bless us. It is true, God is a sovereign, and he gives grace to whom he will; and so he is just as much a sovereign in dispensing the bounties of providence. He gives health and prosperity to one and not another. But yet, if the means are neglected, the end will not be realized. If the farmer does not prepare the earth, and sow the seed, and fence the field, he cannot expect a harvest. If he does this, he may justly expect a crop, and he will rarely be disappointed. And so, if a sinner does not read, believe, and obey the word of God, he cannot expect to be saved. If he does this, he will be saved, he will not be disappointed. (See Isaiah, lv. ; John iii. 14, 15, 16, &c.) And now, my dear brother, seek first the kingdom of God, and all its blessings will be yours.

" May the Lord bless you all."

November 6*th*. The second anniversary of my second marriage; my infant son two months old. With how many benefits art thou loading us, O God of my salvation! Every day adds to their number and to their value. Former blessings continued; new ones bestowed. When shall my soul be all on fire with love and gratitude, and my life show forth thy praise continually?

November 11*th*. A day recommended by the General Assembly to be spent in fasting, humiliation and prayer, in view of the sin of Sabbath breaking, which prevails through the church and nation.

May thy people truly humble themselves in thy sight, and repent and find mercy. May my soul make progress in her own work for eternity. Preached this morning, Jer. xvii. 27, and continued the subject in the evening.

WRITTEN IN A YOUNG LADY'S ALBUM.

" *November 23d*, 1830.

" My dear A.—While friendship and flattery, piety and genius bring their various offerings to fill up the pages of this volume, another book is preparing which contains a faithful history of your life. The present volume you may peruse with various emotions when every hand that has written it shall be in the dust; but the other, you shall examine after *you* are no longer numbered among the living.

" It is preserved, as well as written, on high; and it contains all the facts and the evidence by which the Judge of all the earth will decide when he fixes your *abode* and your *companions* for eternity. In the exercise of memory you can now peruse its principal pages, though many may have become, to you, illegible from the lapse of time.

" As I contemplated the book my mind was arrested and pained by such broken sentences as ' *Neglected the Saviour.*' ' *Received the grace of God in vain.*'

" Another sentence met my observation : ' She was often warned, urged, entreated to accept the blood-bought mercies of the Son of God, but' ———

" It was left unfinished, and it is for you to make out the remaining clause. How would you wish to have it stand? It is important soon to decide; for as the recording angel laid down the pen, another arose. The book will soon be completed. The record will stand for ever! Whatever you desire to add to the history, previous to the day of final reckoning—add it to-day—to-day—to-day!

" My young friend will excuse a subject at once so grave and so personal, and which will lose none of its importance

when the heart which has dictated this effusion, and the hand
that has recorded it shall be cold and still.

"J. S."

December 6*th.* Day never to be forgotten. What hold
is this which the mind retains on objects out of sight? On
beings no longer known among the living? On friends,
from whom death has separated us? O we shall meet again.
Fond idea to my fond and bleeding heart. Those we have
loved on earth shall be loved in heaven. There, they shall
shine in the glory of God, and be like the Saviour, to whose
grace they owe and ascribe their bliss. And why should
not our affection for them be cherished? "Prepare me, Lord,
for thy right hand; then come the joyful day." Lord, sanctify my heart.

December 31*st*, 1830. Here I make my last record for
the closing year. It has been a year of the goodness of the
Lord; but of the ingratitude of men. I am nearer eternity
than ever. Much, very much, of my time has run to waste.
O Lord, quicken me to live and act for thee. To feel that
the time is short, and strive to redeem it. May the view I
now take of the time past, influence me in improving more
diligently the time that may remain to me. May all the
hours of the coming year appear as valuable as the remaining hours of this. And may I wait the close of life as calmly
as I expect the striking of the midnight hour, that shall an-
nounce that the year 1830 is gone for ever, and the year
1831 has commenced.

January 1, 1831. Already I am in another year. God
of my life, thou art the same for ever. "Teach me to number my days, so as to apply my heart to wisdom." Much
of my life is gone. How little may remain to me is known
only to him who holds my time in his hand. God of these
changing seasons, grant thy grace to aid me in duty, in liv-

ing to thy glory, to improve every moment as it flies to eternity, in preparing for my own departure.

January 2d. "The time is short," was the theme of my discourse, this morning, considered in relation to the duration of the world, the whole term of human life, and the sinner's day of grace.

January 28th. Day for special prayer, with humiliation and fasting, in the Presbyterian churches in the city. Have felt some sense of the presence of God. O Lord, repeat and prolong the gracious visit. May my soul be truly and deeply humbled, and then raised up and revived.

"'Tis thine to cleanse the heart, to sanctify the soul,
    To pour fresh life in every part, and new create the whole."

O deliver me from this dreadful spiritual deadness; grant me *a melting view* of the cross and the love of Christ—deeper repentance of my sins; give me faith to lay hold of the hope set before me in the gospel.

February. My birthday. How solemn the recollections of this day. One year nearer the end of my mortal career. Thirty-four years I have already numbered. The mercy of God has continually attended me. How kindly has he cared for me. How condescendingly has he employed me in his service. Oh Lord, I have been an unfaithful servant. How little have I done for God, the great husbandman, whose field I have occupied, and whose bounty has sustained me! May I renew my soul's engagements to be the Lord's. Alas, how often have I renewed them, and as often violated them. Jesus, my divine, dishonoured master, bind my wandering heart to thee. May I now arise to new zeal and fidelity in thy service. Enable me to live, henceforth, with my conversation in heaven.

February 12th. An eclipse of the sun. O how this event,

which is so intelligible to every cultivated mind, but which fills the benighted heathen with such a superstitious awe, is calculated to remind us of the time when the sun shall be darkened in the heavens, not because an intervening orb sends a dark shadow on the earth, which is quickly gone, but because the God that made it shall arrest it in its course and quench its glory. O my soul, prepare for that dread day.

23d. Special prayer and conference in the church; some melting among God's people; deepening impressions of past unfaithfulness. May it prove to be a day long to be remembered. O Lord, revive thy work in my soul.

Feb. 27th. Addressed my congregation, all day, from Ez. xxxiii. 11. Strange that sinners should be willing to die, since it is not desirable, nor necessary; since God does not desire it, nor his glory demand it.

March 6th. " Behold, now is the accepted time," &c. Felt, in preaching to-day, on this subject, as if it is an accepted time, and a day of salvation indeed. Many things concur to make it a most favourable time to seek the Lord. His Spirit is descending on some parts of the city, and on many parts of the land. Glory be to his name.

March 17th. Day of voluntary prayer for the revival of God's work in the city. Had some sense of God's presence. My own mind rather uneasy on account of the indisposition of my child. Lord, I would commit him to thee without reserve. Help me to do so.

18th. This evening had a narrative of the work of grace in Rochester. O that Christians would wake up to do the work of God and plead for his blessing.

20th. Preached this morning, on the necessity of the exaltation of Christ.

P. M. Lord's supper; Dr. Green assisted. Had something of God's presence. The day profitable to some of

God's people. May it be the beginning of good things in the congregation.

27th. Addressed the church on Is. lx. 1. " Arise, shine," considered as a call to prosperity, and joy, and activity, and duty. O that we might arise to do the work of God. Spirit of light and truth, quicken and enlighten us.

April 3d. Concluded the subject on Is. lx. 1. Oh God, may thy set time to favour us come; or is there no time? Hast thou determined to leave this people in their deadness? Lord, my unbelief is enough to bring thy curse on the flock, blasting on the heritage. The deadness has existed long before my unfaithfulness could produce it; and thou canst glorify thy name by affording, even to me, more spiritual life, and success in the gospel of thy Son. Paul might plant and Apollos water, but it would be in vain without thy blessing. O Lord, revive thy work.

April 19th. Meeting of Presbytery. Alas, how little of the spirit of Jesus Christ! And these the ministers of the gospel of peace! Are they animated by the love of God? Actuated by unmingled zeal for his glory, and the prosperity of the church? O thou Spirit of peace, thou Spirit of truth, shed thy light into all of our hearts, and fill them with love, that we may glorify thy name, and strengthen the hands, and rejoice in the labours of all who love Jesus Christ in sincerity.

21st. Presbytery still in session, and no time yet to attend to the spiritual condition of the churches and the state of religion. O when shall the *power* of religion be deemed more important than the mere *form* of it? When shall thy people and thy ministers give more evidence of spiritual life, and feel less jealous of those who are not contented with a name to labour? May the means suggested to raise the tone of feeling, and rouse the professed friends of Christ to activity, be blessed of God?

Wednesday, May 11th. Special prayer for more feeling and faith in my own soul, and in the church. My inmost spirit mourns in view of the desolations of Zion! How long, how mournful! When shall they be built up? O that thy people might begin to take pleasure in the dust and ruins of Jerusalem here. O that we might be convinced that we have wandered far, and fallen low; and that with one accord we might arise and return to our Father. Some tenderness in our evening exercises.

Trenton, N. J. May 17th. How many and how tender the recollections fondly cherished concerning scenes that have passed in this city. Visited the dear spot where Mrs. Jackson lived and died; where I found and loved my A. How precious to my heart is the remembrance of these now citizens of Zion. The house and the garden remain as they were; but, O, how changed the inhabitants! How often have I entered that hall where the arms of loved ones were spread out to embrace me; their voices spoke a welcome which sent gladness to my soul. But now all is still; they are gone; those voices, attuned to the immortal melodies of heaven. I visited the grave of Mrs. J.; the green sod covers it; read the precious text selected by my A. "Blessed are the dead," &c. My gratitude arose that the father and mother of my dear A. had welcomed their daughter to the bliss of heaven. May M. and S. and myself, and all who were dear to them, prepare to follow and join them.

O God, may I live more for eternity, and may the dear partner of my joys and sorrows, and the dear babe thou hast given us, rise, and shine, and sing in that world where all the loved ones, who have died in Jesus, now inherit the promises.

18th. This evening prayer for the blessing of God on the General Assembly now convening, that their visit to our city may be blessed to them and to us. O what an influence

19*

might be exerted through the united prayers of God's ministers and people, on the city, on our whole church, and on
the world.   O thou prayer-hearing God, listen to the cries
of thy children, and visit us in mercy.

22*d.* Dr. Miller, Mr. Proudfit and Dr. Spring, preached
for us.   May the Lord bless his word and his servants.
Evening exercise peculiarly impressive.   Oh how wide is
the gate, how broad is the way, and what a multitude of
travellers!   Lord, may I be led in the right way.

23*d.* Reports of the work of God's grace in the churches.
O how rich the grace.   What hath God wrought!   May the
divine Spirit pervade the Assembly, and give character to
all their proceedings; and, through them, exert such an influence on the United States as shall make the reports presented next year more glorious still.   O Lord, revive thy
work.

24*th.* Anniversary of the American Sunday School Union.
Attempted to call the attention of the friends of Sabbath
schools to the true object of Sabbath school instruction,
and urged the necessity of a higher standard for the qualifications of teachers, the importance of parental co-opera-
tion, of united and unceasing prayer to God for his blessing.

29*th.* Dr. M'Cartee, Dr. Herron and Mr. Kirk preached.

                              " *June* 13*th,* 1831.

" My dear A.—I hoped to see you and your friend E. to-
day, but it has not been in my power.   And, as I leave the
city in the morning, I wish to suggest to you both the inquiry,
Why will you not own and honour Christ?   What more *can*
he do to deserve your confidence, and to fix your warmest
affections upon himself?   Are you making a decision now,
which you will approve on a dying bed, and review with
pleasure at the judgment bar?   You will pardon (and may

I hope, improve ?) this affectionate warning from your friend
and pastor.

" J. S."

During the preceding month Mr. Sanford received a unanimous invitation from the M'Cord Church in Lexington, Kentucky, to become their pastor.   The following is a copy of
a letter addressed to him by many members of that church
and congregation, on that occasion.

" *Lexington, May* 11*th*, 1831.

" REV. AND DEAR SIR,

" We enclose you, under sanction of Presbytery, which is
attached, the call of the M'Cord Church, a copy of which,
without waiting the meeting of the Presbytery, we took early
occasion to send under cover of our letter on 30th April.

" In performing our duty in transmitting this call, we
seize the occasion to renew briefly the expression of the
earnest desires we feel on the subject. The more we have
revolved it over in our minds, the more anxious have we become that success should attend our application.   The more,
dear sir, we have heard of your personal character and
ministerial qualifications, and of their peculiar importance
and suitableness to the present wants of our church, town,
and state, the more ardent and desirous are we to hear of
your favourable answer ; for the persuasions and convictions
on this subject are so vivid and solemn in our minds—without knowing what particular causes might interfere to prevent it—we are ready to persuade ourselves that our heavenly
Father will direct you to us ; and in anticipation we see rising
already from your early labours among us the richest fruits
and most grateful returns : in your timely presence, and accompanied by *His blessing*, without whose aid all human

effort is fruitless, our little Zion, no longer in dust and ashes, will be more than renewed in its beauty; and the moral wilderness around us shall be made glad, and our deserts, hitherto barren or growing with weeds, shall blossom as the rose.

" Not only from our solemn conviction of your eminent suitableness to the field of labour which we deem invitingly open here, but from the weekly, the constant experience of our necessities and wants, and of those which religion bewails in our town and country at large, are we anxious and urgent. For we are solemnly impressed with the opinion, that there are few situations any where in our widely extended country, including the most populous cities of the seaboard, where the devout and able minister of God may plant himself with better hope of reaping a higher and more enduring reward. Most of the reasons for this opinion we have glanced at in our first letter—we should be glad they were fully before you as we conceive them—but the limits of this letter forbid us to enlarge upon them. To our friend Mr. R. J. Breckenridge, a member of the General Assembly, who has promised us to wait upon you, we would respectfully and confidently refer for much information that you might find it interesting to be possessed of: and Mr. Abraham T. Skillman, one of our elders, we hope has made it his business to see you; he left Lexington a few days only before the call was made, but if we mistake not was aware of the intention of the congregation, and has been apprised by letter of their united act and effort.

" The fact of a hearty unanimity and desire on the part of the church and congregation, we think a matter worth repeating to you with some emphasis in this letter; we feel it in this instance cause of particular gratification and joy. And we deem it proper in this place to say, that the subject of your election and call as our pastor has been much spoken of in Lexington since the day it was made, and much desire is felt and expressed on the part of the Christian community, as well as by friends of religion, that it might be accepted. We feel it would not be going too far to say, that an extensive and general desire is felt upon the subject, which we rejoice to think would do much to prepare the way for a prosperous and harmonious career of ministerial duty.

" Should our solicitations receive your favourable regard, and our divine Master direct your steps to labour here, we offer you our most affectionate greetings, and shall joyfully welcome your approach. We give you the assurance of our willingness to co-operate with you to the utmost of our abilities in the work of the Lord, and that we shall be happy to see that you want for nothing in our power to render your situation easy and comfortable among us.

" We pray you may be relieved from any difficulty in this case, and that you may be permitted to see the way clear before you where our adorable Head calls you to work— and we cannot but have a full reliance on the issue. That he may of his infinite goodness grant you the long enjoyment of health, and abundantly prosper your exertions in his cause, in whatever part of his vineyard you may labour, is the devout wish of,

" Rev. and dear sir, your friends."

To this call Mr. Sanford felt it to be his duty to give the following reply, in which he assigned the reasons which induced him to decline its acceptance.

" *Philadelphia, June 6th,* 1831.

" WM. A. LEAVY, ESQ.,

" My dear sir—Through you, as the only individual of the congregation worshipping in the M'Cord Church whom

I know, I wish to reply to the communications of the 30th of April and 11th of May, which came duly to hand.

" On the interesting subject they present, I have carefully perused the representation of your letters, have conversed with several gentlemen members of the Assembly and others, who are well acquainted with Lexington and its inhabitants, its wants, and prospects, and its commanding situation in the bosom of the great valley of the west, and especially have I endeavoured to look up to the great Head of the church, to ask, ' Lord, what wilt thou have me to do?' and now set down to write you the result of my deliberations and prayers.

" My previous opinions, formed on general representations concerning Lexington and the M'Cord Church, have been more than confirmed.   I am persuaded there are few if any situations west of the mountains, more important and desirable; and I do not hesitate to say, that were I disengaged, or could I feel that the Head of the church actually called me to disengage myself from all my Atlantic associations, I should cheerfully set my face toward the setting sun.

" My heart's fondest desires have long been to preach the gospel, either personally or instrumentally, *to every creature.* And that post of duty, whatever be the difficulty or danger attending it, which will enable me to act most efficiently for this object, is the post I choose.

" It was such a prospect as this that brought me to this city, against every dictate of worldly interest and personal comfort, and indeed when every earthly consideration urged me to remain.   I left a people who were to me all that a pastor's heart could desire, and a place, which, from its peculiar situation, and the circumstances attending my residence in it, dearer to my heart than any spot on earth.

" An imperious sense of duty influenced me to the step, and the hope of doing more to attain the favourite object of my heart, and to accomplish which I trust will ever be the ruling purpose of my life, animated me while I took it, in the midst of many regrets and many tears.

" Until I consider the experiment here as fairly tried, and the Head of the church as clearly directing me to a field of wider usefulness and higher promise, nothing could induce me to remove.

" The situation of our Atlantic churches in general, and of those in this city especially, is such at the present time, that in my own opinion, and in the estimation of every man I have consulted, it would be highly inexpedient to disturb my present connexion. Your friends who have been in the Assembly will be better able to appreciate this subject, than those who have not been on the ground. They can see the relation which these churches sustain to the cause of religion in our country, and the cause of missions throughout the world.

" Long and profoundly have they slumbered over the last command of the risen Redeemer, and over the present and the prospective wretchedness of millions of the human race. But here and there a sentinel on the heights of Zion is beginning to awake, and to sound the Master's signal to activity and duty ; and some pastors and congregations do already begin to move. In this work I shall be happy to bear some humble part ; and if this, or any kindred object, should lead me across the mountains, I shall feel a peculiar pleasure in visiting Lexington, and shall hope to find all the pulpits supplied with preachers,

<blockquote>
' Such as Paul,
Were he on earth, would hear, approve, and own.'
</blockquote>

" May the Lord speedily supply you, and may the Shepherd of Israel take charge of his flock, and gather you, and all of your children, into the fold of his mercy."

June 15*th.* Returned from Brooklyn, where I left my dear wife and babe this morning. O Lord, may I see him and his dear mother soon in health. Take them under thy care, O Shepherd of Israel, and carry them in thine ever-lasting arms.

O great Physician, restore and preserve the health of our child ; and may he be a rich blessing to thy church, and to the poor, unworthy parents who have loved him too well ; who have loved the great Giver too little. Lord, I am con-vinced, and have long felt, that this is the case. Lord, for-give, and grant repentance, and may it not become necessary in correcting us, to take away our child.

18*th.* Letter informs me, to-day, that my child is really sick. A physician has been called: active medicines resorted to ; and appearances encouraging. To whom can I go but unto thee, O God. Lord, help me, help me to confide in thee, and to commit all to thee. Lord, forgive ; he is thine, but my faint and fearful heart would fondly cling to this dear, alas, too dear, object of my affections and hopes. O my God, raise him up, if it may consist with thy holy purposes; or help me and my dear companion to bear the bereaving stroke like Christians, supported by thy kind hand. Lord, spare him and bless him for Jesus' sake.

19*th.* Lord's day. God of the Sabbath, meet my soul in mercy to-day. May I be stayed on God, and be aided in my arduous duties. May this day be rendered memorable by thy displays of mercy. My mind much distressed re-specting my child. Tried to cast him on the arms of the Lord. For life and death may he be thine. The day was solemn and the audience attentive. Lord, revive thy work and bless thy heritage. Give it not to a perpetual reproach.

20*th.* Left the city at 6, for Brooklyn, to see my dear child. Lord, give me true submission to thy will. Arrived at 7 o'clock, and found the child better. Bless the Lord, O my soul, for all his benefits. May I regard the child as the Lord's entirely and for ever. May he live to praise thee, O God.

26th. Our little charge more comfortable. God of the Sabbath, receive the gratitude of our hearts. Bless to the people of my charge the message of thy grace this day, and make the day thy Zion's favoured hour.

[In consequence of the illness of our dear babe, Dr. Mitchell desired our journeying with him. My husband accompanied me as far as Albany, and wrote the following letter during his passage in the steamboat to New York, returning to the city of Philadelphia.]

TO MRS. S.

" Steamboat New Philadelphia, June 28th, 1831.

" The rain has descended in torrents for some time, but we make good progress, ' dragging at each remove a lengthened chain.' I have left all my earthly treasures behind— wife and only child. May the Lord have you under his kindest care. It is trying to be separated; but I regard it as the will of the master I serve, and he is a good master. He gives us all our friends and comforts, and has a right to require us to leave them all to serve him. Oh could we feel more ready to do this, how much higher and purer would our joys become! We should enjoy our friends better, and love them more; and yet Christ would be dearer to us than all, and every other friend would be regarded as some faint reflection of his love and goodness.

" Since I came on board, I have been reading a few pages of Bickersteth's Christian Student. He takes an interesting view of the grounds on which false hopes are built; he speaks of a dead faith, excited feelings; *acts of obedience, religious services* and *works of benevolence; the mercy of God with-*

out respect to the merits of *Christ; our own goodness, con-*
joined with the merits of Christ, as among the most common and the most fatal; and which will all be swept away
by the flood of divine wrath.   And then proceeds to state,
with much sweetness, that ' *Christ crucified is the founda-*
tion of the sinner's hope. Christ on the mediatorial throne
is the sovereign of the redeemed. Christ, by his *word* and
spirit, in the heart, is the believer's *life. Christ,* in glory,
is the elevating object of the saints' expectation.'

." Oh, my dear M., may Christ be our foundation, sovereign, life, our hope, and our eternal portion.

" I will hope to finish this line to-morrow, if the Lord
will, and mail it at Princeton—perhaps send it by the boat
in the morning.   May the God of Israel keep you and your
dear little one, this night, in safety and health."

29th. Left Albany for the field of my official duties, leaving my wife and child, my earthly all, behind. Great Shepherd of Israel, carry him in thy bosom.

July 5th, Sabbath. Let me enjoy thy presence this day,
O God of my salvation; and may my wife and child be
kept in the hollow of thy hand.   Preached from the words,
" Stand fast," &c. Gal. v. 1.   May I know the liberty of
the gospel, and stand forth an example and friend of it.

" *Philadelphia, July 15th,* 1831.

" My dear young friends,—Mrs. S. attempted to write
you yesterday, to express her deep sense of the obligations
imposed by your constant, delicate and most gratifying expressions of kindness; but was compelled, in a few moments,
to lay down the pen, which she could no longer guide or see.
She is better this morning, but unable to write, and has requested me to say, for her, that she will write when able;

that she loves you, appreciates your kindnesses, and tries to remember you at the mercy-seat of God.

" Having now executed my commission, I may take the liberty of saying a few words on my own account; or rather, much rather, on the account of that Saviour whom I desire and endeavour to serve; but whom my dear young friends have never publicly acknowledged. Perhaps he regards you as his friends. If so, how must he estimate your public, practical denial of him and his salvation? And, if you indeed love him, how do you estimate it? If either of you had, in some hapless and unguarded moment, wounded the feelings and disobeyed the most reasonable injunctions of the best and kindest of parents, would not the recollection of it plant thorns in your midnight pillow, and bathe it with your bitterest tears? And would you go on satisfied and happy? Would not every favour, lavished upon you by parental tenderness, awaken a more poignant sense of your guilt and ingratitude?

" Now, is not God your Father? Is he not loading you with blessings, which you know not how to appreciate, because you have never known the want of them? Is he making the most reasonable requisitions on your hearts and lives? And are you refusing to comply?

" Pause, ponder well, my dear friends, before you answer. And if you have reason to believe that you have been withholding the very offering God requires; the only one you are capable of making, that he will accept; will you still refuse to make it?

" Will you squander on a creature, or on all creation, that which belongs to God? Oh! if a brother's affection, and a brother's importunity could lead you all, and unreservedly, to Jesus, and bless you with all the hopes and joys of the gospel, the duty should be done, and the consolations should be yours for ever.

"But there is one above all others, who stoops from heaven to be your friend.   May his Spirit incline and enable
you to accept his proposals.

  " Remember me, most affectionately, to your parents, and
believe me, my dear young friends, most fraternally, your
friend and pastor.

" J. S."

Galway, N. Y. Aug. 1*st*, 1831.   Here, as a last resort,
under Divine Providence, we have come to try the benefit of
the air of the country for our dear babe. O God of life, bless
these means for his recovery. He appears somewhat revived,
notwithstanding the fatigue of the journey.   May these encouraging symptoms continue.   Our Father in heaven, thou
art our only hope.   Kindly interpose thy hand.

  Wednesday, 3*d.* Yesterday was cold and rainy.   An
invisible hand can sustain and raise up the little sufferer;
and without this he evidently must sink soon into the sleep
of death.   Jesus, Saviour, let thy blood cleanse his soul of
its native defilement and fit it for thy presence and glory.
What evidence these sufferings give of God's abhorrence of
sin ! Were it in my power, how soon I should relieve them.
But it is in God's power; he is far more compassionate
than I, and yet he permits them.

  August 4*th.* O God, teach me submission.   I cannot understand why an infant should suffer thus.   It cannot atone
for sin, nor produce penitence, nor exercise patience.   Is it
not for the sake of others, that they may learn to hate sin
and forsake it?   I am sure I need thy correcting rod ; and
though I would rather suffer, personally, than see my child
in agony, yet the Judge of all the earth will *do right,*
and I dare not prescribe the method nor the measure of his
paternal stripes.

  P. M. 5 *o'clock.* Our dear babe seems to be revived.

" Who can tell whether God will be gracious to me, that the child may live?"—2 Sam. xii. 22. O thou that hearest prayer, be entreated to say to this disease, " Thus far and no farther." Thou canst glorify thy name; humble me in the dust; bring me nearer to thee; quicken me in duty in this way, as well as by removing him. But, Lord, teach me to say *thy will*, not mine, be done.

Friday, 5th. Nearer and nearer our dear lamb seems to be approaching the last scene. O how fondly his parents' arms would cling to him and detain him; but other arms, I trust, are open to receive, and welcome, and bless him. Lord, may I have a more *vivid impression* of thy presence, and realize the assurance of the acceptance and bliss of my dear babe, through Jesus Christ. Enable me to give him up, actually, at thy call, as readily as I have tried to give him to thee in acts of dedication. ·He is thine, O Lord, may no rebellious feeling dispute thy right or resist thy claim.

TO M. L. B., ESQ., OF PHILADELPHIA.

"Galway, August 5th, 1831.

" I came to this place, on Monday last, as a last resort, under God, for our dear babe. We had intended to go down the river, to New York, but learning of our friends in Albany, that many instances had occurred here of the recovery of children, more reduced than ours, we were induced to try the experiment. We are in the family of a skilful physician, and have the benefit of the purest air. But all will not do. Our little one is sinking, I fear, to the grave. He took a relapse the very day before I left Philadelphia; and, with some days of comparative improvement, has been, I now believe, regularly and rapidly declining. He is now very low, and I should not be surprised to be summoned, at any moment, to see him expire. Yet I know the Lord *can* interpose, and will do it, *if it is best;* and if it is not best, in the view of infinite wisdom, I should not desire it.

" By this time I hoped to mention the time of my return. But I cannot leave my dying child. It seems impossible that he should continue longer in his present state. A change, yes, a decisive change, may now be hourly expected. Children have been raised after being brought as low as ours. But the cases are rare, and though we shall *hope* as long as he breathes, yet all the probabilities are against his recovery. Oh! what an act was that, which has exposed all the millions of our race, to the dreadful consequences of sin! How deadly the energy of that contagion which, after travelling down the stream of ages, pollutes, and poisons, and *destroys* such multitudes of beings, who have never committed one actual transgression!

" How wonderful and rich the grace of God, and the blood of Jesus, that can make our children the heirs of immortal glory, when they are incapable of faith, or penitence, or prayer for mercy! How high the transports of those who only look out upon life's stormy ocean, and are then embosomed by the good Shepherd; who learn the history of their fall and their recovery together; and who are taught the causes of their sufferings and death when every pang is over, and every tear wiped away!   *   *   *

" I am sure I never felt so keenly the depravity of my nature as when I have stooped in agony to change the position of my suffering child; and the imploring, despairing look which he casts upon us, when no mortal hand can relieve him, is enough to strike daggers through the soul. Methinks it would afford consolation, which I could give a world to purchase, had I a world at command, to be able to tell my child *why he suffers;* and to speak to him of Jesus, who is willing and ready to receive him when these days and nights of anguish shall be ended.

" But these lessons he cannot learn from a father's lips.
He will know it all in heaven ; and, probably, know it soon.
I will write you soon.   Mrs. S. unites with me in affection-
ate regards to the family and friends.

" Truly yours, in the gospel,

" J. S."

12th. Still we have to sing of mercy.   O that we might
lie low at the mercy-seat, and live nearer to God.   May
health be restored to our babe, and a sweet sense of a father's love be given back to our souls; and may he, and we
his parents, be conformed entirely to the will of God, and
be changed into his image and brought into his presence. O
to stand, and shine, and sing in his kingdom, monuments of
his glory, reflecting his light and proclaiming his love to a
wondering universe.

Sabbath, **14th.** Preached this day in the church where I
was baptised in childhood; and where, at the age of thirteen,
I made a public profession of religion, from Phil. ii. 16.
" Holding forth the word of life." Felt some tenderness and
comfort in stirring up God's people by way of remembrance.

16th. Attended the meeting of the opening Presbytery
of Albany.   Mr. Kirk preached from Paul's theme to the
Corinthians, " Now, then, we are ambassadors for Christ,"
&c.

THE THINGS WHICH ARE UNSEEN ARE ETERNAL.

" The man who desires his happiness from communion
with God has an object worthy of his love, and suited to his
spiritual and immortal nature.   The soul holds high and delightful intercourse with infinite mind, and with the lofty intelligences of congenial purity and ardour, that throng the
Creator's courts, and worship in his presence.   To discover
more and more of his character and perfections, to watch

the evolution of 'his eternal counsels; to be changed into his divine image, from glory to glory; to trace the wisdom and the righteousness of his darkest dispensations; to dwell in God's immediate presence; to behold his glory without a glass or cloud to intervene; to make new discoveries of the wonders of his love; the depth of his condescension; the riches of his grace; to find the river of life for ever becoming deeper and broader as it rolls; to stand in the ranks of redeemed sinners, and to swell the everlasting song; to find the powers of the mind for ever strengthening, and room for their highest exercises; the capacity for enjoyment for ever enlarging and for ever full. These are some of the things above, which claim the affections, and are suited to the nature of the soul."

19*th*. Returned from the country, after an absence of several weeks of great anxiety. Our child has been dangerously ill, but the Lord has interposed, and, for a few days, we have had high hopes of his recovery. O may I be ready to resign him at any moment; and yet be enabled to bring him up for God. Sustain, guide and sanctify me, and make me more faithful to do and suffer all thy will.

21*st*. Preached from Phil. iii. 8. " Yea, doubtless; and I count all things but loss," &c. May I imitate the apostle, and become savingly acquainted with Jesus Christ. In the afternoon from 1 John ii. 3. " Hereby we know that we know him," &c. Could only give an analysis of the sermon, on account of cold and hoarseness. May I know that I know Jesus Christ, and may the word be made quick and powerful among us.

Sabbath, 28*th*. Read two sermons to-day, unwilling to tax, or even trust my feelings, under the trying circumstances in which I am placed.

Monday, 29*th*. Unfavourable news from my child; he is

much worse again. I fondly hoped his health was improving, but it seems to be far otherwise. Great Physician, undertake for him; heal him; and, especially, renew and sanctify him. Teach me true submission to thy holy will. " I know thy judgments, Lord, *are right*, though they may seem severe." Give me brighter evidence of thy covenant love, and all will be well. Subdue and sanctify my heart.

Sabbath, Sept. 5th. Preached with some freedom to-day, from Rom. ii. 3, and Prov. xxviii. 13. O that sinners might give up their delusive expectations of happiness while they neglect the gospel, and be induced to confess and forsake their sins, and then may they find mercy. Lord, may I practise the duties and embrace the offers I recommend, and feel more of thy presence.

" DO THIS IN REMEMBRANCE OF ME."

" We are accustomed to regard with peculiar sacredness the last expressions of expiring friendship. When the heart has been desolated of all that responded to its throbbings; when the sun of our prosperity has set, and the bright bow of hope and of promise has faded from the clouds that darken our horizon; when a friend sleeps in death, from whose presence the world borrowed its loveliness, and the path of life its flowers, it is the part and the employment of busy memory to recall the looks, the actions, the words of tenderness, and especially the farewell wishes and exhortations of the friend we mourn. Nay, so universal, so deeply seated is this principle of human nature, so constant in its operations, where any thing like sensibility is found, that enlightened communities, not only bow to its influence, but have reared around it, the safeguard of civil law. It is to this principle of our nature that these words are directly addressed.

" The disciples had left all to follow Christ: they had

been his constant companions for several years; 'they had seen his miracles; they had heard his words; they had tasted of his love'; they had espoused his cause; they had embraced him as their Lord and Master. He had pitied their blindness and ignorance; he had borne with their unbelief and their erroneous opinions respecting himself, and the nature of his kingdom. He had adopted them into his family, and loved them as his own.

" They were now assembled in an upper room in Jerusalem, to celebrate the last paschal supper. He was soon to be parted from them, and was desirous of leaving them some dying token of his love, some memento of suffering sympathy; something to cherish in their bosoms the warm remembrance of the object and the accomplishment of his mission to our world.

" But besides the fact of the words being spoken under such interesting circumstances, which give them the charm of a most tender and perpetual obligation, they present themselves to our contemplation, and our faith, and our obedience, in all the majesty of God's authority; in all the uncompromising righteousness of God's requisitions."

" Human life is often compared to the ocean; and the sons of men are voyagers to eternity. Their successive generations, like the mountain billows, are driven onward by the same agency, and dashed upon the same shore; and the various characters, and circumstances of men, may find some striking illustration in the various states and aspects of the mighty deep."

11*th.* Preached once to-day; had some tenderness, and was enabled to rise above the circumstances of the congregation, and to speak in the name and by the authority of the Mediator. Numb. xvi. 48, the text.

Sabbath, 18*th*. Lord's supper. Had some precious views of my Lord at his table to-day. Endeavoured, in the morning, to fix all minds on him as the "*Wonderful.*" Isa. ix. 6. At his table, in the afternoon, felt him near and dear to my soul. O for an abiding sense of his love! How it would smooth every path and sweeten every cup.

25*th*. Preached this morning from Ps. lxxxvii. 3. " Glorious things," &c. May the Lord perform, in his good time, the things he has promised to Zion. Was mercifully assisted in the services. Lord, stand by me, and hold thou me up, and I shall not fall. Give me a forgiving spirit towards those who have risen up against me. May my mind be stayed on thee, and all my goings ordered by thee.

Nov. 2*d*. Lectured this evening from 1 Sam. xxx. 6. " But David encouraged himself," &c. O may I be enabled to imitate him in the trying circumstances in which I am placed. O God, be my God in covenant, and grant me the tokens of thy love.

3*d*. This day I was to have been in Boston, but the providence of God has prevented me. He will take care of the Sabbath School cause.

Dec. 4*th*. Almost all my Sabbaths are days of anxiety and toil, rather than holy rest and enjoyment. May I be enabled, by a more judicious and more successful attention to my duties, to secure time for my own spiritual improvement. To-morrow, the session of Congress opens; and the day after, the Legislature of this state. O God, may their deliberations promote thy glory and the good of Zion.

Friday evening, 9*th*. Had unusually tender and fervent affections in the prayer-meeting this evening; some enlargement in prayer. Lord, inflame me with a more ardent love for souls and thee.

11*th*. Sabbath. Sick with the influenza, and could not preach. Mr. R. preached for the Board of Missions in the morning; church closed in the afternoon; much sickness prevailing. Lord, be our physician, and keep us in the hollow of thy hand, and keep our souls in health.

12th. Visited the sick. Baptized a child of Mr. G. O how precious the hopes of the gospel! How rich the covenant of mercy which includes us and our children! My gracious Master, smile on the little one I have this day baptized in thy name, and make her a monument of thy sparing mercy and renewing grace.

———

But one more record was made by Mr. Sanford, in his journal, and that was a very brief one. It is of the date of the succeeding day, December 13th, and is as follows:

"Our babe is quite sick. Called a physician. Lord, bless the prescription. In many trying hours thou hast spared and upheld him. Do it now, if it is best for him, for us, and for thy dear cause."

But now the time was at hand when it pleased his Lord and Master to remove him from his service on earth to his service and enjoyment in heaven. In the course of a few days afterwards, he caught a violent cold, which brought on a raging fever. His final illness was not of long duration, but was exceedingly severe and distressing. The unremitted services of two of the most distinguished physicians in Philadelphia were rendered in vain. There was no arresting of the disease.

During the last five or six days Mr. Sanford's mind was greatly affected by the sufferings of his body. But, during the few lucid moments which intervened, his thoughts were evidently fixed on heavenly things, and displayed what had long been the habitual state of his soul.

During this time of suffering he had the heart-felt sympathy of many Christians of his own congregation, as well as of the other churches in the city. Many prayers were offered up in his behalf. And many of his dear flock, as well as of other congregations, hastened to proffer any services which they could render.

But although it was distressing to friends not to be allowed to converse with this devoted servant of the Lord, and hear his abundant testimony to the value of the religion of Christ, in a dying hour, yet they had enough to satisfy any mind. They had the testimony of a life of more than twenty years of consistent, devoted piety to assure them that he was prepared to die. Nor were there wanting very sweet and cheering evidences of his eminent preparedness for death, even in that tremendous process of dissolution which seemed, within a few days, to prostrate body and mind in complete ruin. During the few lucid moments which intervened, Jesus and his salvation, were the theme on which he delighted to dwell. One morning he asked Mrs. S. to read to him the thirty-fourth Psalm; and when she had done so, he directed her attention to the following hymn, of which he had been very fond when in health.

> Jerusalem! my happy home!
>   Name ever dear to me!
> When shall my labours have an end,
>   In joy, and peace, and thee?
>
> When shall these eyes thy heaven-built walls
>   And pearly gates behold?
> Thy bulwarks, with salvation strong,
>   And streets of shining gold?
>
> O when, thou city of my God,
>   Shall I thy courts ascend,
> Where congregations ne'er break up,
>   And Sabbaths have no end?

There happier bowers than Eden's bloom,
　Nor sin nor sorrow know:
Blest seats! through rude and stormy scenes,
　I onward press to you.

Why should I shrink at pain and wo?
　Or feel, at death, dismay?
I've Canaan's goodly land in view,
　And realms of endless day.

Apostles, martyrs, prophets there,
　Around my Saviour stand;
And soon my friends in Christ below,
　Will join the glorious band.

Jerusalem! my happy home!
　My soul still pants for thee;
Then shall my labours have an end,
　When I thy joys shall see.

When asked whether he felt heaven to be his home, he replied, with an upward look of the deepest interest, "O yes, I feel it to be my happy home." At another time, in answer to the inquiry whether Christ was precious to his soul, he replied, "Yes, he is the chiefest among ten thousand, and altogether lovely;" and, as well as can be recollected, he added, "I commit my all into his hands, and he will *keep* that which I commit to him."

On another occasion he was asked whether he felt much *joy.* He replied, "My joy arises not so much from a sense of Christ's presence, or my personal union to him, as from a view of the extension of Christ's kingdom in the world." At one time he was overheard repeating those words, so precious to him in health,

> " Jesus, lover of my soul,
>   Let me to thy bosom fly."

He was very partial to hymns, and was accustomed, for years, to spend the moments of twilight, after the labours of the day were closed, in repeating his favourite ones, when it often seemed as if his soul mounted upwards on the wings of faith, and caught something of that ardour and love which animate the happy worshippers above.

During his seasons of delirium, which were protracted and very violent, the state of his church and congregation was the absorbing and painful theme, on which his distracted mind continually dwelt; and his exclamations in regard to that subject were truly heart-rending.

But why should we dwell on this mournful point? Death soon did his appointed work; and this devoted servant of the Lord was released from his sufferings, and entered into rest! The manner of his death is a matter of comparatively little importance. He was prepared to die. What if his disease was painful; and the mind, under its violent influence, deprived of the use of the faculty of reason? The ever-blessed God has no where, in his word, assured us that his children, whom he most tenderly loves, shall not die of the same diseases as other men; and of such diseases, too, as their physical constitution and temperament, or their situation in life, may expose them to. Let it be enough for us that the Lord has done it. What more does the heart that is filled with faith and love desire?

Mr. Sanford died on the morning of the 25th of December, 1831. On the 28th, the funeral solemnities were performed. A numerous procession of ministers and other citizens moved from his late residence to the church of which he had been the pastor. The corpse was deposited in front of the pulpit; and the house was filled with deeply solemn auditors. The Rev. Dr. M'Auley, after having conducted the introductory services, delivered an appropriate address from Revelation xiv. 13 : ". And I heard a voice from heaven, saying unto me, Write, Blessed are the dead which die in the Lord from henceforth : yea, saith the Spirit, that they may rest from their labours; and their works do follow them." After the services had been terminated by prayer, by the Rev. John Breckinridge, the corpse was deposited in the family vault of Alexander Henry, Esq., where it remained until it was taken to Brooklyn, and deposited by the side of the remains of his first wife. On which occasion an appropriate sermon was preached by the Rev. Mr. Carroll, which was afterwards published.

Thus ended the mortal career of this servant of God, before he had completed his thirty-fourth year. It now remains that we give some brief notices of his character, his attainments, his labours, together with some facts which could not well be introduced into the foregoing portion of the volume.

1st. *Mr. Sanford's talents were of a very respectable order.* We speak here of the qualities of his mind. These qualities were not so brilliant as substantial. His judgment was uncommonly sound and discriminating. His perception was sufficiently ready. His memory was good; and his taste was refined. His mind was well balanced; proportioned, if we may so speak, and disciplined.

2d. *His attainments in knowledge were highly creditable.* His situation, during the greater portion of his youth, was not favourable to the acquisition of knowledge. But although he did not begin his classical studies until he had nearly entered the period of manhood, yet by means of such application to study as a state of health, never very vigorous, enabled him to make, he obtained a very respectable standing in his class at college, in almost every branch of study. The same remark may also be applied to his theological education. He always maintained an honourable standing among his fellow-students in the Theological Seminary at Princeton. And many of the themes which he composed whilst there, as well as during his college course, display very considerable attainments, united with a sound judgment. We are not aware that he published, over his own name, any thing more than one sermon, addressed to his church at Brooklyn, when called to leave them; extracts from which have been given in another part of this volume.* He wrote a considerable number of anonymous articles for the religious journals and reviews. He had made some progress in the preparation of a Catechism on the Evidences and Divine Authority of the Christian Religion, when death put an end to his earthly labours. This work was intended to embrace the substance of a course of lectures which he had delivered on this subject, and was in preparation for the benefit of Bible Classes and Sunday Schools. Indeed, his labours as a pastor, to which he most assiduously devoted himself, allowed him little time for writing works for publication.

It was, at first, intended to give a few of his sermons in this volume; but this part of the plan was found impracticable, inasmuch as it would have increased its size too much.

3d. Mr. Sanford's manners were eminently those of a Christian gentleman. No one could have known him, we think, without being struck with the dignity of his appearance, and his habitual freedom from every thing resembling an unbecoming levity. His whole demeanour was marked by that seriousness which ought to characterize a minister of Jesus Christ. And yet it was not studied, or acquired as a habit. He was far from being morose. In his intercourse with his fellow men he was habitually calm, self-possessed, cheerful and agreeable. " His spirit," said Dr. M'Auley, in his address at his funeral, " was eminently a spirit of great meekness. I can freely say that I never heard from his lips one unkind word, one harsh epithet, one unbrotherly expression, nor imputation of any motives not avowed by their authors. His meekness, and charity, and innocence were so blended and triumphant, that the accuser stood forth the culprit, and the accused desired no advantage, and seemed unconscious of the generous feelings and graces which he exercised. Of his brethren in the ministry, he always spoke as *brethren*; some of them, indeed, not perfect as yet, but brethren still; whose name and reputation were sacred; whose character, precious; whose influence, vastly important, and not to be diminished. Of his brethren, in his own session, he always spoke with perfect respect, and generally called them *venerable fathers.* Of his people he spoke as his *dear people;* and as a man should, who knows he must give an account of his flock, of which God has made him overseer, of which he is a servant for Jesus' sake, but of which he neither is nor may be, hireling, slave, or sycophant."

In a word, Mr. Sanford's whole deportment was penetrated by a spirit of benevolence, purity, and propriety, which impressed, in the most favourable manner, all with whom he came in contact. He was an example of that " sober-mindedness" which an apostle enjoins, and which is so becoming those who profess godliness, and especially those who minister at the altar.

4th. In the various intimate relations of life, Mr. Sanford was emphatically exemplary. These pages bear witness to the truth of this assertion. As a *son*, how bright is the example which he set! For his father, he cherished and manifested, so long as that parent lived, the most profound and truly filial respect, which was indicated by actions on all proper occasions. To his venerable mother, who survives him, he was all that a dutiful and affectionate son could be. He spared no pains to render her situation as comfortable as it was in his power to do; and he was indeed a source of great comfort to her in the lonely period of her widowhood, so long as God spared him to her.

As a *brother*, he was all that could be desired in that endeared relation; and his affection will never be forgotten by his brother and sister. He felt a very deep interest in their spiritual interests, and rejoiced greatly in seeing his prayers answered in regard to them.

As a *husband*, it would hardly seem necessary to say a word in addition to what his letters and his journal have so abundantly uttered. He was one of the most devoted and excellent of husbands. Such conduct as his gives a dignity and happiness to married life, which the Author of marriage designed to attach to that tender, affectionate and exalted union.

There is no lesson which this volume is more calculated to give than that of the beauty, purity, affection, and happiness of married life, when pervaded and governed by the genuine spirit of christianity.

As a *father*, his letters and his journal bear testimony to the deep parental solicitude which he felt for his infant son. Indeed a large portion of his journal, after the birth of that son, is nothing else than a series of recorded prayers on his behalf. And the last sentence which he wrote was the record of an invocation of the divine favour over its infant head. May these earnest and heart-felt prayers prove indeed to be a richer legacy than all that wealth and worldly greatness could bequeath!

As a *friend*, many among the living can bear testimony to his excellence in this respect. Mr. Sanford was not hasty in forming friendships. He was naturally reserved. If he had a prominent fault it was that of too great reserve. But he was not cold-hearted. He was not a doubtful friend. Where his affections were once enlisted, they were permanent, ardent, faithful. There was, with him, however, no empty profession of friendship. His was the silent, deep, lasting feeling of the heart, and was displayed in acts rather than in words, though there were not wanting times in which he gave way to the spontaneous gush of ardent affection in his letters to his chosen, his bosom friends.

5th. Mr. Sanford was a man of eminent piety. This was his crowning excellence. His piety was early, uniformly progressive, enlightened, consistent, beautifully symmetrical, and fruitful. He was a man of far more than ordinary piety. He was a very holy man. His conversation and deportment invariably made this impression on the minds of those who became acquainted with him. In all situations, and under all circumstances, he was the same holy, devoted man. His very look indicated that he was a man conversant with eternal things.

He was a man of much *prayer.* He evidently spent much time in his closet. This was the secret of his remarkable gift of prayer; or, rather, of the gift and grace of it united. His prayers, in public, possessed great fervour, propriety of expression, solemnity, unction. They were the prayers of a man of a most devout spirit—of one who was familiar with the blessed, the solemn work of addressing God. His life seemed to be truly what archbishop Leighton calls the heavenly life—that of ascending to heaven by prayer, to obtain spiritual blessings, and descending to the earth to scatter them among his fellow mortals.

We have said that Mr. Sanford's piety was symmetrical. It was emphatically so. His piety was uncommonly per-feet, in this, the scriptural sense of the word perfect. It shed its hallowed influence on all his actions. It was a holy principle which pervaded every thing which he did. He carried his religion with him, wherever he went. It was this which rendered him a *conscientious* man, and fearless too, in the discharge of ascertained duty. During the last two years of his life, his conscientious adherence to principle, and to what he deemed to be duty, was often put to a severe test, especially in the distressing discussions and acts of the ecclesiastical bodies of which he was a member. Actuated, as he felt himself to be, by principle, he was not slow, however, to admit that those who were opposed to his views of duty might be influenced by just as conscientious a regard for duty as himself.

Mr. Sanford's piety was evidently progressive. From the outset in the divine life, he seemed to advance steadily, and was a striking illustration of the truth of the divine declaration, that the " path of the just is as the shining light, which shineth more and more unto the perfect day."

" During his last illness," remarks Dr. M'Auley, in the discourse to which we have already referred, " and as he rapidly approached the melancholy catastrophe, in all the agonies and wanderings of a mind overwhelmed with trouble, not a murmuring, nor unkind, nor harsh expression escaped his lips. Instead of this, his prayers were constant, and painfully interesting, for grace, and mercy, and peace upon all his congregation; his church-members, especially the lambs of his flock ; his friends, his brethren, and his very dear family. There was scarcely any wandering here. The living oracles of God were lively in his heart, and, in every lucid moment, came with life from his dying lips. Heaven seemed let down to earth, and filled the privileged chamber where the good man yielded up the ghost."

6th. Mr. Sanford possessed uncommon advantages as a

public speaker. Few men are capable of producing so deep an impression on the minds of a public assembly. To the possession of an uncommonly melodious voice, were united a commanding person, a serious but agreeable countenance, perfect self-possession, and a vigorous but chastened imagination. He had cultivated, with considerable care, the whole art of public speaking, and few men of his age were his equals in it. Those who sat under his ministry will never forget the powerful appeals of his eloquence. Nor will those who heard his occasional addresses at the annual meetings of the American Bible Society, and other religious and benevolent assemblies of New York; or at those of the American Sunday School Union, and other societies of Philadelphia, soon forget the deep and holy impression of his eloquence on those occasions. He spoke emphatically with the view of doing good, of giving proper views of duty, of exciting to holier and higher resolutions, and to a determination, in reliance on divine grace, to execute them. There was, with him, no speaking for mere effect. It was always a conscientious and prayerful effort to advance the glory of God and the kingdom of the Lord Jesus Christ. And unless he believed that there was a reasonable prospect of accomplishing this great end, he declined accepting the invitation to make a public address on such occasions. He was also very distinguished for his speeches in the Presbytery and other ecclesiastical bodies of which he was, from time to time, a member. He did not ordinarily speak very often; but it was seldom that he did speak without producing a manifest effect.

7th The work of the ministry was the sphere in which Mr. Sanford delighted to move. This was his chosen, his appropriate field of labour. To preach the gospel from the pulpit, and to perform the work of pastoral visitation, was the highest enjoyment which earth could yield him. No other employment, however interesting, or however useful it might be, could be compared with that of directly labouring to convert souls, and to assist them to prepare for a holy heaven. To fit himself for the work of the ministry, he had spent several years of preparation. And when, in the good providence of God, he was allowed to be " put in trust of this ministry," he entered upon his work with a deep sense of its solemn importance and responsibility, and also with great delight. Even long before the completion of his college studies, he had commenced labouring, as opportunity was afforded, for the salvation of men. Many of the churches around Schenectady will long remember his visits of love during that signal outpouring of the Spirit, in the years of 1819 and 1820. And when he entered upon his office, as an ambassador of the Lord Jesus Christ, in Brooklyn, he consecrated himself wholly to the work. This engrossed his soul. His studies all had a direct bearing upon it. Nothing was pursued which did not have this great end in view. He " preached the word in season, and out of season." And he was among his people as an overseer who watched for their souls; as one who " sought not theirs, but them." And his ministry there was eminently successful. Under his ministrations, the church increased very greatly. Within the period of five years and three months, during which he was pastor of their church, nearly four hundred persons were added to its communion. And, during the time of his pastoral labours in the Second Presbyterian Church, in Philadelphia, which was less than three years, upwards of one hundred and fifty persons were added to the number of its members. Thus, exclusive of the good which he did by occasional labours in other places, more than five hundred persons were brought to the knowledge of the Saviour in the two congregations to which he ministered as pastor, during a period of little more than eight years. This fact demonstrates that his ministry was a successful one.

Mr. Sanford was an affectionate, faithful pastor. He visited his people much, and was especially attentive to the poor and the sick. To the afflicted he was a most suitable minister. He could truly say,

"Haud ignara mali miseris succurre disco."*

The couch of the afflicted was a spot which had many attractions for his sympathising heart. He hasted thither as often as his other duties permitted. To the young of his flock, and especially to the young converts, he was greatly attached. He watched over them with more than parental solicitude, counselled them, shared their joys and their sorrows, and helped them, by every means in his power, in their upward journey to the skies. Nor did he cease to feel an interest in a people because he ceased to be their pastor. He frequently revisited Brooklyn, after his removal to Philadelphia, and laboured, as he had opportunity, for the benefit of the people of his former charge, and witnessed with delight the successful labours of his successor.

That such a pastor should be loved, dearly loved, by a people in whom he took so lively an interest, and to many of whom he had been, under God's blessing, an instrument of the highest spiritual blessings, is not wonderful. This affection he shared until the day of his death. We select two or three letters, from among many, which he received from members of his former charge, at Brooklyn, written to him at Philadelphia, and which show how highly that people valued him. The first is from a gentleman in that congregation, in whom Mr. Sanford had long felt a very deep in-

---

* Having myself experienced misfortune, I have learned to help the miserable.

terest, but who had not become a decided Christian when he removed to Philadelphia. During one of the visits which he made to Brooklyn he sought an interview with this gentleman, and had a faithful conversation with him, which, with the divine blessing, was the means of leading him to decision on the subject of religion, and to the Saviour. Soon after he had found peace in believing he addressed the following letter to his former pastor, to inform him of the happy change which he had experienced. The second is from a young lady who had received much benefit from his instructions. The third is from an excellent Christian in that church, who has long been a blessing to it, and to the church of Christ throughout our country, by his beneficence.

" Brooklyn, April 26th, 1830.

" REV. AND DEAR SIR,

" You will be reminded by this, of the request you made me to write you. Although I felt, then, as though I should like to write, still did not believe I should.

" I, however, bless God that I am now, not only enabled to discharge a duty which ought long since to have been acknowledged and performed, but experience a pleasure in communicating the goodness and mercy of God to my soul. If you were not well acquainted with my former views and feelings on religious subjects, and had not heard me recently express them, I should be particular in the relation of them; but you have too well and too long known them to make it either necessary or interesting. Suffice it to say, that I believe the interview at my house was, under God, the means of leading me to the Saviour; and, while I sincerely thank you for that short visit, I desire to render to God all the glory of my salvation.

22

"I shall never forget the expression you then made use of, '*Look to Jesus, look and live.*' Nor the manner you pointed that finger to him. I was convinced, by your remarks, that my then state of mind was the effect of the strivings of the Holy Spirit. And, as I was convinced of *sin*, I had but '*to look and live.*' And these thoughts were so impressed on my mind, that the day you left us, I was enabled to believe, and see, and feel, that although I had been a great sinner, yet the blood of Christ was sufficient to cleanse me, even me, and on that alone I rested, and desire to rest, my only hope of salvation.

"Oh, my dear sir, I know not how to thank God as I ought for his long-suffering kindness and forbearance to me. You, too, well know the many mercies and bounties of Divine Providence, which have literally been heaped upon me. You know, too, how often, under your ministry, I was convinced of sin, and yet how often I grieved the Spirit and said, 'Go thy way for this time.'

"If I am not deceiving myself (and I verily believe I am not) I pray that I may be a sincere, devout, humble Christian, rejoicing with trembling, and showing to the world, by my walk and conversation, that I love Jesus my Saviour, and desire the salvation of all mankind.

"As you feel a lively interest in the spiritual concerns of your late, and, I trust, still dearly beloved people, I will say that the day you left, there was a meeting at the house of Mr. Carroll for those under conviction of sin, and who were anxious about the salvation of their souls. There were then twenty present, under different degrees of conviction; some of whom are now rejoicing in the hope of a glorious immortality, others halting, waiting, perhaps, for the same reasons that I did; and others, I fear, have lost their serious impressions. At the next meeting there were, in addition to the former number, five others; and, as far as I can judge, from their solemnity, and what I learn of their views, they have set their faces Zionward. Surely the Spirit of God is in our midst, and I hope for a great harvest of souls as the fruit of your, and your brother Carroll's sowing.

"I have been enabled (not in my own strength) to erect a family altar, and, morning and evening, to call my family around it, and there offer up my thanks to the Almighty for the manifestations of his great goodness, and supplicate his continued blessings.

"I now desire to thank you, in the Lord, for your faithfulness and kindness to me and my family, and to request, as a further obligation, on my part, that you would soon write me a long letter, and give me that Christian advice which your own experience so well qualifies you to do. And do not forget to pray for me. I desire to be affectionately remembered to your wife, and then unite with my wife and sister, in testifying our love and esteem, both towards you and yours.

"That the Lord may prosper and bless you abundantly, in that whereunto he hath called you, is my sincere prayer."

" Brooklyn, Jan. 6th, 1830.

"The kind congratulations of my dear pastor* were received on the morning of the new year, and excited emotions which I know not how to describe.

"I was musing upon days and scenes for ever fled, and my heart felt sad indeed, when your unexpected favour was handed me, and in a measure dispelled the gloom, although it brought the past more vividly to remembrance.

"How painful the retrospect of seasons misemployed. Oh my pastor, the view is an overwhelming one! What

* Thus she always addressed him.

cause have I for gratitude, that I have not been cut off in the midst of my unfaithfulness. I am permitted to behold the opening of another year. May the wish expressed in your dear letter be answered, that ' God would make it a happy year by granting his presence and the light of his countenance.' Will you not frequently put up this petition for me at the throne of grace, for my days of darkness are many."

" Deprived of the privilege of attending the sanctuary, this evening, I will devote it to answering the affectionate inquiries of my much loved pastor. You express the hope that I am living in the light of God's countenance, and rejoicing to see his work prospering around us. Moments, sweet and precious, are granted, during which I am enabled to say, *My Father*, with an unfaltering tongue. These are green spots in my pilgrimage through this wilderness, and demand my warmest gratitude.

" I trust I do rejoice to see those around me enjoying the presence of God; and there is much cause for rejoicing at present. Many are inquiring the way to Zion, and some have submitted to the Saviour. The little cloud, we trust, is increasing still. Yes, my dear pastor, the seed you have sown we trust is now springing up, and will yield an abundant harvest. Our meetings are all well attended. At the prayer-meeting, on Friday evening last, every seat in the lecture room was occupied, and several around me were in tears. I had thought Mr. C. too sanguine in his expectations; but was now led to exclaim, ' The Lord is in the midst of us, and I knew it not.' Mr. C. has an inquiry-meeting every week: the number present at the last I do not recollect.

" If the professed followers of the Lamb will be united and unceasing in their petitions at a throne of grace, I do think we shall experience a season of refreshing from the presence of the Lord.

" My dear pastor, I do wish you could be with us, that both the sower and the reaper may rejoice together.

" Your request shall certainly be complied with ; but do not imagine that you are forgotten. O no, there are those who oft present you in the arms of their affection, at a throne of grace, and whose earnest prayer is, that your present labours may be abundantly blessed.

" When shall we be permitted to welcome you at Brooklyn ? Do you not intend coming this spring ? That you may have your heart encouraged and revived by seeing the work of the Lord prospering under your present ministrations, is the ardent prayer of your affectionate friend."

" *Brooklyn, April 11th*, 1831.

" REV. AND DEAR SIR,

" Knowing that you feel deeply interested in all the concerns of our church, I hasten to communicate some of the particulars with which our hearts were cheered yesterday. It was the communion Sabbath, (session having, on a former occasion, found it inexpedient to celebrate that ordinance on the *first* Sabbath, by a permanent regulation, have substituted the second.) Before the appointed hour, 3 o'clock, the church was filled to overflowing ; benches and chairs were placed in the aisles, and were all occupied. One hundred and three names were then called off ; the Confession of Faith, penned by yourself, was then read and assented to. Thirty-two individuals were baptized ; and the covenant, according to the form you left with us, was then solemnly entered into. The whole body of the church, except the part immediately under the front gallery, had been reserved for the communicants, and every seat was crowded. A committee, consisting of three deacons, had been appointed to, superintend the seating and accommodating the various classes of communicants and visiters. The galleries, filled beyond any former occasion, maintained the most profound silence; and, although the exercises took up more than two hours, no impatience whatever was manifested, but every thing was done with decency and order. I could delight in describing this scene, but the outline must suffice. I know you can fill up all that is necessary to bring the spectacle before you. Your mind's eye will discern many countenances that have, in times past, been fixed on yours, when imparting the tidings of salvation, and inviting them to close with the offers of mercy—at length they have yielded.

" To God's rich, and free, and sovereign grace, through the gift of his dear Son, and the influences of his Holy Spirit, we would ascribe all the praise. The human instrumentality employed in this work, has been the incessant labour of our beloved pastor, somewhat more engagedness on the part of the elders and deacons, and of individual Christians; and of the assembling together of the congregation for morning prayer. This was begun on Monday, the 28th of February, at 6 o'clock, and continued *precisely one hour.* The experiment was tried for holding these meetings every other morning, for one week, but the plan was abandoned. It was found the best to meet every morning. These meetings continue to be well attended. The lecture room has, at some periods, been crowded; and this morning, although the weather was cold, and the hour of meeting half past five, the room was nearly full. On Friday, the 11th, and Saturday, the 12th of February, public services were held in our church, at which some of the clergy from the city, attended. These we have every reason to believe were attended with beneficial effects. I have only to add, that our brethren of the Dutch, Episcopal, Baptist, and Methodist churches, are more or less stirred up at this time.

" Mr. M'Ilvaine (now bishop of Ohio) has regular meetings for religious conversation, and is much encouraged in his labours. There is a most excellent state of feeling amongst the respective denominations of this place. Our morning prayer meeting has been attended by individuals of all these several persuasions ; and it is a delightful circumstance, that the voice of prayer has ascended in our lecture room from the Episcopalian, the Dutch Reformed, the Baptist, the Methodist, as well as the Presbyterian."

But not only was Mr. Sanford greatly beloved by his people in Brooklyn, he had many warm friends wherever he was known. In Philadelphia, there were not a few by whom he was greatly beloved. The following is one out of many letters addressed to him by members of his church, in that city, which exhibit the great affection entertained for him. It was written by a person who is every way qualified to form an opinion of what constitutes profitable preaching.

" Pardon me, dear sir, for so long retaining the book you kindly lent me last summer, which I read with peculiar interest ; and, I hope, with profit. The doctrines it presents to view are the only foundation on which my soul can rest with confidence of pardon and acceptance before God. They are well calculated to bring relief to the conscience labouring under a sense of guilt, and feeling the necessity of a better righteousness than sinful human nature can possibly render.

" I cannot deny myself the gratification afforded by this opportunity, of expressing, though it be but feebly, our grateful sense of the kindness you have evinced toward us, under the severe afflictions through which we have been called to pass. You have been truly the minister of consolation to us; and though we have experienced much of the loving-kindness of our heavenly Father in sustaining us, while suffering beneath the righteous inflictions of his hand, we have especially felt our faith confirmed, our hopes .excited, and our wounded spirits soothed and elevated while we accompanied you in your fervent addresses to the throne of grace, and poured out our prayers and our sorrows, where only we could obtain relief and support.

" I pray God that the consolations wherewith you have been enabled to comfort others may be abundantly administered by his gracious Spirit to your own heart, in your *present painful circumstances.* I have most sincerely sympathized in the varied afflictions you have been called to endure ; and my constant, earnest prayer has been that you might be sustained and comforted, guided and blessed by him, to whom having, in faith, committed your way, you have his certain promise that he will direct your steps.

" Ever since, in the providence of God, I was first permitted to attend upon your ministry, I have found your mode of presenting divine truth peculiarly adapted, if I may be allowed the expression, to my spiritual taste ; and, if not deceived in the humble hope I indulge, that I have been brought into the way of life and peace, I feel that I am greatly indebted to your instrumentality for any progress I may have since made in the divine life, any measure of comfort or edification I have experienced. Your faithful admonitions have frequently been brought home with resist-less energy to my heart, and, through the divine blessing, which, I trust, has attended your ministrations, I have been instructed, reproved, humbled, and animated to greater diligence in Christian duty by the message of his grace, which

I doubt not God has commissioned you to deliver. My languid affections have often received a new and upward impulse, while influenced by his Spirit, in your prayers you have led us into the immediate presence of God.

"Forgive me for dwelling so long on the expression of my own feelings. But to a heart in some degree sensible of its obligations, there is pleasure in acknowledging a debt of gratitude which it feels it can never discharge. And among the richest blessings which God confers, the privilege of receiving the instructions of a faithful pastor is one which claims our most fervent thanks.

"Assure Mrs. S. of my affectionate remembrance. I rejoice to hear that her health is in so great a degree restored. Remember me with sincere respect to your mother.

"With sentiments of most grateful esteem,

"Yours."

Nor was the circle of those who loved him, and who consulted him, confined to his own church, or even his own denomination. The following two letters were addressed to him by persons who occasionally frequented his lectures. The first is from a gentleman belonging to the Episcopal church. The second is from a most estimable individual, who was then under the awakening influences of the Spirit, and whose case needed that judicious advice which the spiritual and experienced teacher, whom she consulted, knew so well how to administer.

"*Sunday night.*

"May God bless you, my dear sir, by making you the means of turning many to righteousness!

"Your sermon, this evening, was exactly what I wished

for my dear wife. The doctrine of God's sovereignty, as
she has understood it—and understood it so long, that I fear
it will be very difficult to eradicate it from her mind—has
been lying as an impassable barrier before her; and had
been, (so far as I could see) the cause of the gradual decay
of her earnestness, and the origin of an apathy the most
dreadful.

"It is to no purpose that God's word, so full, so universal in its offers, is preached to her by me, or by any one
whom she has been accustomed to consider heterodox upon
the point of predestination. I have assured her that I dif-
fered, upon that subject, with the teachers to whom she has
been accustomed, only in so much that I considered them to
waste their time, and to confound their hearers, by prying
into what must, from the nature of the human mind, be dark
to us, while in the present state of being. I have assured
her that, *practically*, there was no difference among the
mass of Christians. Some are more metaphysical than
others—and metaphysics are not intelligible to any congregation. It really does appear to me that injury is done,
whenever a sermon of that kind is preached.

"Excuse me, dear sir, my only object in enlarging upon
this point is, to testify to the correctness of your apprehensions upon the extent of the impediment which it was, to-
night, your object to remove.

"Come and see us whenever you can, and I confidently
look for the blessing of God to my wife and sister, through
your hands.

"I am anxious to be better acquainted with you; and I
shall be glad, whenever you can make useful to yourself the
gratitude and confidence of

"Your friend."

" Sunday night.

" You have, to-night, dear sir, expressed a wish that any of your congregation who wished to consult their pastor concerning their eternal interests, would call upon you to-morrow.

" Not having a claim upon you as one of your flock, I do not feel at liberty to intrude upon you at that time; but, feeling a strong desire to have some communication with you, I have chosen this method. But first let me state, as some excuse for encroaching upon your time, that I am one of Dr. W.'s congregation, and, of course, have no pastor, at present, to whom I could apply.

" My complaint is *hardness of heart,* and an utter indifference of *feeling,* to the things of most importance. Having sat under Dr. W.'s preaching, during my whole life, I have never, for a moment, had the excuse of ignorance of duty to plead; but have gone on, from my earliest recollection, to the age of twenty-eight, deliberately sinning against my own conscience. I *think* I never have laboured under any self-delusion in this respect. I do not remember ever having persuaded myself that what I was doing was right. Indeed I do not remember having ever attempted it; but, having seen right and wrong clearly set before me, have calmly, and without trembling, chosen the evil—have deliberately turned away my thoughts from sacred things and turned them unto sin. All my life long I remember seasons when my reason would so strongly represent the irrationality of pursuing a course which would so certainly eventuate in misery, that I would make a few faint efforts to free myself, but evil habits were too strong upon me, and I willingly yielded to Satan's powerful influence. After a while, I found that his service, even the service I had chosen, was, indeed, bondage; but every failure to release myself only made my bonds stronger. I have found by actual experience, what reason had always told me, that even without reference to a hereafter, a pure and holy life, with all its self-denial, must be infinitely happier than living in sin. I think that, for some time past, it has not been so much the *pleasure* of sin, as the force of powerful habits, long indulged—too powerful for any but Almighty force to overcome, that has kept me in bondage. My *understanding* has lately felt this slavery so much, and the consequences to be so inevitable, that I have been making my *heart* also affected with the subject. In this I have as yet failed. I know that no power can effect a change but the Spirit of God; but I also know that it will be a *certain* evidence that I have not this Spirit if I sit down to wait for it without making any effort. I have prayed—how weakly, and, no doubt, wickedly, God knows—still I have never entirely given it up; for it would be deliberately dropping the only hold I have, however insecure a one. My difficulty is, that I am in no distress of mind; or, rather, in no distress of heart. I set in array before me the attributes of a holy God; but my heart is deadened by long indulgence in sin, and the contemplation produces no awe, no emotion. I, therefore, though perfectly conscious of sin so great that only his restraining hand has prevented me from being the worst of *actual* transgressors, have no feeling of the inexpressible guilt of sin, as committed against a pure and perfect being. As a consequence of this, I do not *feel* my need of a Saviour, though perfectly *conscious* that I can do nothing of myself; and, of course, cannot see the excellence and all-sufficiency of Christ, as a Saviour.

" Your representation of the love of Christ, to-night, I found had no effect upon my hard and stony heart. The most trivial things will turn my thoughts away from these all-important subjects; and it requires a constant effort of the mind to pay what little attention I do. And yet I cannot be content to give the matter up. I think I can say that I have not the slightest expectation of ever gaining the least ad-vantage by any righteousness of my own. I am fully con-scious of my own utter inability to raise myself from the depths wherein I am sunk. And, I think, also, that I have none of the pride of heart which would make me object to owe *all* to Christ. I think, as far as I have any command over my own feelings, that I am perfectly willing to submit, but I find that I cannot repent and believe. I know that the obstacles have been created by myself; and that, therefore, I have no right to any assistance. But, as God has promised that he will give bread, and not a stone, to those that ask him, I cannot but entertain some faint hope that he may grant me his Holy Spirit to enlighten and warm my heart. In the meantime I know that I must ' stretch forth the withered arm.'—But how to do this l

" I have generally attended on your preaching on Sun-day and Wednesday evenings, for some weeks past, and have found that what I heard from you tended, more than any other preaching, to keep alive the faint determinations which I had formed. I know that God has given us, in the Scrip-tures, a full revelation of the way of life; but as my heart seems closed against the truth contained therein, he may, perhaps, bless some explanation or advice which you can give me."

———

Even strangers were indebted to him for his faithful in-structions in the journeys which he made. The following extracts from a letter, written by a young lady who had heard from his lips " a word in season," state an instance of this sort.

———

" In the year 1826, my dear mother consented that I should visit New York for the first time. My feelings, on

leaving home, were rather sad. This first excited the attention of a lady on board, who entered into conversation
with me. In hopes of diverting my thoughts from self, and
those I was leaving behind, she made remarks on the individuals around us. Your dearly beloved, and much lamented
husband was one among them. He had, at that time, been
to visit his parents ; and, if I mistake not, to attend the last
mournful rites of a beloved father. This circumstance, with
others mentioned, excited in me a deep interest for one so
afflicted.

  " After a short time, a gentleman, with whom I had a
slight acquaintance in Albany, came and took a seat by me.
He made many remarks on serious subjects, somewhat de-
ridingly ; and at last concluded by saying, ' Well, if there
is any hereafter,' &c. In reply to this, I said, ' Could I
believe in annihilation I should be comparatively happy.'
This remark did not escape the observation of your husband, who was engaged at that moment in conversation
with a gentleman very near me. They had no sooner
finished, than, turning to me, he inquired: ' Did I rightly
understand you, Miss ——, in saying that you believed in
annihilation ?' ' I said, if I could believe in it, I should be
comparatively happy.' ' You are not happy, then,' replied
Mr. S., and immediately commenced a conversation of the
deepest interest. First, by general remarks ; then, by degrees, more and more pointed, until personal feelings were
spoken of. Being made somewhat acquainted with my history, from myself, he alluded to the death of my father ;
the promises made to the orphan, and a heavenly Father's
care. The mercies of a suffering Saviour. Particular providences. The various calls of sinners. The astonishing
forbearance of God in sparing them, and granting them opportunities to turn and live, &c. He then adverted to the
pleasures of New York ; the many temptations that would

surround me on all sides; entreated me to consider this, and see if I could resist all these allurements. I replied, that I hoped that duty to my mother would not be so far forgotten as to allow me to do any thing out of her presence which she could not sanction at home. Thus ended this interview for that day. It was resumed as we came in sight of New York, the following morning; after which, in the most so-lemu and impressive manner, Mr. S. bade me farewell.

"What an effort I then found it to appear cheerful! I was determined, at that time, never to let any one know what fires raged within. After my arrival in the city, having a letter of introduction to a most pious, and, afterwards, intimate friend, I was in a measure shielded from many temptations. This friend improved every opportunity to warn and admonish me; and is now, no doubt, reaping the reward promised to the faithful amid the heavenly host.

"Could Christians only feel more that it was their privilege, as well as duty, to seek out opportunities for doing good, we cannot say what blessed results would follow.

"I staid in New York five weeks. During that time, heard Mr. Sanford preach once. I desired much to see him; he took my address before parting at the wharf, with the intention of calling on me; but I afterwards learned indisposition prevented him until the very day I left the city for home.

"On arriving at Albany I found the church, of which my mother was a member, awakened to a sense of their obligations, and inquiring meetings were established. The first was held on Tuesday evening—one of deep interest to me. Many of my intimate friends were present. All of them since united with the church militant.

"I have not, even in a faint manner, done justice to an event which, to me, was one of so much moment. Oh that I could give you to understand the *manner* in which all was said; but I should fail did I make the attempt.   I can only, therefore, say it was the spirit of Jesus that spoke to me through him."

If it were proper, or necessary, to give the letters of con-dolence which his family received, upon his death, every reader would say that he was greatly beloved.   But we must close these remarks.

Such was the Rev. Joseph Sanford—a man of God; a faithful ambassador of Jesus Christ.   May the contempla-tion of his life, of his faith, his example, of his usefulness, be rendered profitable, through the divine blessing, to all who read this volume; and to God alone shall be the praise.

THE END.

Printed by BoD™in Norderstedt, Germany